The Essential Controller

Second Edition

Founded in 1807, John Wiley & Sons is the oldest independent publishing company in the United States. With offices in North America, Europe, Asia, and Australia, Wiley is globally committed to developing and marketing print and electronic products and services for our customers' professional and personal knowledge and understanding.

The Wiley Corporate F&A series provides information, tools, and insights to corporate professionals responsible for issues affecting the profitability of their company, from accounting and finance to internal controls and performance management.

The Essential Controller

*An Introduction to What Every
Financial Manager Must Know*

Second Edition

STEVEN M. BRAGG

WILEY

John Wiley & Sons, Inc.

For general information on our other products and services or for technical support, please contact our Customer Care Department within the United States at (800) 762-2974, outside the United States at (317) 572-3993 or fax (317) 572-4002.

Wiley also publishes its books in a variety of electronic formats. Some content that appears in print may not be available in electronic books. For more information about Wiley products, visit our web site at www.wiley.com.

Library of Congress Cataloging-in-Publication Data:

Bragg, Steven M.
  The essential controller : an introduction to what every financial manager must know / Steven M. Bragg. — 2nd ed.
      p. cm. — (Wiley corporate F&A series)
  Rev. ed. of: Controller's guide. c2005.
  Includes index.
  ISBN 978-1-118-16997-1 (pbk); ISBN 978-1-118-22685-8 (ebk);
ISBN 978-1-118-23973-5 (ebk); ISBN 978-1-118-26443-0 (ebk)
    1. Controllership.   2. Chief financial officers.   3. Corporations—Accounting.
4. Corporations—Finance.   I. Bragg, Steven M. Controller's guide.   II. Title.
  HG4026.B662 2012
  658.15′1—dc23

                                                                        2011042681

Printed in the United States of America

10 9 8 7 6 5 4 3 2 1

Contents

Preface

THE TITLE OF *The Essential Controller: An Introduction to What Every Financial Manager Must Know* clearly specifies its purpose; a person newly hired into the controller position needs this book in order to understand the demands of the position and to succeed in the role.

The book describes the role of both the controller and chief financial officer within the corporation, as well as how these roles vary between companies of different sizes. These issues are addressed in Chapters 1 through 3. Chapter 4 describes a variety of efficient practices for managing the accounting department. Chapter 5 turns to internal accounting, also known as cost accounting; it takes the new controller through traditional costing concepts, such as job and process costing, as well as the most recent costing systems, such as throughput, target, and activity-based costing.

Chapter 6 shows the new controller how to analyze information through the use of ratio and trend analysis, which is also a good way to pinpoint the control problems that can be resolved through the control systems changes noted in Chapter 7. It is also useful to understand the process required to issue reliable financial statements, which is covered in Chapter 8. The new controller may work with an internal audit department; Chapter 9 describes the composition and role of the audit committee, as well as the general functions of the internal audit group.

The book then moves on to more general management topics. Chapter 10 turns to the accounting department staffing—how to recruit, hire, promote, and motivate employees. Chapter 11 delves into the new controller's role in dealing with company investors—the information needs of the various investor groups, various methods of communication with them, and the use of a standard disclosure policy. The book concludes with an analysis of tax strategy in Chapter 12, where the impact of a number of key issues on a company's tax liability—the cash method of accounting, inventory valuation, acquisitions, net operating loss carryforwards, transfer pricing, and so on—are covered.

In sum, the book is designed to give the new controller a firm foundation in the concepts of managing the accounting department, analyzing and knowing what to do with key accounting information, and setting up control systems that reduce a company's risk of loss. Knowledge of these core issues is central to the new controller's success in the position.

Steven M. Bragg
Centennial, Colorado
March 2012

CHAPTER ONE

Accounting in the Corporation

Importance of This Chapter

Though this chapter is relatively short, the new controller should read it carefully and ponder the key topics of discussion. We point out that the accounting function is extremely complex, both in terms of tasks and global reach as well as in its impact on other parts of the business. In many respects, the controller position has the most far-reaching impact of any management position, so the new controller must spend time considering how he or she will fit into the complex gearing of the modern corporation in order to achieve the greatest positive impact. Further, ethical issues arise more frequently in the accounting field than in most other areas, so the controller must be aware of these issues and understand the process for dealing with them.

The role of the accounting staff used to be simple enough—just process a basic set of accounting transactions and convert them into financial statements at month-end. The role has undergone a vast change in the last few decades, as technological improvements and a shifting view of management theory have resulted in a startlingly different accounting function. This chapter describes how the accounting function now incorporates many additional tasks and can even include the internal auditing and information technology functions in smaller organizations. It then goes on to describe how this functional area fits into and serves the needs of the rest of the company, and how the controller fits into the accounting function. Finally, there is a discussion of how ethics drives the behavior of accounting employees, and how this shapes the way the accounting staff and controller see their roles within the organization.

In short, this chapter covers the high-level issues of how the accounting function and its controller fit into the modern company, not only to process its transactions, which was its traditional role, but also to provide additional services.

TASKS OF THE ACCOUNTING FUNCTION

The accounting function has had sole responsibility for processing the bulk of a company's transactions for many years. Chief among these transactions have been the processing of customer billings and supplier invoices. Though these two areas comprise the bulk of the transactions, there has also been a long history of delegating asset tracking to the accounting function. This involves all transactions related to the movement of cash, prepaid assets, inventory, and fixed assets. Finally, the accounting staff has been responsible for tracking debt, which can involve a continuous tracking of debt levels by debt instrument, as well as the payments made to reduce them.

A multitude of changes in the business environment have altered the role of the accounting function. One change has been the appearance of the information technology function. In a larger company, this function is managed within its own department and does not fall under the responsibility of the controller. However, it is common for the information technology group to fall under the management umbrella of the controller in a smaller company. Likewise, the internal auditing function frequently falls under the controller's area as well. This function has expanded in importance over the last few decades as companies realize the benefits of having an internal watchdog over key controls. Though it should report directly to the board of directors or the chief financial officer (CFO), it is common for a small internal auditing staff to report instead to the controller.

Besides adding new functional areas, the accounting staff has other new responsibilities that have arisen due to the increased level of competition. With worldwide barriers to competition crumbling, every company feels the pinch of lower competitive prices and now asks the accounting staff to provide analysis work in addition to the traditional transaction processing. These tasks include margin analysis on existing or projected product lines, geographic sales regions, or individual products.

Targeted Financial Analysis

One of the controller's key tasks is proactively analyzing company issues and recommending changes. In one case, a new controller solved a company's low-profitability problems by preparing a one-page grid showing the sales volume and profitability of every customer. The president promptly dropped most of the customers having low volume and low margins, resulting in the company deliberately losing 1/3 of its customers—and raising its profitability. ▪

Also, different organizational structures complicate the job of the controller. For example, there may be a number of subsidiaries that were created specifically to reduce the taxes on newly acquired businesses, or to take advantage of tax rates in different government jurisdictions. These situations greatly complicate the accounting work of the accounting staff, particularly in regard to consolidating the results of the various entities.

There are also continuing changes to the various accounting frameworks, such as generally accepted accounting principles (GAAP) or international financial reporting standards (IFRS), which require considerably more complicated accounting for some situations. For example, the controller may be called on to capitalize the interest expense associated with a fixed asset under construction, or to accrue a liability for an asset retirement obligation.

In addition, the accounting staff may even be asked to serve on new product design teams, so that they can determine the projected cost of new products, especially in relation to target costs. Further, the accounting staff must continuously review and report on nonproduct costs, which can range from advertising to utilities. This level of cost review and reporting calls for highly trained cost accountants and financial analysts, almost always with college degrees and professional certifications, to conduct the work.

The world of business has become more international. Many companies are doing an increasing volume of business with companies based in other countries. This greatly increases the complexity of accounting, for a company must now determine gains and losses on sales to other countries. In addition, if there is no separate finance function, the accounting staff may be called on to handle letters of credit and hedging transactions that are designed to reduce the level of risk that goes with foreign exchange dealings.

In the face of more intensive competition, many companies are also merging or acquiring subsidiaries. This adds a great deal of complexity to the accounting staff's work, for it must now coordinate a multitude of additional tasks in other locations. This includes setting up standard procedures for the processing of receipts, shipments, and cash. Also, closing the financial books at the end of each reporting period becomes much more complex, as the accounting staff must now coordinate the assembly and consolidation of information from multiple subsidiaries. Even if a company decides to consolidate all of its accounting facilities into one central processing location to avoid all this trouble, it still requires the management expertise to bring together the disparate accounting systems into a smoothly operating facility. This is not an easy task. The environment of mergers and acquisitions greatly increases the skill needed by the accounting staff.

The tasks of the accounting function are itemized below. The tasks that belong elsewhere—but are commonly given to the accounting staff in a small company—are noted under a separate heading.

- *Traditional accounting tasks*
    - Accounts payable transaction processing
    - Accounts receivable transaction processing
    - Asset transaction processing
    - Debt transaction processing

- *New accounting tasks*
    - Coordination and consolidation of accounting at subsidiaries
    - Currency translations
    - Margin analysis
    - Nonproduct cost analysis
    - Selection, implementation, and operation of accounting software and related systems
    - Target costing

- *New tasks assigned to the accounting function of smaller companies*
    - Information technology systems installation and maintenance
    - Hedging, foreign exchange, and letter of credit transactions
    - Internal auditing programs

Given today's highly volatile and ever-changing business environment, the only safe statement to make about the new activities presented in this section is that they will only become more complex, requiring even greater levels of skill by the accounting staff and its management team.

ROLE OF THE ACCOUNTING FUNCTION

Having noted the expanded number of tasks now undertaken by the modern accounting function, it is important to also note how the role of the accounting staff has changed in relation to the rest of the company.

When the number of accounting tasks was more closely defined around transaction processing, it was common for the accounting staff to be housed in an out-of-the-way corner of a business, where it would work without being impeded by other functions. Now, with a much greater number of tasks, the accounting staff finds itself involved in most major decisions. For example, the cost accountant is expected to serve on product design teams and to let other team members know if new designs will have costs that will meet targeted cost goals. An accounting analyst may be asked by the sales manager to evaluate the profitability of a lease deal being extended to a customer. The controller may be involved in integrating the accounting functions of an acquired business. The accounts receivable clerk may work with the sales staff to collect overdue invoices from customers. And in general, the entire accounting staff may be called on to issue financial reports to other parts of the business, possibly with accompanying formal presentations. For these reasons and others, the accounting function now finds itself performing a variety of tasks that make it an integral part of the organization.

A particularly important area in which the role of the accountant has changed is related to processes. When another area of the company changes its operations, the accounting staff must devise alterations to the existing accounting systems for processing transactions that will accommodate those changes. For example, if the manufacturing function switches to the just-in-time production methodology, this has a profound impact on the way in which the accounting staff pays its bills, invoices customers, monitors job costs, and creates internal reports. Also, if the materials management staff decides to use material requirements planning or integrated distribution management systems, the accounting software should be interfaced to these new systems. To alter its processes, the accounting staff must first be aware of these changes, requiring the accounting staff to engage in more interaction with other parts of the company to find out what is going on.

A company may find that it has to streamline various aspects of its operations in order to lower its costs and remain competitive. This can be a problem for the controller, who may find key controls being eliminated at the same time. This requires a fresh view of which controls are really needed to mitigate risks, and a considerable amount of diplomacy in extending the viewpoint of the controller regarding this issue to the rest of the company. The result may be that some controls must be modified, replaced, or eliminated.

It is very important to develop strong relationships with key suppliers and customers. These business partners will demand extra services, some of which must be fulfilled by the accounting staff. These changes may include the online submission of invoices, providing special billing formats to customers, or paying suppliers by electronic transfer. If these steps are needed to retain key business partners, then the accounting staff must be willing to do its share of the work. Too frequently, the accounting staff resists these sorts of changes on the grounds that all transactions must be performed in exactly the same manner with all business partners. The accounting department must realize that altering its way of doing business is sometimes necessary to support ongoing business relationships.

In short, altering the focus of the accounting staff from an introverted group that processes a few traditional transactions to one that actively works with other parts of a company and alters its systems to accommodate the needs of other departments is required in today's business environment.

ROLE OF THE CONTROLLER

The controller has traditionally been the one who supervises the accounting department, reviews systems, and delivers financial statements. Though the details of the position are covered in Chapter 2, suffice it to say here that the position has expanded to a great extent. As noted earlier in this chapter, the accounting function as a whole is now required to take on additional tasks, to work with other departments more closely, to continuously offer advice to senior management, and to alter systems and controls to match the changing needs of other areas of the company. All of these changes have had a massive impact on the role of the controller within the organization.

The key factor is that, due to the vastly increased interaction with other departments, the controller must be highly skilled in interdepartmental dealings. This involves constant interactions with fellow department heads, attendance at meetings, and the issuance of opinions on a variety of topics regarding the operation of functions with which the controller previously had no connection. Because of this changed role, the controller must now have top-notch interpersonal and management skills—the former to deal with other departments and the latter to oversee the expanded role of the accounting department.

Forming Alliances

The controller position impacts nearly every part of the company. If the new controller is to succeed in the position, it is extremely important to build strong relationships with the managers of other departments. For example, if there is a large inventory investment, be sure to form a strong bond with the warehouse or materials manager. Also, do not ignore informal lines of communication; in many instances, a very senior person in an innocuous job may have considerable informal control over key functions. In one instance, the author found that the person in charge of developing sales proposals had the best overall knowledge of company operations!

In addition, the controller must govern a group of employees that is much more educated than was previously the case. This requires constant attention to the professional progress of each person in the department, which requires goal setting, mutual discussion of training requirements, and continuous feedback regarding employee performance. This clearly calls for management skills of an order far higher than formerly required of a controller that presided over a clerical function.

Also, the wider range of functions managed by the controller now requires a wider range of knowledge. A controller now needs at least a passing knowledge of computer systems, internal auditing, and administrative functions, because this area frequently falls under the controller's area of responsibility. In addition, traditional accounting functions have now become more complex; a controller must know about all of the following:

- The costs and risks associated with outsourcing various accounting functions.
- The impact of tax laws on how the department collects and aggregates information.
- Changes in accounting standards and their impact on accounting reports.
- Changes in the reporting requirements of the Securities and Exchange Commission (for publicly held companies).

It would take a perpetual student to have an in-depth knowledge of all these areas, so it is more common for the controller to manage a cluster of highly trained subordinates who are more knowledgeable in specific areas, and who can provide advice as problems arise.

In short, the role of the controller has expanded beyond that of a pure accountant to someone with broad management and interpersonal skills who can interact with other departments, as well as manage the activities of an increasingly well-educated group of subordinates, while also working with them to further their professional careers. This is a much more difficult role for the modern controller, requiring someone with at least as much management experience as accounting knowledge.

 ## IMPACT OF ETHICS ON THE ACCOUNTING ROLE

With the globalization of business, competition has become more intense. It is possible that the ethical foundations to which a company adheres have deteriorated in the face of this pressure. There have been innumerable examples in the press of falsified earnings reports, bribery, kickbacks, and employee thefts. There are vastly more instances of ethical failings that many would perceive to be more minimal, such as employee use of company property for personal use, "smoothing" of financial results to keep them in line with investor expectations, or excessively robust sales or earnings forecasts. The controller and the accounting staff in general play a very large role in a company's ethical orientation, for they control or have some influence over the primary issues that are most subject to ethical problems—reported earnings, cash usage, and control over assets. This section discusses how the accounting function can modify a company's ethical behavior—for good or bad.

The accounting function can have a serious negative impact on a company's ethical standards through nothing more than indifference. For example, if the controller continually acquiesces to management demands to slightly modify the financial statements to achieve certain targets, this may eventually lead to larger and larger alterations. Once the controller has set a standard for allowing changes to reported earnings, how can the controller define where to draw the line? Examples of such modifications are:

▪ Allowing sales from the next period to be included in the preceding accounting period.
▪ Not charging an inventory item to expense, knowing that it is obsolete.

- Spreading recognition of an expense over multiple periods, when it should be recognized at once.
- Maintaining an inadequate allowance for doubtful accounts.

Another example is when the accounting staff does not enforce control over assets; if it conducts a fixed-asset audit and finds that a television has been appropriated by an employee for several months, it can indirectly encourage continuing behavior of this kind simply by taking no action. Other employees will see that there is no penalty for removing assets and will then do the same thing. Yet another example is when the accounting staff does not closely review employee expense reports for inappropriate expenditures. Once again, if employees see that the expense report rules are not being enforced, they will include more expenses in their reports that should not be included. Thus, the accounting staff has a significant negative influence over a company's ethical standards simply by not enforcing the rules.

The previous argument can be turned around for an active accounting department. If the controller and the rest of the accounting staff rigidly enforce company policies and procedures and acquire a reputation for no deviations from these standards, the rest of the corporation will be dragged into line. It is especially important that the controller adhere closely to the *highest* standards, for the rest of the accounting staff will follow the controller's lead. Conversely, if the controller does not maintain a high ethical standard, the rest of the accounting staff will have no ethical leader and will lapse into apathy. Accordingly, in a sense, the controller is a company's chief ethics officer, since the position has such a strong influence over ethics. It is a rare week that passes without some kind of ethical quandary finding its way to the controller for resolution.

Drawing the Line

A new controller may have been specifically hired due to lack of experience, with the management team hoping they can steamroll ethically suspect business practices past the new hire. Thus it is useful to promptly inquire into the reason for the last controller's departure, and to also call the internal and external auditors to discuss their views of how far the company has stretched accounting rules in the past.

It is not sufficient to merely say that the accounting staff must uphold high ethical standards, if the standards are not defined. To avoid this problem, the controller should create and enforce a code of ethics. This document may not originate with the controller—many chief executive officers (CEOs) and CFOs prefer to take on this task. However, the controller can certainly push for an ethical code to be developed higher in the organization. Some illustrative topics to include in a code of ethics are:

- Bidding, negotiating, and performing under government contracts
- Compliance with antitrust laws
- Compliance with securities laws and regulations
- Conflicts of interest
- Cost consciousness
- Gifts and payments of money
- Leave for military or other federal service
- Meals and entertainment
- Preservation of assets
- Restrictive trade practices
- Use of company assets

Once the code of ethics has been created, it must be communicated to all employees. Once again, this is the CEO's job, but the controller should constantly reinforce it with his or her staff. It is especially helpful if the controller visibly refers to the ethical code whenever an ethical issue arises, so that the accounting staff knows that the controller is decisively adhering to the code.

A code of ethics becomes the starting point in the series of judgments a controller must follow when confronted with an ethical issue. The decision tree is:

- **Consult the code of ethics.** Use the code of ethics as the basis for any ethics-related decision. A senior company officer would have difficulty forcing the controller to adopt a different course of action than what is prescribed by the code. If the controller feels it is necessary to take a course of action contrary to what is stated in the code, then document the reasons for doing so. If there is no code, then proceed to the next step.
- **Discuss with immediate supervisor.** The controller's immediate supervisor is probably either the CFO, chief operating officer (COO), or CEO. Consulting with them for advice is a reasonable second step in the absence of a code of ethics. However, if the supervisor is the one causing the ethical problem, then skip this step and proceed to the next one.
- **Discuss with a trusted peer.** There is usually someone within the company in whom the controller places a great deal of trust. If so, consult with this person in regard to the proper course of action. Be more

circumspect in doing so with a person outside the company, since this runs the risk of spreading information elsewhere, with possible deleterious consequences. If there is no one with whom to discuss the issue, then proceed to the next step.

▪ **Discuss with the company's ethics committee.** If there is an ethics committee, this is a good forum for discussion. Unfortunately, many companies do not have such a committee, or it meets so infrequently that the immediate needs of the controller may not be met through this approach. In either case, proceed to the next step.

▪ **Discuss with the board's audit committee.** Many boards have an audit committee, which should be comprised entirely of independent directors. If so, the controller should take his or her concerns to this group. Keep in mind that this is a serious step, since the controller is now going around the corporate reporting structure, which may have unenviable consequences later on if the controller chose not to tell senior management of this action.

▪ **Consider leaving the company.** If all these avenues are untenable or result in inadequate advice, the controller should seriously consider leaving the company in the near future. Reaching this final step probably means that the ethical issue is caused by senior management, and also that there are no outside checks on their ethical behavior, such as an audit committee.

Deciding When to Quit

It is exceptionally damaging for a new controller to be involved in any situation that has even the slightest taint of accounting scandal, since it is nearly impossible to be hired into a succeeding job where this problem is known. Unfortunately, it is frequently better for the new controller to leave a new position where ethical concerns are rampant, rather than to stay on the job and attempt to fix the underlying issues. To assist in making the difficult stay-or-quit decision, consider finding a senior-level mentor who can offer unbiased advice on the correct course of action. ▪

In summary, the accounting staff has a large role in enforcing ethical standards throughout a company, since it has such strong influence over several key areas that require ethical judgments, such as the quality of reported earnings, control over assets, and the uses of cash. Accordingly, it is very much in the controller's interests to have a code of ethics that the accounting staff can adhere to in enforcing the appropriate ethical standards.

EVOLVING ROLE OF ACCOUNTING

Though there are many variables that can impact the direction of the accounting function and the controller's role in the future, there are a few broad trends that are likely to continue, and from which you can predict the evolving role of accounting.

The accounting function is in the midst of a fundamental change from being a clerical group without significant training to a cadre of experienced technicians and managers. Though there will always be a need for clerical help (indeed, this group will continue to comprise the majority of the department), there will be an increasing focus on hiring more experienced personnel. This prediction is based on the technological trend that brings continued levels of automation to the accounting function, thereby reducing the need for clerks. Also, the same trend toward more technology means that a greater proportion of the accounting employees must have better training in how to use the new hardware and software.

The accounting department is likely to become a more common route to top management positions. The accounting area has always been a fertile one for training people in the nuts and bolts of transactions and how they must function. This is useful for a lower-level manager, but now that the department also handles a multitude of additional tasks, such as cost analysis, target costing, and advanced finance functions, it becomes a much better training area for higher-level managers. The company of the future will not only see large numbers of well-trained people advancing out of accounting, but they will also see a large proportion of new recruits clamoring to get into it, so that they too can receive the necessary training and experience.

This section discussed some evolutionary changes to expect in the role of the accounting function and the controller. It is likely that there will be a decrease in the proportion of purely clerical positions in the accounting area in favor of more senior personnel with extra technical and management skills. Also, because of the greater breadth of responsibility to be obtained in this area, it will become more common for senior management personnel to come out of this area.

CHAPTER TWO

Controller's Responsibilities

Importance of This Chapter

This chapter contains a detailed job description for the new controller. If you are new to the position, the number of tasks may at first seem overwhelming, since they cover so many subject areas. The best way to handle the situation is to first address crucial short-term issues like cash forecasting and meeting debt requirements, and then delegate tasks to the more capable staff, such as assistant controllers.

A controller's job can vary dramatically based on a company's size and whether it has other managers who handle related functions. If a company is small and there are few other managers, the controller may end up with a formidable list of tasks on the job description. However, as a company grows in size, the role becomes more precisely and narrowly defined. This chapter covers the full range of the activities that may be assigned to a controller, beginning with the classical management areas of planning, controlling, reporting, and maintaining key accounting processes, and expanding into ancillary functions that may become part of the controller's job, depending on the circumstances. In addition, the chapter touches on variations in the controller's title and why the term *controller*, though most commonly used, is perhaps not the best description for the job. The chapter concludes with a review of the relations between the controller and chief financial officer (CFO), the future job description of the controller, and how to manage in an explosive growth environment. This wide-ranging discussion gives the reader a comprehensive view of the controller's job.

VARIATIONS ON THE TITLE

Numerous titles can be applied to the position of the chief accounting officer (CAO); however, the most common title used is controller. The duties are sometimes assumed by a chief accountant, office manager, comptroller, treasurer, assistant treasurer, or secretary. However, with the increased emphasis on accounting control, increased management duties, and for additional statistical and financial decision-making information, the duties of the position are more frequently being segregated into the role of a separate manager called the controller. This is especially true in larger organizations, where there is much more specialization. The term controller is an unfortunate one, for it seems to emphasize the control function only; as the reader will find after reading this chapter, there are a number of other basic functions this person performs, such as planning, reporting, and management, that are just as important as the control function.

The CAO title is a more complete description of the position. However, in some organizations, the CAO is considered a separate and higher-level position than the controller, so we do not use that title in this book in reference to the controller position.

The term comptroller is a more old-fashioned term for the controller, whose use is declining. It is seen in somewhat greater concentrations in government and not-for-profit entities.

PLANNING FUNCTION

The establishment and maintenance of an integrated plan of operation is a major function of the controller. The business objective is usually to earn a profit, and planning is necessary to fulfill it, for profits are difficult to create. Visualize, then, the role of the modern controller in business planning.

First, there is a responsibility to see that a plan exists and that it is supported by all levels of management. The implication of an integrated plan is that all parts will link together to support the business objective. For this reason, all members of management must participate willingly and contribute to the information in the plan. It must be the company's plan and not the controller's plan. The controller's primary task is to act as the coordinator who assembles and maintains the plan. The result is a master budget and a number of supporting schedules. In more detail, the following points describe the controller's key tasks related to the plan:

- Verify that the revenue plan can be achieved, given the number and productivity of the sales staff, the presence of any bottlenecks within the company, the impact of product life cycles, and so forth.
- Verify that the production plan supports the sales schedule. This involves comparing the amount projected to be sold to the amount to be produced, while factoring in the amount of finished goods inventory already on hand. This also requires judgment regarding the ability of the production operation to increase its output, as necessary, based on skill levels, bottlenecks, raw material sources, and so on.
- Verify that expense levels are in proportion to other activities. For example, the utilities expense must go up if the company is adding a facility, while the travel expense must increase if there will be a larger sales staff. You should also address the need for any step costs, which involve the addition of entirely new expenses at certain activity levels, such as adding a shift, a machine, a facility, or an employee.
- Verify that the organization is spending an adequate amount on the correct set of research and development projects, which includes an adequate mix of low-risk and high-risk projects.
- Verify that there is sufficient funding for the projected activity. If there is not a sufficient amount of debt or equity funding, the plan must be recast on a smaller scale.

Once the plan has been completed, the controller should test or appraise its adequacy and report to the CFO or chief executive officer (CEO) on the results of this analysis. It must be judged based on the following concerns:

- In light of past experience, is it realistic?
- Does it reflect economic conditions that are expected to prevail in the period of the plan?
- Does it include the expected cost of commodities during the budget period?

- Is there a reasonable probability that actual results could vary from the budget, and if so, to what extent?
- Does it meet the company's requirements for return on investment and such other ratio or other tests as may be applicable?

Some of the testing and analysis will be accomplished as preliminary plans are formulated, and the rest will await the total picture. However and whenever it is done, the controller is the counselor and coordinator, extending advice and suggestions to all who need it during the plan preparation. Final responsibility for the plan rests with the CEO, and responsibility for each operating function must be that of the manager in charge of each function. Nonetheless, though responsibility for the plan lies elsewhere, the controller should be deeply immersed in the underlying mechanics and assumptions of the plan.

CONTROL FUNCTION

The controller is responsible for the system of controls used to monitor accounting transactions. This is of considerable importance if the company's books are audited, since the outside auditors may rely to some extent on the system of controls when designing their testing procedures. Controls are of particular importance for a publicly held company, since a robust control system is required, and the company must attest to its adequacy.

The controller should map out all control points in the company and periodically monitor them to ensure that they are operating as planned. Further, these controls may have to be changed from time to time to reflect changes in the operations of the business. These changes may involve the addition of new controls, or possibly the elimination of old controls that are now redundant. For example, if the business were to acquire another company, the controller would need to assess the control systems of the acquired business and integrate them into those of the parent company.

Controls can negatively impact the efficiency of company operations, so the controller should periodically assess the cost and benefit of maintaining each control, and decide whether some controls can be eliminated without increasing the risk of loss to a significant extent.

Control systems should be modified with considerable deliberation, since controls are generally considered to be the responsibility of the controller, and so control failures do not reflect well upon the perceived performance of the accounting department. Thus, most controllers are quite cautious when altering these systems.

REPORTING FUNCTION

The reporting function is closely related to both the planning and control functions. Reporting is essential to make planning and control effective. Yet the reporting function is not merely one of presentation of tabulations and is not wholly routine. Moreover, the management that makes decisions often cannot be kept adequately informed solely from periodic statements regardless of how well designed they may be. The reporting function encompasses the *interpretation* of the figures, and the controller's duty is not discharged until management actually understands what is being presented. At a minimum, this means that the controller should include an interpretive cover letter with the monthly financial statements, describing key changes during the month, and possibly also noting events that are expected to occur in the near future. If there are particularly important items to bring to the attention of management, then the controller should meet with those managers able to act on the information and ensure that they are fully aware of the issues.

In addition, the controller may be required to report to outside entities, which usually calls for some reformatting and expansion of the internal reports. Typical recipients of reports are shareholders, creditors, the general public, customers, and the Securities and Exchange Commission (SEC).

Using Reports to Meet Fellow Managers

In many companies, the only product the rest of the management team sees from the controller is periodic reports. Knowing this, the new controller should use a discussion of the delivery, format, and content of reports as an excuse to meet and gain feedback from the management team. Review their reporting needs with them and make sure they promptly receive the revised information. There is no better way to make a good first impression. ▪

ACCOUNTING FUNCTION

The systematic recording of financial transactions is often regarded as the principal function of the controller. The controller is expected to apply sound accounting principles and practices within the company, as well as to stay current on the latest technological advances, so that this can be done in the most effective and efficient manner possible. For example:

- **Benchmarking key practices.** Regularly compare the performance of the accounting department for various tasks against the results of other accounting functions at other companies, not necessarily in the same industry, to see if anyone else is doing it better, and, if so, to copy their practices into the accounting department.
- **Using electronic transactions.** It is possible to send and receive most business transactions and payments with business partners by electronic means, which introduces a variety of efficiencies.
- **Installing new systems.** There are a broad array of systems that can improve the efficiency of the accounting department. These include a company-wide enterprise resources planning system, centralized accounting software, automated timekeeping solutions, and warehouse management systems.
- **Reducing cycle time.** The controller should actively engage in cycle time reduction, so that the time required to complete the primary transactions is greatly reduced. This allows a company to act more quickly, as well as to generate information about the results of its actions, both of which allow it to compete at a higher level.
- **Outsourcing accounting functions.** The controller should look into handing some or all accounting functions over to suppliers who are better equipped to handle key transactions. For example, many companies now outsource their payroll processing to suppliers that calculate taxes, make tax deposits, and pay employees by direct deposit. The controller should review this option for other accounting functions, too.

All of these new methodologies ensure that today's controller will be armed with enough tools to greatly improve the operational effectiveness of the accounting function.

ADDITIONAL CONTROLLER FUNCTIONS IN SMALLER COMPANIES

The controller of a smaller company will find that the position includes a number of additional tasks besides those already enumerated in the last section. This is because a small company cannot afford to also hire a CFO, an office manager, an information technology manager, and a human resources director. Consequently, all of these functions may fall on the controller.

The most common additional functions that a controller will take on are those in the finance area. These tasks are normally handled by the CFO, which is a position that many small companies dispense with if they have minimal funding needs or are not publicly held. The primary tasks of the finance function are:

- Acquiring insurance coverage
- Conducting public offerings
- Dealing with investors
- Dealing with lenders
- Determining customer credit levels
- Entering into hedging transactions
- Investing pension funds
- Investing surplus funds

Of the tasks normally handled by a CFO, the controller usually has little trouble in managing insurance, credit, and investment decisions. However, conducting a public offering is usually well outside the experience of most controllers, and so it would behoove a controller to recognize this inadequacy and bring in qualified help if a company decides in favor of a public offering. In particular, going public requires an inordinate amount of work to prepare the quarterly Form 10-Q and Form 10-K, as well as dealing with auditors for quarterly reviews and annual audits. Thus, going public will likely require a significant increase in the staffing of the accounting department.

A small company, usually one with less than 100 employees, frequently does not have a human resources manager. This means that the function, once again, must be managed by the beleaguered controller. Many of these new functions are administrative and procedural in nature—tasks for which most controllers are amply qualified. However, others, such as career planning and recruiting, are not. These latter tasks are sometimes shifted elsewhere in the organization, depending on who is most qualified to handle them. The most typical human resources functions are:

- Administering changes to the pension plan
- Administering new-employee paperwork
- Monitoring employee bonus plans
- Conducting employee safety training
- Conducting recruiting for all positions
- Devising a career plan for key managers

- Operating stock purchase plans
- Maintaining employee files
- Monitoring employee benefit plans
- Processing workers' compensation claims
- Updating the employee manual

Given the large proportion of clerical tasks in the human resources function, which are similar to the clerical functions of the accounting area, most controllers are fairly comfortable in administering this department. Some tasks, such as safety training and administering the pension plan, require some extra knowledge to handle.

Taking Additional Tasks to an Extreme

In one of the author's first positions as a controller, there was no janitorial staff—everyone cleaned up after themselves. One day, a toilet overflowed in the bathroom next to the author's office. While he was mopping up the water, the phone rang—a venture capitalist was calling to inquire about investing funds. The author took the call with a mop in one hand. ▪

The most common additional function for the controller to manage is administration. This includes the secretarial pool (if any), the reception function, all office equipment, and the telephone system. Because this area impacts all functions, it is common to have a disproportionate volume of complaints about it that take up an excessive amount of a controller's time. Accordingly, it is frequently handed off to an assistant controller. In addition, it is wise to outsource the repair and maintenance of all office equipment and the telephone system to a qualified supplier. This reduces the controller's day-to-day management to contacting suppliers and ensuring that the administrative staff is supplemented by a sufficient number of temporary help to complete short-term projects, such as special mailings, that pass through this area. The most common administrative functions are:

- Answering incoming calls
- Ensuring that all office equipment is operational
- Ensuring that the telephone system is operational
- Managing administrative staff
- Planning for the timely replacement of aging office equipment

- Handling incoming and outgoing mail
- Working with temporary help agencies to bring in personnel for special projects

Finally, the controller sometimes manages the information technology function. Most small companies maintain only the minimum number of computer applications, and these are usually packaged software, which allows them to avoid having a full-time department to handle this function. Instead of a separate department, the controller is in charge of backing up the computer system, ensuring that it is repaired promptly, that the system is expanded as the situation requires, and that new software is implemented in an efficient manner. Due to the highly technical nature of this work, a controller is well advised to outsource as much of this work as possible rather than dealing with it internally; not only does this approach reduce the controller's workload, but it also brings in much more qualified personnel than most small companies can afford to keep in-house. The main computer services functions are:

- Backing up the computer system
- Enforcing computer security standards
- Expanding systems as needed
- Maintaining all hardware and software
- Maintaining and repairing the computer network
- Providing system training to employees

The controller must be especially careful to make provisions for system crashes. This means that there must not only be daily backups of the database, but also offsite storage of the backups to ensure that they are not damaged if the main facility is destroyed. This should also include power backup systems to ensure that the computers remain operational even if the main power source goes down. The controller should also consider a disaster recovery plan that details how to make the system operational again as soon as possible in the event of a major problem. Though other parts of the information technology function can be outsourced, this one must be handled internally and correctly—if the controller does not prevent a serious computer crash that renders key systems inoperable, this may have a major—and negative—impact on senior management's view of how the controller is performing.

There are additional areas that the controller of a smaller company may find him- or herself supervising. The most likely areas are human resources, administration, computer services, and finance. The controller is well advised to outsource as much of this extra work as possible in order to put it in the hands of experts from suppliers, while also handing off selected tasks to other members of the organization who may be more qualified to perform them. The remaining tasks must be managed by the controller or a subordinate. Because these are areas in which most controllers are only partially trained, this can involve a very rapid and intensive learning experience.

 ## CONTROLLER'S JOB DESCRIPTION

Though the previous sections briefly discussed a number of the main aspects of the controller's job, they do not show a complete view of the position's responsibilities. This section answers that need by showing a complete controller job description. The description is summarized into subheadings, so that tasks are noted under such categories as finance, human resources, or information technology, which allows the reader to ignore those broad functional areas that do not apply to him or her. The tasks are noted in the order in which they are most likely to be the controller's responsibility, starting with accounting, finance, and administration, and then progressing through the information technology and human resources functions. Also, the description assumes that there is a staff handling all transactions, so it does not refer to actually handling specific transactions, only ensuring that they are correct. The description is as follows:

- *Position Title:* Controller
- *Reports To:* Chief Financial Officer or Chief Executive Officer
- *Supervises:* All accounting, finance, administration, information technology, and human resources personnel (varies by size of company and presence of other managers).
- *Tasks:*
  - *Accounting*
      Assist in the annual audit as required.
      Assist in the quarterly review as required (for public companies).
      Ensure that accounts payable are not paid earlier than required.
      Ensure that accounts receivable are collected promptly.
      Ensure that all reasonable discounts are taken on accounts payable.
      Ensure that customer billings are issued promptly.
      Ensure that job costs are calculated.
      Ensure that the monthly bank reconciliation is completed.

Issue interim management reports as needed.
Issue timely financial statements.
Issue timely reports to the SEC (for public companies).
Maintain an orderly accounting filing system.
Maintain the chart of accounts.
Manage outsourced functions.
Manage the accounting staff.
Update the accounting reports for any changes in accounting standards.
Manage the production of the annual budget.
Process payroll in a timely manner.
Provide financial analyses as needed.
Maintain a robust system of accounting controls.

- *Finance*
  Arrange for banking services.
  Arrange for debt financing.
  Conduct public offerings.
  Invest excess cash.
  Invest pension funds.
  Issue credit to customers.
  Maintain insurance coverage.
  Maintain lender relations.
  Manage the finance staff.
  Monitor cash balances.
- *Administration*
  Bring in temporary personnel for special projects.
  Ensure that mail is properly distributed and issued.
  Ensure that office equipment is operational.
  Manage outsourced maintenance work.
  Manage the secretarial staff.
  Upgrade office equipment as needed.
- *Information Technology*
  Back up the computer system.
  Implement hardware and software.
  Maintain a disaster recovery plan.
  Maintain computer security systems.
  Manage the information technology staff.
  Manage outsourced functions.
  Provide system training.
  Select hardware and software.

Human Resources
Administer safety training.
Administer the pension plan.
Monitor employee bonus plans.
Monitor employee benefit plans.
Maintain employee files.
Maintain employee manual.
Manage career planning.
Operate stock purchase plans.
Manage the human resources staff.
Process workers' compensation claims.
Recruit employees.

This generic and very wide-ranging controller job description can be used as the basis for a more customized description that is tailored to individual circumstances.

RELATIONSHIP OF THE CONTROLLER TO THE CHIEF FINANCIAL OFFICER

In a larger company, there is a clear division of tasks between the controller and the CFO. However, there is no clear delineation of these roles in a smaller company, because there is usually no CFO. As a company grows, it acquires a CFO, who must then wrestle away some of the controller's tasks that traditionally belong under the direct responsibility of the CFO. This transition can cause some conflict between the controller and CFO. In addition, the historical promotion path for the controller has traditionally been through the CFO position; when that position is already occupied and is likely to stay that way, there can be some difficulty with the controller. This section addresses these issues.

In a small company, the controller usually handles all financial functions, such as setting up and maintaining lines of credit, managing cash, determining credit limits for customers, dealing with investors, handling pension plan investments, and maintaining insurance policies. These are the traditional tasks of the CFO, and when a company grows to the point of needing one, the CFO will want to take them over from the controller. This can turn into a power struggle, though a short-lived one, because the controller always reports to the CFO and will not last long if there is no cooperation. Nonetheless, this is a difficult situation, for the controller has essentially taken a step down in the organizational structure upon the arrival of the CFO. For example, the CFO replaces the controller on the executive committee. If the controller is an ambitious one, this will probably lead to that person's departure in the near term. If the controller is a good one, this is a severe loss, for someone with a detailed knowledge of a company's processes and operating structure is extremely difficult to replace.

The controller should take a job elsewhere if he or she perceives that the person newly filling the CFO position is a roadblock to further advancement. However, this does not have to be a dead-end position. The controller should talk to the CFO about career prospects within the company and suggest that there may be other responsibilities that can replace those being switched to the CFO. For example, a small minority of controllers manage the materials management department; this will become increasingly common as controllers realize that much of the paperwork they depend on originates in that area and that they can acquire better control over their processes by gaining experience in this area. There may also be possibilities in the areas of administration, human resources, and information technology, which are sometimes run by controllers. The fact that there is a new CFO does not mean that a controller should immediately quit; there may be other opportunities involving related tasks that can shift the controller's career in other directions.

Finding a New Role Under a CFO

One of the reasons why a CFO is hired is to acquire other companies. If so, the new controller not only does not have to worry about being in a dead-end job, but even has a large number of new positions to choose from, since the acquiring company has the right to staff the accounting management positions of all acquired companies in any manner it chooses. At worst, the acquired accounting departments may be centralized, leaving the controller with the massive chore of creating a single large accounting function for the entire conglomerate. ▪

The CFO position is one with an extreme emphasis on money management, involving such tasks as determining the proper investment vehicles for excess cash, dealing with lenders regarding various kinds of debt, making presentations to financial analysts, and talking to investors. None of these tasks are ones that the controller is trained to perform. Instead, the traditional controller training involves handling transactions, creating financial statements, and examining processes and controls. The requirements for the CFO position and the training for the controller position are so different that it seems strange for the controller to be expected to advance to the CFO position, and yet that is a common expectation among accountants. As noted in the next section, the controller may not want to assume that the CFO position is an obvious next step, and that perhaps the controller position may now lead into other management areas.

 ## FUTURE CHANGES IN THE CONTROLLER'S ORIGINS AND RESPONSIBILITIES

The accounting function has changed drastically over the last half-century, and the controller has changed along with it. Where the position used to require someone with a tight focus on processing transactions and financial statements, the job now requires much more managerial skill, as well as a general idea of such diverse bodies of knowledge as taxation, business process improvement, outsourcing, and information technology. This calls for a controller with a much more diverse skill set than was previously the case. It also points toward a different career direction for the controller of the future.

The controller of the future will come from a different educational and experience background. Most companies currently call on the "Big Four" auditing firms for their controllers, and many auditors enter the Big Four on the assumption that they will eventually be hired by their clients into that role. However, auditors only are trained in the areas of accounting standards, verifying the accuracy of financial statements, and reviewing underlying accounting processes to ensure that they function correctly. Though these tasks are still part of the controller's job description and will remain so for the foreseeable future, an increasing proportion of the controller's job now includes tasks for which an auditor is not prepared. These new tasks include computer systems selection, implementation, and management, as well as outsourcing, cycle time reduction, benchmarking, and process reengineering. Because of these new tasks, company management will find that it can fill the position with more thoroughly qualified personnel from other sources. The better companies will look to consulting firms for people with a detailed knowledge of process improvement and systems management, as well as to people who have spent their careers in corporate accounting, rather than in auditing. Finally, top management will eventually realize that controllers do not have to be certified public accountants (CPAs); on the contrary, it will be more important to have good management skills and be surrounded by a team of highly qualified accounting professionals who can advise on the more technical accounting issues. In short, controllers will come from other sources than auditing firms, because that source no longer provides people with a complete set of skills.

The future direction of the controller position is probably toward something with much more responsibility. Companies are competing more and more on such issues as rapid cycle times and low costs, and the controller is an integral part of the work required to improve them. As management realizes that the controller has an enormous impact on these most critical competitive areas, it will place the controller in charge of them. This means that the controller of the future will become more of a chief process officer (CPO), with general authority to alter processes. This function will cross department lines as much as the processes that the controller is fixing, so the position must have added authority to make changes. This added authority may raise the controller in the management hierarchy to a point above those of other department heads. We may also find that the controller will be more likely to manage new areas that are heavily driven and influenced by processes, especially materials management.

As the controller position adds companywide processes to its area of authority, the controller will find that, due to this extra responsibility, promotional opportunities will veer away from the CFO position and toward the chief operating officer (COO) position. This does not mean that there will be a wholesale abandonment of the CFO position, since that remains the goal of most controllers, but controllers will have such an in-depth knowledge of a company's operations that they will be contenders for promotion to be COO.

There are changes already underway that are preventing many controllers from reaching the coveted CFO position, and which may provide further impetus in the direction of promotions to the COO position. The trouble with the CFO position is that its job requirements are significantly different from those of a controller, and few controllers are trained to take over the job. It involves lender and investor relations, investing activities, risk management, and taking a company public. Thus, the job requirements for the CFO position really call for someone with treasury or Wall Street experience, not accounting experience.

If we do see CFOs being promoted from directions other than the controller position, this also calls into question the traditional reporting relationship that has the controller reporting to the CFO. If the CFO does not have a background that yields any knowledge of the accounting field, then it does not make much sense to have that person control the function. Instead, it may become more appropriate to have the controller report straight to the CEO alongside the CFO.

■ MANAGING RAPID GROWTH

A controller sometimes finds him or herself in a situation in which a company has just released a "hot" product, it embarks on a massive expansion of sales territories, or it goes on an acquisition binge, which results in a phenomenal rate of growth. This frequently causes a difficult situation for the controller, because there are never enough resources to handle the flood of transactions swamping the department. This section discusses how to prioritize tasks in such an environment, and how this fundamentally changes the controller's job. It also notes the same issues for the finance and human resources functions, in case the controller is in charge of those areas as well.

In a rapid growth environment, the key focus of the accounting staff is on the conservation of cash. This is because a growing company is constantly investing cash in working capital and facilities, leaving little cash available for further growth or as a reserve in case of a sudden downturn in company fortunes. The controller plays a major part in cash conservation. For example:

- **Send invoices promptly.** It is difficult to collect cash from customers if they have not yet been billed. To avoid this problem, the controller must pay strict attention to the billing process, especially the speed with which invoices are created and sent. This may also involve a switch to electronic invoicing, an alteration in payment terms to encourage faster payment, or delivery of the invoice with the shipment. Any of these system modifications will result in a faster cash flow.
- **Collect accounts receivable promptly.** Increasing the speed of collections also improves the cash flow. The controller can do this by adding more staff to the collections effort, concentrating the bulk of the collection effort on the largest overdue invoices, working closely with the sales staff to obtain payments, concentrating on issuing accurate invoices that customers cannot complain about, and tightening the terms of credit being offered.

Eliminate Errors to Conserve Cash

A major cause of delayed cash flow is billing errors. If an invoice is perfectly constructed and delivered to the correct customer contact, it will probably be paid approximately within terms. However, if anything goes wrong, the payment interval will likely double the standard terms. To avoid delays, double-check the larger invoices before they go out and verify contact information with the sales staff. ■

▪ **Conduct cost accounting promptly.** A growing company must know immediately if it is selling a product that is not returning enough of a profit; otherwise, it will not spin off enough cash flow to sustain a high rate of growth. The controller can push for a very rapid costing review of new products, both before they are issued as well as after they have been produced for a short time, to see if there are significant variances from expected margins. The results of these costing studies should be immediately communicated to upper management, so that steps can be taken to revise the product costs or prices to yield better profits.

If the controller also manages the finance function, there are several additional issues to consider in a rapid-growth environment. The main one is predicting future cash flows. This is because an accurate cash forecast tells management how much extra cash it will need from outside sources, as well as the timing of that need. This becomes the foundation for efforts to acquire additional debt or equity funding. In addition, the controller should keep a close watch over the risk and return of any investments, in order to maximize the company's investments while maintaining as low a risk profile as possible. Finally, the controller must devise an orderly system for clearing incoming payments through a system of lockboxes, funneling these payments into a central account, and then disbursing the money back out for accounts payable through outlying banks that take extra time to clear payments. This system of lockboxes and controlled disbursements maximizes the amount of a company's cash on hand, as well as the time period during which it can be used.

A controller may also be responsible for the human resources function in a rapid-growth situation. If so, the primary focus is on where to find qualified candidates for positions throughout the company. Without enough staff, no company has a chance of continuing its growth, so this is absolutely crucial. There are a variety of techniques available for finding new staff, such as the Internet, recruiting firms, paying bonuses to in-house staff to bring in acquaintances, and using targeted publications that are distributed to specific trade disciplines. Also, since the human resources staff is usually overwhelmed by its recruiting work, the controller can ease the work burden by outsourcing other tasks. For example, benefits and pension administration can go to a supplier.

This section summarized the controller's management functions in a rapid-growth situation. The controller function changes drastically in this environment. For example, th e accounting and finance areas must focus on cash management, while the human resources staff must focus on recruiting new employees, to the exclusion of any other activities.

CHAPTER THREE

Chief Financial Officer: From Controller to Facilitator of Change

Importance of This Chapter

The new controller needs to know all about the chief financial officer (CFO), not only because she reports to this position, but also because becoming a CFO may be the next logical step in the controller's career track. This chapter gives insights into the motivations and responsibilities of the position.

Years ago, chief executive officers (CEOs) were satisfied with finance chiefs who could manage the analysts on Wall Street, implement financial controls, manage initial public offerings (IPOs), and communicate with the board—in other words, possess strong financial skills. However, in today's business climate in which competitors appear out of thin air, where e-commerce has changed entire industries, and global competitors abound, the ability to change quickly has become a necessity for growth, if not for survival. CEOs are no longer satisfied with financial acumen. They are demanding more from their finance chiefs. They want individuals who can fill a multitude of roles: business partner, strategic visionary, communicator, confidant, and creator of value. Bottom-line CEOs want someone who will drive improvement quickly—a facilitator of change. This chapter focuses on how to drive change in an organization. It is not about running a meeting or facilitating groups, but about implementing critical management practices that will help CFOs implement major business changes.

UNDERSTANDING WHAT CHIEF EXECUTIVE OFFICERS WANT

Facilitating change sounds simple until you are in the trenches trying to make significant improvements in how a business operates. Chief executive officers want creators of value, but often do not see that redefining the role of finance. In some organizations, line managers see finance as a necessary but unpopular support function. In other organizations, norms have developed within the senior management group where there is an unwritten rule: "You don't ask too many tough questions about my area and I won't ask you too many questions about your area." In one case, a new CFO saw large opportunities for improvement. These opportunities were in the operational areas, and the president of those businesses did not need "the new guy" telling him what to do. Even though the new CFO had a good relationship with the CEO, any immediate improvement efforts became mired in political turmoil. Thus, moving from controller to facilitator of change is not an easy transition. However, it can be done if CFOs focus on several key concepts.

TASK OF THE CFO

In today's business climate, the quote "There are the quick and then there are the dead" is quite true. How does a CFO drive change quickly? Creating value and becoming a business partner to the CEO means facilitating change that not only affects finance but also directly impacts the operating units. To accomplish this end, CFOs must become skilled in several key management practices. The CFO must:

- Develop and communicate a compelling finance agenda.
- Build a commitment to change within finance.
- Change executive management practices.
- Enlist the support of the CEO.
- Mobilize the organization.
- Institutionalize continuous improvement.

By applying these concepts, CFOs can begin to accelerate the implementation of major organizational changes, as seen in Exhibit 3.1.

DEVELOP AND COMMUNICATE A COMPELLING FINANCE AGENDA

CEOs say they want finance chiefs who can bring their organization to another level of performance. They want CFOs who are strategic thinkers and aggressive implementers, who can execute successfully. Because the finance agenda may affect the operating groups, an important skill is creating commitment around what is to be accomplished. One of the key reasons that change often fails is a decrease in organizational commitment. This often occurs when senior executives continuously change priorities, do not focus, or do not show their personal commitment to an effort by spending time managing the effort. To implement and then institutionalize change, senior executives need a constancy of purpose over a long period of time. The question becomes: How do you create stability and yet stay sufficiently flexible and dynamic to address market changes?

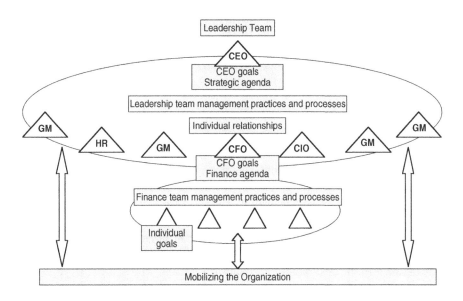

EXHIBIT 3.1   Becoming a Facilitator of Change

The first step in creating a constancy of purpose and building commitment is developing a clear finance agenda. The finance agenda describes the five to seven key outcomes to be accomplished in the next 12 months, stated in crisp, definitive language where there will be no doubt when they have been accomplished. Essentially, the finance agenda is a set of objectives that the CFO has memorized and can describe succinctly. For example, a strategic agenda may be:

▪ A fully functional shared services group for finance in the Americas
▪ A simplified and focused rolling budget process
▪ Books closed within three days
▪ A simple value-based scorecard and a value-based measurement system for each business
▪ Return-on-investment (ROI) calculations for any software implementation and a process for measuring the ROI on subsequent module installations
▪ Accurate monthly financial summaries for each of the business units

Sources of the Agenda

The CFO cannot run the risk of trying to lead the organization to achieve a set of goals that they do not care about, since this carries a high risk of failure. Instead, talk to the various company constituencies—managers, staff, creditors, investors, and so on—and determine what key problems are of major concern to them. By sprinkling these topics throughout the agenda, there will be much more commitment to accomplishing the total list. ▪

Interestingly enough, creating this agenda sounds simple, and many executives say they already have clear objectives. But the key questions are: Are you fluent in your ability to describe them from memory? Is your organization clear about them? When asked specifically, "What are the five to seven key outcomes that you need to accomplish this year?", few executives can explain what they need to accomplish from memory in specific, crisp language in only a few minutes. Even more troubling, the knowledge of corporate objectives drops rapidly, lower down in the organizational structure.

How does this affect organizational behavior? Competing priorities is a reality in today's organizations, yet it is an executive's job to help focus the energy of the organization on what is important and build commitment around those objectives. The first question people ask is whether the executive is personally committed. They draw their conclusions by observing his or her behavior.

Communicating a clear set of objectives is critical in telling the organization what is important. However, in today's information-overload work environment, a few presentations will not suffice. Communication experts say that senior executives often need to use every opportunity to repeat their messages to the point where they are literally "sick of repeating themselves." Only then do people begin to remember the message. Furthermore, this begins to reinforce the executive's personal commitment to the objectives.

Forcing yourself to memorize the strategic agenda allows you to communicate continuously. Imagine a CFO is standing in the elevator and a new business analyst asks him a question about the finance department. Or the CFO is in the cafeteria and a manager wonders whether what he is doing is adding value. If within two minutes the CFO can clearly, simply, and specifically cite what finance is trying to accomplish, the analyst in the elevator knows the focus. That person can then communicate the focus to peers with little translation error. Furthermore, a manager can immediately determine if what he or she is doing contributes to the overall direction of the finance organization, because the manager knows exactly what the CFO is trying to accomplish. This type of clarity, constancy of purpose, and reinforcement helps individuals commit to a direction.

Another benefit is that by keeping the agenda focused, specific integration among functions is much easier. For example, if a key objective for finance is implementing a balanced scorecard in the businesses, it is easy to determine whether the line executives also have that on their strategic agendas. If not, there is a disconnect, and it can be addressed immediately. If a CFO is having lunch with one of the business unit presidents, who asks if the organization could design a new supply-chain reporting mechanism, the CFO can immediately mentally scroll through his or her strategic agenda and understand the implications of this request. If this is not part of the agenda, the CFO can tell the unit president that this will not be possible in the near term. Because many decisions happen during such informal dialogues, people can determine the value of activities immediately since if something does not contribute to the overall finance agenda, it may not be worth doing. This discussion process makes the organization more flexible in its thinking.

Several years ago, a general manager strongly believed in this model. He knew exactly what he needed to accomplish and could state his objectives anywhere, anytime. He would use any and every opportunity with people in his organization and his peers to reinforce his message. Over time, everyone knew exactly what the business needed to accomplish. People began to realize how committed he was to accomplishing those objectives. They knew exactly what he wanted to achieve and could make a personal decision on whether they wanted to be on board. The majority decided to stay and help him meet those objectives; some who did not like where the organization was headed decided to leave. However, no one questioned the direction or his commitment to change. Also, because he was fluent about his objectives and his focus, any time another general manager or the senior vice president asked for help or additional work, he immediately knew how this would affect his goals. Because everyone knew what he was trying to accomplish, any time his organization was asked to do other work, he could use the strategic agenda to negotiate, because there would always be trade-offs. By observing his behavior, the organization began to mobilize around the required changes. There was no question about leadership spending enough time, no question about leadership driving change, and no question about what was important to the business. This organization consistently surpassed its financial, customer satisfaction, and employee satisfaction targets.

BUILD A COMMITMENT TO CHANGE WITHIN FINANCE

Once some thought has been given to the strategic agenda, it is time to build commitment around what the CFO wants to accomplish. If the CFO has developed a compelling finance agenda, the most important step toward commitment has already been taken, clearly describing what the CFO and the function need to accomplish. It is amazing how often this type of clarity is neglected, either because of not understanding how powerful this can be, political maneuvering that keeps accountabilities hazy, or too little time to be specific. Yet when people are asked to commit to something, the more they can understand the specific implications, the easier it is for them to make a decision about commitment.

A common misunderstanding is that people will only commit to something in which they have been involved in every step. This is not necessarily true. People want to be able to influence the direction (what needs to be done) and the approach (how things will be done) and have an open, authentic dialogue around the realism of the objectives. They do not always need to be involved in every step. Some executives exhibit reluctance in communicating their agenda and providing direction because they want it to "evolve from the team." This often leads to several consequences. First, people often become frustrated by the lack of direction and then make comments like, "He's not managing this department" or "She's getting the executive salary, but we always have to figure out what needs to get done." Second, people believe that most executives must be goal-driven, and therefore managers know what they want to accomplish; by not stating it explicitly, people begin to wonder. They wonder if the manager has a hidden agenda, if it is a test, or they begin to doubt the manager's leadership skills. It is much more effective to know what one wants to accomplish, use a straw model to begin the discussion, and openly listen to the staff and allow them to influence the agenda.

Another attempt to build commitment is often labeled "team building." Managers often believe that if they conduct a series of team-building exercises or off-sites, their team will suddenly be committed to driving change. Unfortunately, in most cases, people engage in the team-building exercises, but under the day-to-day pressures the new behaviors are most likely forgotten and rarely reinforced—especially if the senior executive only talks change, but does not reinforce the message with his own behavior. There is a mountain of evidence in the learning and training literature about how little learning transfers from external or simulated learning events back to on-the-job behaviors. Team building can be much more effective if it is integrated into day-to-day work. For example, several years ago, an executive requested team building to increase commitment for his staff. The conversation went like this:

Consultant: "I'm sure we could help, but before talking about team building, let's talk about what are you seeing that suggests team building is the answer. What do you want them to commit to?"

Executive: "Our meetings are totally unproductive—all we do is talk and talk with no decisions; no one is on the same page, and we can never wrap up."

Consultant: "What has been the impact of this?"

Executive: "We keep revisiting decisions, never coming to closure. Last time, we talked about whether we were going to assemble parts in Taiwan for almost two hours with no decision."

Consultant: "It sounds like there is a lot going on and not something we're going to address with one team-building session. It sounds like we need to begin addressing how the executive team works together. I have found that most managers hate dealing with all this touchy-feely stuff. They see no value in it. However, if we begin to address some of these issues as part of trying to accomplish an objective, people tend to be more open about the process. What's pressing right now that you need to accomplish in the short term?"

Executive: "We need to finalize our strategic marketing plan."

Consultant: "Now there is something people can probably sink their teeth into. We can address some of these behavior issues that you've cited as part of developing the strategic plan."

A prerequisite to many of these activities is the CFO's ability to explain what he wants to accomplish and why. The CFO needs to understand his personal motivations for why he wants to achieve certain goals. What drives him? Why is he passionate about these goals? If he is not passionate about a certain goal, why is he pursuing it? What will he do to ensure success? After he has had time to develop his agenda and the reasons why it is important, the CFO should think about and practice how he will tell his staff. There are a variety of ways that this can be done. The most critical factor is that the CFO engage in genuine dialogue with the staff, listening to their views and allowing them to influence his opinions. Some executives conduct an off-site in which they discuss the strategic agenda; others embed the discussions in their regular staff meetings. Having an open dialogue with the staff is critical. The following is an adaptation from a director of finance's (George's) off-site meeting.

"As you see on the agenda, we are going to spend most of our meeting talking about the agenda for finance and specific goals. Realize that this strategic agenda is what finance needs to accomplish this year. I'd like to spend the next few minutes describing each goal and why I think it's important. After that I'd like us to have an open discussion on whether these items make sense, since your individual and department goals will be tied to this agenda." The director goes on to explain each of his seven goals. The dialogue around one particular goal is worth highlighting. "One of the goals is to create tighter financial controls." One of the other directors challenges the goal. "George, is that really something we want to focus on? We just spent months decentralizing some of the processes because we were constantly getting complaints that we're like the audit police, always saying what the business could and could not do." George replies, "Bill, I understand your reluctance. I struggled with this one myself. But look at our numbers, almost everywhere you look we're struggling. Look at our new product development, over 50 percent of our new products produce little to no profit. Our travel expenses and miscellaneous expenses are totally out of sync with industry standards. I truly believe that successful businesses

have fiscal discipline and rigorous controls. The challenge will be in how we help our operating managers take more accountability for the numbers. We can't remain in the cop role. That's why this objective is tied to my second goal, which is the reconfiguration of finance so that we have our best analysts dedicated to different business units providing analytic support." Bill responds, "I still don't like it, but I can understand your point." "Absolutely," says George. "We need to think of this as version one, and that's why I wanted your input. We will probably have to revisit this after my discussions at the upcoming executive committee meeting."

Time to Build Support

The director of strategic planning at one Fortune 500 company claims that she spends 25 percent of her time determining the appropriate strategy and 75 percent convincing the rest of the company to follow it. The CFO is in a similar position—be prepared to budget a very large amount of time for communicating with the company about strategic issues. This is the single largest difference between the CFO and controller positions. ▪

This type of dialogue is important in building commitment. The key factor is how well the CFO maintains the balance between setting a definitive direction and letting the staff have input. The CFO should also help his staff understand that this is not a linear process. After his discussion with them, the finance agenda still needs to be discussed at the executive committee meeting, where the focus might change. However, it is important to solicit their input prior to that meeting.

A key element in obtaining commitment is the CFO's own behavior. Everyone has heard the cliche, "It's not what you say, but what you do." Too often, we forget. In one project, a senior vice president told his team that he would dedicate at least 50 percent of his time to the effort. One week after the effort started, he was spending at most two hours per week on the project. People started to question his leadership and his commitment. His reaction was, "They should know I'm committed. I authorized the effort, and I am providing the budget." Unfortunately, that is not enough. In many organizations, commitment is measured by how much time people spend on what they say is important. In this case, people interpreted the executive's behavior as a lack of leadership, they never fully committed themselves, and the effort stumbled.

CHANGE EXECUTIVE MANAGEMENT PRACTICES

Changing the finance organization is often hard work, but because the CFO has direct responsibility for that function, it is often easier than driving change across the operating units. Yet in many cases, change also needs to occur in those units. To begin this process, the executive team must develop a set of management practices that allows the CFO to implement his or her finance agenda and begin to function as an advisor and consultant to not only the CEO but also the operating units. Unfortunately, many executive teams develop management practices that are often counterproductive to implementing change quickly. Following is an example of several executive meetings that highlight how patterns often develop:

- **Team 1.** The group rarely gets together to discuss operations. When they do assemble, there is an unwritten rule that no one points out a deficiency in someone else's area. The prevailing climate is "don't mess with mine and I won't mess with yours." Executive meetings are characterized by a lot of dialogue, but little or no action. Rarely are action items or decisions documented. Individuals rarely challenge each other and almost never challenge the CEO
- **Team 2.** This team does get together to discuss operations. However, everyone needs to fully agree with a recommendation before it is acted on. The constant drive to consensus often takes so long that participants turn off and agree just to move on. Rarely is substantive conflict present. The meeting is characterized as nice and cordial. Meeting minutes may be taken, but they are lengthy and difficult to understand.
- **Team 3.** This team also meets, but many one-on-one meetings have taken place before or outside of the meeting either between the CEO and other executives or between executives. There is no common database of knowledge; no one is on the same page. The CEO or senior executive drives the meeting, pushing forward through the agenda. Others participate when their area is up for discussion and spend the time reading e-mail or finishing administrative tasks. Minutes might be taken.
- **Team 4.** These meetings are brawls. Managers get together and fight. Conflict rules the session; people challenge each other and debate each other. Debates are often subjective interpretations of data or opinions. There are no clear processes on how to work through information and come to resolution.

For a CFO, the focus is on ways in which to help the management team understand his or her new role, what he or she wants to accomplish, and how they need to contribute to those objectives. Therefore, understanding the management practices of the executive team is important. Changing these practices and the dynamics of the executive team is the first challenge in moving into a change agent role. Executive teams that are able to drive change through the organization, who operate and work toward a common agenda, and are able to work through many organizational challenges have the following characteristics (practices):

- **Regular meetings.** The executive team meets regularly to discuss operations. Research and practice have shown that if management teams do not meet on a regular basis to discuss work, the group slowly begins to splinter. Individuals may still be able to run their areas effectively, but cross-boundary issues become harder to resolve.
- **Constructive confrontation.** Because all individual executives are accountable to meet the business or function goals and are accountable as a team to meet the overall business goals, there is a clear expectation to question and challenge one another's operations.
- **Listening.** All executives actively listen to and are able to stimulate substantive and honest dialogue about issues and potential solutions.
- **Shared agenda.** The executive group reviews and challenges one another's strategic agendas to ensure consistency and integration across organizations. All of their goals directly and clearly reinforce the CEO's goals.
- **Clear feedback.** Managers have clear review processes in which they review operations, make course corrections, provide feedback, and ensure accountability.
- **Decisive, fast-paced meetings.** Meetings are held regularly to discuss operations in which it is expected that each participant provides input and advice to other areas and solicits input for his or her area. The pace is fast, yet the meeting is comprehensive. Decisions are made; actions are determined, documented, and communicated in a comprehensive manner.

Preventing Comfortable Meetings

The primary reason for a meeting is to reach a decision, which may require very little time. A long meeting is possibly a sign of a small amount of productive decision-making surrounded by a thick blanket of unnecessary chatting time. Managers use a variety of techniques to keep meetings short, such as removing chairs from the room, scheduling meetings in five-minute increments, and locking the doors as soon as a meeting has begun (thereby encouraging promptness).

- **Consensus with qualification decision-making.** Participants debate and look at all angles of a recommendation or impending decision. If consensus cannot be achieved after listening to all the options, the most senior individual will make the decision and everyone will be committed to its outcome. The decision is data driven and made quickly.
- **Data driven.** Decision-making is driven by data, and clear procedures and templates for the type of data needed are developed for decision-making purposes.
- **Role of support functions.** Support functions act as consultants to the operating units, challenging and working with them to improve performance.
- **Continuous improvement.** The executive team periodically reviews its own management processes to assess effectiveness. Based on these assessments, continuous improvement actions will be taken.

If an executive team does not operate in this manner, if finance is not given the liberty to challenge operations, or if finance is not seen as a strategic partner, changes in how the executive team operates may be in order. To begin this change, it is important to remember that this is the boss's team. The CFO is one of several peers, and in some cases, depending on the relationships, the power may be unequally distributed. The CFO might be able to influence some of the behaviors, but few major changes will take place unless the CEO is aware of the improvement potential and is willing to play a role. So how does the CFO begin the process of changing the practices of the management team?

ENLIST THE SUPPORT OF THE CHIEF EXECUTIVE OFFICER

An important step in change is creating the awareness that change is necessary. One of the most difficult areas to change is management process. Most successful executives have honed their managerial skills over many decades and have strong opinions of what works and what does not. Therein lies the opportunity. Today's business environment is quite different from that of just a few years ago. Often, the management team has new players, or the challenges confronting the organization are more intense. Those organizations that are able to change their management practices are those that have a greater likelihood of success. And those practices start at the top. Consequently, enlisting the support of the CEO in reshaping the management practices of the executive team will be critical. To begin this process, the CFO must find a way to create awareness about required changes. One way to do this is:

Step 1. Lay out the agenda for finance.
Step 2. Determine what will be required to implement the strategic agenda.
Step 3. Determine how the executive team will need to change and what is required from them to manage the implementation of the finance agenda.
Step 4. Develop an action plan on helping the CEO see the team's current dynamics, how they may need to change, and his role in that change effort.
Step 5. Meet with the CEO to discuss the strategic agenda and what will be needed from the executive team and from the CEO.
Step 6. Jointly develop a way to raise any issues with the executive team.

One approach to help create awareness is to look at best practices or use white papers, articles, or other print material as a way to help educate the CEO on what could be. Begin creating an awareness on how to improve the senior team dynamics. Discussing an article or summary can be a powerful way to begin the dialogue around change. In some cases, it may be effective to bring in an outsider to counsel the group on how it can be even more effective. Once the CFO understands the CEO's reaction to reshaping the executive team's management practices, he or she can jointly develop an action plan on how to introduce these changes. Following is an example of how one finance executive addressed the issue. The CFO met several times with his boss to discuss his observations and used an article as a neutral way to begin questioning some of the management practices. After several discussions, the senior vice president understood and agreed that there were improvement opportunities. Given the formal authority of the senior vice president and his ownership of the meeting, they decided that he would introduce the topic and lead the discussion at the next staff meeting.

Andre, the senior vice president, starts the meeting.

You'll notice one of the first items on our agenda is about our management practices. Several weeks ago, Cathy came to me with an article that she saw in a recent CFO magazine. Based on her reading, she thought that this would be of value to all of us. After a few discussions and after looking at the article myself, I think she's right. There are some interesting concepts in here. I don't necessarily agree with all of them, but I think it is something we should discuss implementing. There are some ideas I definitely want to put in place. So, I'd like each of you to spend five minutes reading this article and then we'll spend another 15 minutes talking about what elements we will implement.

After everyone finishes reading, he talks about the management practices he wants to put in place and solicits people's input and opinions. The executive group decides to bring in an outside advisor to talk to individual executives, assess the team's management practices by observing several key meetings, and then facilitate a workshop in which they will decide on some of the recommendations.

◾ MOBILIZE THE ORGANIZATION

Results can be achieved quickly when a large part of the organization is mobilized. Mobilization goes beyond communication, which is often characterized as a two-way exchange of information, to enlisting the active involvement of individuals. Communication is necessary, but not sufficient, in driving major organization changes quickly. Unfortunately, in many change efforts, this concept is misused in several ways:

- ◾ A project team spends weeks or in some cases months preparing a business case, a new design (new processes, new systems, new structure), and an implementation plan. These are then communicated to the organization through an elaborate communication plan that often involves challenge sessions or other activities to "involve" the organization. The assumption is that the organization is then mobilized and committed to the effort. Unfortunately, this is rarely so. In many cases, the executive team has never had the opportunity to clearly debate the plan in detail, they have not come up the learning curve together, and the most senior executive does not clearly demand that operating executives take accountability for the implementation. Consequently, it is often unclear whether the executive team is fully committed, and this message filters throughout the organization, causing a hesitancy to proceed and a lack of commitment. The organization is not mobilized.
- ◾ In other large change efforts, organizations spend weeks preparing elaborate communication plans incorporating the most advanced delivery mechanisms. In some cases, senior executives will give one or two presentations to show their commitment to the project. Yet the strategic agenda and how the project fits into the agenda are not clear. Maybe the executive

team went through several executive education sessions, but few executives have integrated the project into their objectives. Even fewer regularly talk about the project in their regular operations reviews. In some cases, the implementation is managed by a separate steering committee, further separating operating executives from accountability for project results. The project may or may not be discussed at the executive meetings. The organization intuitively senses these disconnects, and mobilization becomes much harder.

- In some change efforts, communication is often seen as a separate activity. There is a separate communication team with their own charter and work plan. The logic is that if this is not done, communication does not occur. There is some truth to this, and therefore having people focus on communication is important. However, more important is the fact that managers are responsible for communication. Communicating to the organization is one of the primary responsibilities of management, and if managers neglect this task, the organization cannot be mobilized.

Mobilization occurs around a specific purpose and specific individuals. People do not mobilize around a communications team. The communications team supports, with the exchange of information, an executive's efforts around mobilizing his or her people around a strategic agenda. People also become mobilized if they see the executive team devoting their attention to these objectives.

The CFO has already completed the first steps in mobilizing an organization by clarifying the strategic agenda, using every opportunity to communicate his or her objectives, and working with the executive team to create shared understanding and common management practices.

Once the organization understands what the CFO is trying to accomplish and is mobilized, he or she will need to sustain that momentum. This is usually accomplished by ensuring operating executive accountability and involvement, determining specific measures, having clear operations review processes in which the projects are discussed, providing feedback, and communicating as a normal course of action. As mentioned earlier, communication is often seen as a separate activity. To maintain momentum, communication must be seen as an integral part of the managerial process. Communication should not be seen as separate from managing the daily operations, and a key success factor is how well the CFO integrates communications.

Several years ago, the general manager of a small $100 million business firmly believed in integrating communications into daily operations.

Although she did have a communications manager, she set a clear expectation that communications was the responsibility of each director. This organization had one of the best communications efforts around—measurement-driven, clear expectations around communication, regular senior management involvement, communication events, communications integrated in performance reviews for supervisors and managers, and so on. Because this organization was measurement-driven, they could tell how well they were doing. Communication, however, left some room for improvement. After a brief analysis, it was determined that the issue was the way in which information received was actually communicated. There was a breakdown in communications after executive team meetings. People wanted to know what was decided. How often are decisions captured from executive team meetings in a way that people can immediately understand what was decided? The decision was made that during the executive meeting all major decisions would be documented, and then prior to the end of the meeting the decisions would be reviewed and the group would decide what could be posted. In some cases, because of the highly confidential nature of discussions or because of the timing of decisions, not everything could be posted. This information was then posted on the intranet, and directors would review these decisions in their staff meetings. By integrating communications as a part of normal operations and making it a managerial responsibility, this organization dramatically improved its communication effectiveness.

INSTITUTIONALIZE CONTINUOUS IMPROVEMENT

Facilitating change is an ongoing process—the more effective a CFO is at instituting a continuous improvement mentality and process, the easier it will be to keep driving change. A continuous improvement mentality suggests that we are constantly reviewing and questioning how we are doing and using a systematic measurement-driven approach to improving performance. Many organizations have implemented processes such as total quality management, Six Sigma, and continuous improvement to help sustain changes. The most common methodology is characterized by the following approach: define, measure, analyze, improve, and control. This approach was developed by the manufacturing industry to improve efficiencies given ever-shrinking margins, but it is now expanding into other industries. The philosophy of continuous improvement is:

- Define a problem to solve; it should be realistic and doable.
- Measure current performance to set a baseline and determine measures.
- Analyze what is causing the gap.
- Determine a realistic target and then implement the improvements.
- Implement control mechanisms to ensure that the new activities become institutionalized.

The most effective teams also use this process to continuously improve their management practices. One group of executives periodically reviewed their management practices in an effort to improve how they managed the business. They reviewed how well they made decisions, how well they held each other accountable, how open they were to other opinions, whether their meetings included substantive dialogue, how well they communicated expectations to presenters, and so forth.

Driving Change Through Performance Reviews

Companies have a tendency to focus on a few performance improvements, complete them, and then return to complacency with no further change efforts. To prevent this, give the human resources staff a mandate to incorporate process improvement into the primary performance review criteria for every employee. By doing so, the message is clearly sent—"Continue to improve or your pay level will not increase." ▪

By institutionalizing a process by which management openly and honestly questions not only what they are doing, but also how they are managing, implementing changes quickly and effectively becomes a core competency.

CHAPTER FOUR

Operational Accounting*

Importance of This Chapter

We have thus far discussed what the controller does, but is there a best way to do it? In this chapter, we address a variety of techniques for assigning responsibilities, streamlining workflow, correcting errors in a methodical manner, and so forth. By following this approach, the controller can achieve a high-performance accounting department within a relatively short period of time.

This chapter focuses on how to upgrade the accounting function so that it runs as a world-class department should. First we define the jobs of everyone in the department, then describe the creation of a very specific work schedule and staff meetings to follow up on particularly difficult problems. Then we move on to the proper treatment of accounting errors and how to avoid them, followed by a lengthy discussion of how to use best practices to improve operations. We also review the pluses and minuses associated with outsourcing selected functions within the department. By following these guidelines, a controller can

---

* Adapted with permission from Chapter 17 of Steven M. Bragg, Controller's Function, 4th Edition (Hoboken, NJ: Wiley, 2011).

create a confident accounting department that is thoroughly capable of quickly and accurately processing all assigned tasks.

 CREATE DEPARTMENTAL JOB DESCRIPTIONS

The first step in running an accounting department is to determine who is responsible for each task. Without such a determination, there is no way to control the flow of activities or to know whom to talk to about fixing problems. The typical departmental structure is for there to be one or more assistant controllers who are responsible for a selected set of functional areas, such as accounts payable and accounts receivable, or cost accounting and the general ledger. Below these personnel are a number of accountants and clerks.

Once the controller has determined the reporting relationships of the accounting group, it is time to define the exact job description for each position. These descriptions should be set up in a standard format by job title, not by individual, since the descriptions must otherwise be constantly restructured as employees come and go or are promoted within the department.

Billing Clerk

This position is accountable for creating invoices and credit memos, issuing them to customers by all necessary means, and updating customer files. Principal accountabilities are:

- Issue invoices to customers.
- Issue monthly customer statements.
- Update customer files.
- Process credit memos.
- Update the customer master file with contact information.
- Track exceptions between the shipping log and invoice register.
- Enter invoices into customer invoicing web sites.
- Submit invoices by electronic data interchange.

Collections Clerk

This position is accountable for collecting the maximum amount of overdue funds from customers, which may include a variety of collection techniques, legal claims, and the selective use of outside collection services. Principal accountabilities are:

- Stratify collection activities to maximize cash receipts.
- Issue dunning letters to overdue accounts.
- Contact customers regarding overdue accounts.
- Issue payment commitment letters.
- Negotiate the return of unpaid merchandise.
- Monitor cash on delivery or COD roll payments.
- Issue credit hold notifications.
- Recommend that accounts be shifted to a collection agency.
- Process small claims court complaints.
- Recommend bad debt write-offs.

Payables Clerk

This position is accountable for verifying proper payment approval, processing payments in a timely manner, and ensuring that discounts are taken. Principal accountabilities are:

- Match supplier invoices to authorizing purchase orders and proofs of receipt.
- Take all economical supplier discounts.
- Obtain payment approvals for non–cost of goods sold invoices.
- Process expense reports.
- Process procurement card payments.
- Issue stop payments and void checks.
- Issue reminders to suppliers regarding uncashed checks.
- Pay supplier invoices when due.
- Research supplier requests for payment.
- Process value-added tax (VAT) reclamations.
- Monitor supplier W-9 form submissions.
- Issue positive pay data to the bank.
- Update the supplier master file.

Payroll Clerk

This position is accountable for collecting timekeeping information, incorporating a variety of deductions into a periodic payroll, and issuing pay and pay-related information to employees. Principal accountabilities are:

- Collect and summarize timekeeping information.
- Obtain supervisory approval of time card discrepancies.

- Obtain overtime approvals.
- Calculate commissions.
- Process garnishment requests.
- Process employee advances and paybacks.
- Process and close periodic payrolls.
- Print and issue paychecks.
- Process direct deposit payments.
- Process paycard payments.
- Calculate and deposit payroll taxes.
- Process employment verifications.
- Process and issue annual W-2 forms to employees.

After each job description is created, the controller should review it in detail with each person whose job it describes, since there may be missing line items that the controller has overlooked. Once it has been finalized, each employee should be given his or her own copy, and the controller or one of the assistant controllers should go over it with him or her at each performance review to ensure that all tasks are being completed and that the description is still accurate.

CREATE A DEPARTMENTAL TRAINING PROGRAM

Once the controller has decided which employees are supposed to complete which tasks, it is time to see if they are capable of doing so. The best method is a combination of sitting with them to see how they complete work and reviewing their error rates and time needed for completed work. It takes time to form an accurate opinion of the abilities of each person, so a controller should allot at least a month, and probably longer, to this task. Once the controller has completed this initial review, the next step is to create a matrix of training programs needed to bring the accounting staff up to an expert level in all assigned areas of responsibility.

This matrix is an extremely important tool, for it precisely delineates the training requirements for each person, as well as when the controller expects training to be completed. Exhibit 4.1 presents an example of such a training matrix. It lists the names of accounting employees across the top of the report and the names of training modules down the left side. The training grid has a shaded area for those training classes that have not yet been completed, with a due date inside it. For those training classes that an employee *has* completed, the shading is removed and the completion date is listed. For cases where the employee is not required to complete a class, there is no shading or due date.

EXHIBIT 4.1 Sample Employee Training Matrix

[Correct score of at least 80% required to pass training]
[Shaded areas indicate required classes and due dates]

Training Description	Anderson, B. (Assistant Controller)	Draston, Q. (Cost Accountant)	Dudley, F. (Accounts Payable)	Ephraim, J. (Accounts Receivable)	Jones, J. (General Ledger)
Accounting Software Training:					
A/P - Entering a credit	July-01		July-01		
A/P - Entering an invoice	July-01		July-01		
A/P - Entering an invoice	July-01		August-01		
A/P - Matching documentation	July-01		August-01		
A/R - Applying cash	August-01			July-01	
A/R - Creating a credit	August-01			July-01	
A/R - Creating an invoice	August-01			August-01	
A/R - Deleting an invoice	August-01			August-01	
G/L - Alter report format	May-01				July-01
G/L - Create chart of accounts	May-01				August-01
G/L - Enter a journal entry	May-01	July-01			September-01
G/L - Enter the budget	May-01				October-01
Accounting Seminars:					
Acquisitions seminar	September-01				
Archiving	April-01				
Bank reconciliations	October-01				November-01
Closing the books	November-01				December-01
Consolidations	December-01				December-01

Training Description	Anderson, B. (Assistant Controller)	Draston, Q. (Cost Accountant)	Dudley, F. (Accounts Payable)	Ephraim, J. (Accounts Receivable)	Jones, J. (General Ledger)
Cost accounting, activity-based	March-01	August-01			
Cost accounting, direct	March-01	August-01			
Cost accounting, job cost	March-01	September-01			
Cost accounting, process	March-01	September-01			
Foreign currency translation	January-02				
Incorporation documentation	February-02				
Outsourcing	March-02				
Payroll taxes	April-02				
Personal property taxes	May-02		September-01		
Sales taxes	June-02		October-01		
Target costing	March-01	October-01			
PC Software Training:					
Beginning Access	June-01		June-01		March-01
Intermediate Access		October-01			
Advanced Access	July-02	November-01			
Beginning Excel			May-01	April-01	
Intermediate Excel	April-01	December-01		May-01	July-01
Advanced Excel	August-02	December-01		August-01	August-01
Beginning Word	March-01			September-01	September-01
Intermediate Word				October-01	February-01
Advanced Word					

Source: Steven M. Bragg, Controller's Function: The Work of the Managerial Accountant, 4th Edition, Copyright © 2011 John Wiley & Sons. Reprinted with permission of John Wiley & Sons, Inc.

An important point in regard to the use of a training program is that the required classes be targeted specifically at the current or prospective job functions of each person. It is useless to force employees to train for a skill that they cannot use, because they will forget the skill soon, and their time has been wasted. Similarly, if the controller expects employees to take on a new job function in the near future, the training should be assigned *immediately* prior to the assumption of the associated new job functions, so that the employees have no chance to forget what they have learned.

Training is made easier if there are prepackaged training programs available, either within the company or through an outside service, that meet the needs of the controller's training program. Because training for accountants frequently involves the company's accounting software, much of this training may be through seminars offered by the software provider. The other most common area of training for accountants is in specialized accounting topics, perhaps involving changes in Financial Accounting Standards Board (FASB) standards. For training updates in this area, it is best to arrange for seminar notifications from the local certified public accountant (CPA) organization or from the Institute of Management Accountants (IMA). If the staff needs to learn more about PC-based software packages, such as Excel, Word, or PowerPoint, many training organizations provide this service.

Training is an area to which the typical controller assigns a low priority, because the benefit may not be immediately obvious, and employees usually do not push for it either. However, given the long-term benefit of having a highly trained and competent staff, the controller should schedule some time once a month, on a recurring basis, to meet with the accounting staff and go over their training accomplishments from the last month as well as their goals for the next month. Only by ingraining training into the fabric of the department in this manner can the controller be assured that the staff will follow a consistent and targeted training program.

CLEAR OUT EXCESS DOCUMENTATION

For a new controller who is trying to attain control over an accounting department, the sheer quantity of paperwork can seem overwhelming—piles of documentation related to taxes, billings, supplier invoices, cash receipts, and on and on. There seems no end to the paperwork and nowhere to start. To avoid this problem, one of the very first acts of any controller should be to clear as much paperwork out of the department's confines as possible. This means going through every filing cabinet, every drawer, and every box, and determining the age and value of the papers contained inside. The main point is to get extra copies and information not currently needed off the premises, so that the controller can clearly see the tasks that still need to be done. This does *not* mean throwing out any documents. The objective is strictly to move out the documentation, not get rid of it permanently. Instead, box all the unneeded items, carefully label the boxes, and create an index that lists what is in every box, so that the accounting staff can easily find it again.

STREAMLINE THE ACCOUNTING WORKFLOW

There is the potential for an endless series of improvement projects within the accounting department. Being a department that handles large quantities of paper, the accounting area can rapidly become choked with clutter, which greatly impedes the flow of work. Also, certain employees are more comfortable with clutter than others, and so will allow unusual quantities of materials to proliferate. The controller can attack this problem by focusing on the ongoing elimination of the following items, all of which interfere with the orderly flow of work:

- Unneeded chairs, desks, filing cabinets, and carts
- Unneeded computers, printers, phones, copiers, and fax machines
- Unneeded posted items, such as outdated labor law posters, whiteboards, corkboards, and old messages on those boards
- Excess quantities of office supplies at employee desks, such as printer paper, staplers, tape, and so on

It is particularly important to search in all possible areas for these items: in corners and behind desks, and especially in drawers, cabinets, and closets, where such items tend to accumulate. To keep accumulation from occurring in these areas, consider removing all doors and drawers in the department. This means that all items are out in plain view, where they can be more easily monitored and therefore eliminated.

Whenever these items are removed from the accounting area, do not immediately throw them out or send them back to a storage area. Instead, pile them in a holding area that is readily accessible to the staff, so they have a few days to retrieve anything they really need. Then remove the remaining items from the holding area. It may be necessary to tag each item in the holding area, to identify where it came from and how long it should stay there until it is removed. If it is unlikely that an item in the holding area will be used within the next year, don't even consign it to storage—instead, put it in the trash or donate it. Otherwise the storage area will become excessively cluttered.

There is the particular problem of what to do about those employees who persist in piling up vast quantities of paperwork and supplies in their work areas. One possibility is the complete rebuilding of a work area. This involves *completely* emptying out someone's work area, even removing computer equipment and related cables. Then clean the entire area and put only the most necessary items back. All other items are removed to a location well away from the employee, who then spends a week deciding how many items that were shifted elsewhere are actually needed. This process will likely liberate a startling number of supplies, and also allow a great deal of paperwork to be filed away.

This process is by no means an annual event—think more in terms of a weekly or monthly review of the accounting area. Clutter increases constantly, so only continual attention will keep it in check.

In addition to clutter reduction, consider reviewing workflows within the department. To do so, create a map of the department, noting all cubicles, office furniture, and equipment. Then note on it the travel paths taken by employees for *all* activities and note their frequency of travel. A likely result will be the repositioning or removal of furniture and equipment. Also, if the department relies on high-capacity, centralized office equipment, such as printers, faxes, and copiers, it will likely make more sense to acquire a large number of lower-capacity units to position very close to individual employees or small groups of staff. Further, the map will clarify which employees need to be clustered together, along with certain document storage areas. By making these changes, travel times within the department can be substantially reduced.

A key detractor from optimum workflow is the filing cabinet. It is a central source of documentation, and because it is extremely heavy, it cannot be moved. Instead, employees must travel to it—possibly many times over the course of a day. An alternative is to buy a number of office carts with wheels; employees load these carts with the files they will need for that day and position the carts nearby in their work areas. The amount of travel time reduction can be astonishingly high.

The cubicle can be a considerable detriment to an efficient department, because it cannot be easily moved. Instead, swap out cubicles for desks, which can be easily reconfigured to match workflows. For example, group together the desks of the billing, cash application, and collection employees, so they can more easily discuss payment issues. If there is an increased need for more staff in this area, then simply move another desk into the group. If there is no way to avoid cubicles, then at least reduce their wall height, so that employees can more easily interact. High cubicles walls are the bane of employee communications.

Another issue that is frequently overlooked is the storage and replenishment of supplies. There is usually a central storage area for the department, but this is not always the best way to position supplies. For example, consider positioning printer and copier supplies right next to those items, so that users do not have to travel anywhere to find them. Also, assign replenishment responsibility to a single individual, and make sure that person uses a standardized checklist to update supplies on a daily basis. Otherwise, the department will lose valuable time searching for supplies that do not exist. The result of these activities should be a reduction in the accounting department's required amount of square footage, which in turn results in less travel time within the department. Thus, a good metric for departmental improvement is either total square footage or (better yet) square footage per person. This metric can be taken to an extreme, since the staff could end up packed together like sardines in a can, so don't use it as an exclusive metric.

In summary, the accounting department can be continually streamlined to improve its efficiency. The top improvement considerations are to move high-usage items as close to the users as possible, and to remove anything that physically gets in the way.

DOCUMENT ALL MAJOR PROCESSES

Although the controller has now determined the skill levels of the accounting staff and organized them along functional lines, he or she still has no knowledge of how the department operates. This problem can be solved by undertaking an in-depth review and documentation of all processes.

The best way to begin a process review is to sit with the most knowledgeable person who is involved with each function and document every step of the process in great detail. The documentation should itemize the exact file locations used, both in the computer and in filing cabinets, as well as the precise keystrokes needed to complete each step. The reason for this level of detail is that the controller probably will incorporate the written procedure into a departmental procedures manual that will be used by new recruits who must learn the system from scratch. After the first draft is complete, review it with the most knowledgeable staff person and perhaps also distribute it through the department, with a request to highlight errors and then return the corrected document.

Once the initial process documentation is complete, review the workloads required to complete each process with either the assistant controllers or the most experienced staff people available, with a particular emphasis on peak work periods of the month, additional staffing requirements, particular areas in which errors are endemic, and changes that will smooth the flow of work. Of particular interest is the concept of process centering, which means that much of the move and queue time inherent in most processes can be eliminated by centralizing as much of the work as possible with one person, rather than only allowing one person to complete a small task out of the entire process, with many other people completing their small, specialized tasks later in the process flow. For example, the accounts payable process can switch to process centering by having a single person conduct all documentation matching, supplier contacts, research, and data entry, rather than keeping these functions separated among different specialists.

CORRECT THE UNDERLYING CAUSES OF ERRORS

Depending on the level of experience, training, and procedural accuracy in an accounting department, it is possible that the accounting staff spends up to 50 percent of its time just correcting errors from earlier transactions. For example, a fixed asset may have been recorded in the fixed-asset register with an incorrect depreciation period, or an expense may have been charged to the wrong account number, or a customer may have been billed twice, or a supplier may have been paid twice. All of these transactions must be corrected, and each one may take hours to fix properly. Furthermore, because the adjustments are exceptions to the normal routine that someone (i.e., an auditor) may not understand when he or she reviews it at some point in the future, the reasons why the corrections have been made also must be fully documented, which takes up still more time. Finally, if the corrections are large enough, they may even have a material impact on the financial statements, which results in additional explanation as footnotes in the statements. This also takes time, not to mention being an embarrassment to the accounting department. Unless the controller corrects the core reasons why these errors continue to occur, the accounting department will never have time to work its way out from under the workload related to error correction.

When correcting errors, follow a specific set of steps that greatly assist in focusing attention on those errors that arise most frequently. The first step is to keep a log of all errors found. This log should include the nature of the error, when it occurred, who caused the error, and the underlying reason for the problem. Exhibit 4.2 shows an example of this log. Compiling this log can take some work, as the accounting staff may hide its errors from the controller and fix the problems without publicizing their mistakes. To find these errors, create error-spotting systems, such as a monthly review of all credits issued to customers, all journal entries, and all unvouchered accounts payable, which are the most common locations for error corrections. Then research each item found and insert it into the log. The next step is to create a Pareto analysis (i.e., 20 percent of the problems cause 80 percent of the total errors) that groups the errors by quantity of occurrences, so that the controller can see which problems arise the most frequently. Then target those errors causing the bulk of the problems, outline a correction plan, and implement it, which will rapidly reduce the incidence of errors. Error correction should be one of the key functions of the controller, because it has such a major operational impact on the efficiency of the accounting department.

EXHIBIT 4.2 Example of an Accounting Error Log

Date Error Found	Date Error Occurred	Person Causing Error	Error Type	Cause of Error
06/11/11	03/04/11	Smith, J.	Incorrect pricing	Due to special deal by salesperson.
06/10/11	06/09/11	Novak, K.	Incorrect supplier cost	Due to incorrect accounts payable entry, shifting dollar amount by one decimal.
06/10/11	05/31/11	Orson, P.	Incorrect payroll accrual	Due to not using standard journal entry calculation to compile month-end expense.
06/09/11	06/09/11	Dudley, F.	Incorrect property tax accrual	Did not include cost of assets at secondary location.
06/09/11	06/01/11	Johnson, A.	Incorrect pricing	Due to customer service overriding standard price in computer.

(continue)

Date Error Found	Date Error Occurred	Person Causing Error	Error Type	Cause of Error
06/08/11	02/28/11	Smith, J.	Incorrect cash book balance	Did not complete bank reconciliation last month.
06/08/11	01/13/11	Johnson, A.	Incorrect supplier cost	Due to incorrect accounts payable entry, shifting dollar amount by one decimal.
06/08/11	05/15/11	Anderson, L.	Tape inventory too high	Due to unit of measure change by engineering that switched tape quantity in inches to quantity in rolls.

Source: Steven M. Bragg, *Controller's Function: The Work of the Managerial Accountant*, 4th Edition, Copyright © 2011 John Wiley & Sons. Reprinted with permission of John Wiley & Sons, Inc.

An additional column that could be added to the example is one for the size of the error, in case the controller wants to focus on fixing problems of great magnitude, rather than those with the highest incidence of occurrence.

The reason for the "Date Error Occurred" column in the example is that the controller may have already fixed a problem that has only now been discovered. For example, if the error is dated three months previously, but the controller fixed the underlying problem the week before, then it can be safely ignored. However, if the problem occurred in just the past few days, then the underlying problem is clearly still an issue and requires further action.

It is also important to create a feedback loop to the accounting staff regarding the elimination of errors, because this system will have a major negative impact on staff morale if it is not presented to them properly.

Wrong Use of Error Logs

A general manager implemented an error logging technique to spot every conceivable problem in a company and used it to target employees for firing, rather than focusing on the problems that the system had highlighted. As a result, employee morale disintegrated, many staff left the company, and those remaining decided not to inform the general manager of any new problems, since they eventually received the blame for the problems. ▪

Staff members should be included in the decision-making for resolving errors; their participation will give rise to more fruitful ideas than any controller could originate alone.

 ## USE BEST PRACTICES

Even after documenting the accounting department's workflow, positioning employees in the correct jobs, and setting them up for the appropriate training programs, there is no assurance that the department will operate in a sufficiently effective manner. The controller may compare the work done by his or her accounting staff and find that it falls well behind the efficiency level of the accounting department of a competing company. The reason for the difference may be that the competition is using best practices to improve its operations. A best practice is any operational improvement that allows the accounting staff to generate more work with an equal or less amount of effort. A constant stream of innovation is coming out of companies all over the world, so there is no end to the number of best practices one can implement. The main problem is finding them. One source is the author's *Accounting Best Practices* (Hoboken, NJ: John Wiley & Sons), for which a new edition is released every few years; the book lists and explains a large number of best practices, including implementation issues, control problems, and related costs.

Once a controller has discovered a best practice that may fit into his or her organization, it is very important to research the issue thoroughly to ensure that these points have been covered prior to commencing with an implementation:

- **Cost-benefit analysis.** A best practice may seem extraordinarily "sexy" in concept, but the controller always must ensure that the cost of installing it does not exceed the savings from using it. For example, a document imaging system may eliminate virtually all the paperwork from an accounting department, but the only identifiable savings from doing so may be the storage costs that are perhaps a few hundred dollars per month or year.
- **Control issues.** A new best practice improvement may result in a major reduction in the volume of work, but it also may eliminate a key control point in the old system that is being replaced. If so, there is now a control risk that may result in a loss that greatly exceeds the potential savings from using the best practice. For example, using procurement cards to replace

the bulk of a company's small purchases will avoid the use of purchase order authorizations, thereby allowing procurement card users to abuse small purchases, secure in the knowledge that no one is reviewing what they buy.

▪ **Capacity.** If a controller is contemplating a mammoth project that will vastly improve the efficiency of the accounting department, it would be useful first to determine the capacity of the department to perform the installation, because it must find the time among its other work to complete the project. It is unrealistic to assume that the existing staff, which is usually overworked, can also complete additional work related to best practice installations. Accordingly, often it is necessary to schedule additional help, either from other departments or consultants, who can assist with or even manage the work.

▪ **Murphy's law.** The controller always should expect that something will go wrong with the installation of any best practice and be prepared for the worst possible case. For example, if switching to an automated vacation accrual tracking system that lists accruals on employee pay stubs, what must be done if some of the accruals are incorrect? The controller should prepare a plan for this contingency and expect to use it.

▪ **Time requirements.** The longer an installation project runs, the worse its chances of succeeding, because there inevitably will be other work that will take priority, the spirits of the implementation team will drop, and it will be more difficult to continue to obtain both funding and the support of senior management.

▪ **Track record.** If the controller has a poor track record for installing best practices in the past, for whatever reason, it will be very difficult to convince the staff to participate in yet another project with any degree of enthusiasm. In such cases, it is best to start with an extremely small project that can be completed in the shortest possible time period, in order to build up the trust of the department.

▪ **Personnel issues.** If a proposed best practice will require the approval or participation of someone who does not have a good record for assisting in previous implementations, then the controller must fix the problem with this person—through replacement, presenting a convincing argument, or shifting responsibility to a different person—before beginning to think about any other implementation-related issues. Without total personnel support, a best practice cannot be installed.

▪ **Support by top management.** If a best practice can be installed without any involvement from other departments, then the chance of success is much higher than if another department must be brought into the process, because this other group may have an entirely different agenda and therefore not want to cooperate. Given the level of difficulty when other departments are involved, the controller always should be sure that the top management group has fully bought into the best practice concept and will be fully supportive if other departments cause difficulties.

If the controller has reviewed the preceding items and finds no roadblocks that could seriously interfere with implementation efforts, it is time to determine which best practices to install first. The key issue here is not to immediately go after the one item with the biggest potential payback, because it may also be the most difficult or expensive one to implement. Instead, focus on creating an accounting organization that is used to always working on the implementation and maintenance of just a few best practices at a time, so that there is a tradition of improvement woven into the fabric of the department.

▣ OUTSOURCE SELECTED ACCOUNTING FUNCTIONS

Once the controller has straightened out the accounting process flow, eliminated recurring errors, and installed best practices, it may become evident that the department is spending too much of its resources on those accounting activities that do not create value for the company. For example, there may be a large workforce of hourly personnel that requires a numerous in-house payroll staff and lots of management attention, whereas the main value driver from the accounting perspective is generating cost accounting reports for the management team regarding the margins being earned on company products. In a situation such as this, the controller may want to review the cost-benefit of shifting some of the less important accounting functions to a supplier, who will run them on behalf of the controller.

All of the accounting functions can be outsourced, but the most common one by far is payroll. A number of national-level payroll suppliers perform the payroll processing for tens of thousands of companies. The reason why this function is commonly outsourced is that it is a combination of being a non-value-added activity and one that can result in significant government fines if tax remittances are not made by specified dates. Thus, with lots of downside risk and no upside potential for doing the job better, many controllers elect to hand this painful chore to a supplier. Other accounting functions are not so clear-cut, however. Smaller firms can have a supplier process their billings and accounts payable off-site, while outside bookkeepers can process the month-end close for a very small company. There are also a few cases where a supplier will take over the entire accounting department. However, there are also good reasons for treading carefully in these nonpayroll areas, because the cost of using a supplier may greatly exceed the cost of performing the same tasks in-house. Also, relations between the company and its supplier can become strained if the outsourcing deal does not work out well, and the controller may be constantly bogged down in contract revisions, when he or she thought there would be more time available for other activities. Accounting functions that can be outsourced include:

- Check printing
- Collections
- Internal auditing
- Payroll
- Period closings
- Tax form preparation
- Transaction processing

If a controller decides to proceed with outsourcing an accounting func-tion, there are several contractual issues to consider. In the case of payroll processing, the main variable is the price of the service, which is divided into a variable fee per person, plus a fixed monthly charge. Both fees are nego-tiable, although other terms do not vary much. The outsourcing of tax form preparation can be negotiated on the price of the service provided, as well as the specific people used by the supplier to complete the work. A controller usu-ally can specify that the same group of people work on all tax forms, so that there is a base of experience and consistency. The main focus of collections outsourcing is the price, which can be either a fixed fee per invoice collected or more commonly a percentage of the dollars collected. Giving a supplier a higher volume of collections work can be used as leverage to reduce the per-invoice cost to the company. From a contractual standpoint, internal auditing is similar to tax form preparation in that the primary items for negotiation are the hourly rate and the personnel to be used. Another issue is what type of internal auditing methodology will be used, which the controller can specify. The contract for transaction processing requires the largest amount of nego-tiation. The single largest issue here is to avoid add-on fees (which tend to be very high) by rolling as many tasks into the monthly baseline fee as possible. Also, if company personnel are being transferred to the supplier, the minimum period for which they will be retained or the severance pay they will receive must be specified. In addition, the minimum period over which key personnel will be retained on the company's account before they can be moved to other supplier work sites must be determined—this keeps experienced personnel working on company business for as long as possible. Finally, the controller should be sure to retain approval control over any efficiencies the supplier wants to implement, because these may change the flow of information to other parts of the company and thus have political consequences. Given the number of negotiable items, it is apparent that a controller must be prepared to negotiate transaction outsourcing at some length in order to arrive at an advantageous contract with a supplier.

When outsourcing accounting functions, there are a few transitional issues to be aware of so that the shift to a supplier is as painless as possible. First, no matter what function is given to a supplier, there must be a functional coordinator who is in charge of the move, so that there is a single responsible person who can monitor the process. This person anticipates problems, deals with supplier and personnel issues, and tracks the progress of the transition against a time and activities budget. If payroll is being outsourced, then the key issue is the timing of the transition, for it is easiest for the supplier if it takes place on January 1 of the new year, when the year-to-date records for all employees are reset to zero. Otherwise, the supplier cannot guarantee that the information that will appear on each employee's annual W-2 form will be correct. Also, a payroll supplier offers a number of add-on services, such as check stuffing, direct deposit, and automatic vacation accruals; however, it is best to transition to the most basic functions first to ensure that they work properly and then incrementally add on the other options later. If the controller is shifting the preparation of financial statements to a supplier, then the main issue is to verify with the supplier the individual accounts that will roll up into separate line items on the financial statements and to monitor this information for several months to ensure that the correct roll-up is occurring. When outsourcing the internal audit function, there are several extra steps to complete. Because the auditors will be meeting with many employees throughout the company, it is important to screen them for a minimum level of experience, then walk them through all relevant policies and procedures, train them in the use of the in-house auditing procedures (if they are to be used), negotiate the details of the audit plan for the upcoming year, and set up a monitoring plan to ensure that the audits are being conducted to the controller's satisfaction. Tax form preparation is much easier to begin, because the controller only has to authorize the auditing firm to begin work, which it can then do based on the audit work papers it has already prepared; however, if the tax work is to be done by a different supplier, then the controller must send written permission to the auditing firm for it to copy all relevant audit work papers and send them to the tax preparation firm. The transition of transaction processing is the most difficult task of all. It involves transferring the accounting staff to the supplier, training any additional staff or supplier managers, either shifting the company's accounting database and application programs to the supplier's location or shifting the database to the supplier's software, and testing to ensure that the data have been moved successfully. The transition for transaction processing can be so complicated that a controller should assign one or more senior staff members to oversee this process.

Another part of outsourcing is maintaining proper control over the suppliers who are now running parts of the accounting department. A key issue is to keep the outsourcing of the internal audit function away from any suppliers who are handling other parts of the accounting department; otherwise, the supplier's auditors will be reviewing their own activities, which is a poor way to control the department. Another good control is to set up separate general ledger accounts for each supplier who is handling accounting department functions, summarize all their billed expenses through these accounts, and compare the expenses to the contractual amounts that were originally agreed on. Also, consider building bonus and penalty clauses into the contract with all suppliers, so that they have an incentive to complete required work both accurately and on time. Finally, there should be a periodic review meeting with supplier management, preferably quarterly, to go over problems that have arisen since the last meeting and how to resolve them. By keeping the lines of communication open between the controller and suppliers, most problems can be quickly resolved.

Setting up adequate controls over suppliers of accounting functions is not enough, however. The controller must be able to measure their performance to ensure that predetermined standards are being attained, which may result in bonus payments or penalties, depending on the outcome. In the case of collections, the controller's main concern is the supplier's ability to collect the highest possible proportion of overdue accounts receivable. Accordingly, the best measure is the percentage of collected funds from the dollars of billings that were assigned to the supplier. If a supplier is creating financial statements for the controller, the two main concerns are accuracy and timeliness. Accordingly, the controller should measure the accuracy of all accruals made, the number of material irregularities that must be adjusted in later financial statements, and the time required to issue the statements. If internal auditing is outsourced, then the controller should be most concerned with the supplier's ability to complete a high percentage of the audits that were originally agreed on. Another good measure is the average cost per audit. If payroll is being outsourced, then appropriate measures are the timeliness of the supplier in paying payroll taxes to the government, the average transaction cost per employee paid, and the number of payroll payments sent by the supplier to the wrong company locations. If a supplier is handling tax form preparation, then the controller certainly wants to know about any tax penalties paid that are due to incorrect or late tax filings. Finally, if the controller outsources transaction processing, several review measures should be used. The most important is the average cost per transaction, which should be compared to the cost prior to using the supplier, to ensure that costs are in line with expectations. Another is the supplier's error rate in completing transactions, although this is a difficult one to measure (because the supplier can easily cover up any errors). A major measurement from the perspective of the rest of the company is the supplier's timeliness in completing transactions, especially when this involves the processing and payment of employee expense reports. Finally, if the supplier is responsible for accounts payable, then a significant measure is ensuring that 100 percent of all possible early payment discounts have been taken. A controller should consider these measures to be nothing more than the bare minimum set of measures to use when dealing with suppliers; add as many as necessary to track their performance adequately.

A final issue is the management of outsourced functions. Although suppliers are technically responsible for their output, the controller is held responsible for all aspects of his or her department by senior management and so must stay in close touch with the activities of all suppliers. To do this, there must still be tight management control of the outsourced functions from within the company. This means that the controller should assign one or more assistant controllers the task of supervising all suppliers. These people should receive extra help from the company's legal counsel or purchasing staff in the matter of negotiating and reviewing contracts. Their typical job descriptions will be to negotiate supplier contracts; authorize payments to suppliers; measure suppliers' performance; monitor supplier service levels and discuss any changes needed to improve them; review and approve all supplier outputs, such as financial statements or completed tax forms; and manage the transfer of functions to the suppliers. These are significant changes from the typical role of accounting managers, who tend to specialize in particular accounting areas, so some extra management training may be necessary for these employees before they are fully equipped to take on the task of managing the suppliers to whom accounting functions have been outsourced.

Outsourcing is a possibility for most accounting departments, but it must be investigated properly and used with care in order to achieve the maximum benefit at a minimal cost to the company.

CHAPTER FIVE

Cost Accounting and Costing Systems*

Importance of This Chapter

Though the new controller will initially be judged based on the quality and timeliness of his financial statements, he can bring considerable value to the company over the long term with a thorough knowledge of the cost accounting concepts described in this chapter. By applying different costing systems to different situations, there is an excellent opportunity to focus management attention on the systematic improvement of profitability.

Cost accounting is one of the most crucial aspects of the accounting profession, for it is a key means by which the accounting department transmits company-related performance information to the management team. A properly organized cost accounting function can give valuable feedback regarding the impact of product pricing, cost trends, the performance of cost and profit centers, and production and personnel capacity, and it can even contribute to some degree to the formulation of company strategy. However, many controllers rarely give due consideration

---

*Adapted with permission from Chapter 26 of Steven M. Bragg, Accounting Reference Desktop (Hoboken, NJ: Wiley, 2002).

to the multitude of uses to which cost accounting can be put. Instead, they think only of how cost accounting will feed information into the financial statements, since their primary focus is on the financial statements. In this chapter, we will focus on how you can collect data, summarize it, and report it to management with the goal of helping the management team to run the business.

PURPOSE OF COST ACCOUNTING INFORMATION

The cost accounting function works best without any oversight rules and regulations, because it tends to result in hybrid systems that are custom-designed to meet specific company needs. For example, a company may find that a major requirement is to determine the incremental cost that it incurs for each additional unit of production, so that it can make accurate decisions regarding the price of incremental units sold (possibly at prices very close to the direct cost). If it were to use accounting standards, it would be constrained to only use a costing system that allocated a portion of overhead costs to product costs— even though these are not incremental costs. Accordingly, the cost accounting system used for this specific purpose will operate in contravention of generally accepted accounting principles (GAAP), because following GAAP would yield results that do not assist management.

Because there are many different management decisions for which the cost accounting profession can provide valuable information, it is quite common to have several costing systems in place. To extend the previous example, the incremental costing system used for incremental pricing decisions may not be adequate for a different problem, which is creating profit centers that are used to judge the performance of individual managers. For this purpose, a second costing system must be devised that allocates costs from internal service centers to the various profit centers; in this instance, we are adding an allocation function to the incremental costing system that was already in place. Even more systems may be required for other applications, such as transfer pricing between company divisions and the costing of inventory for external financial reporting purposes. Consequently, cost accounting frequently results in a multitude of costing systems, which may follow GAAP guidelines only by accident.

Any cost accounting system is comprised of three functional areas: the collection of raw data, the processing of this data in accordance with a costing methodology, and the reporting of the resulting information to management in the most useful format. The remainder of this chapter is split into sections that address each of these three functional areas. The area that receives the most coverage is the processing function, for there are a number of different methodologies available, each of which applies to different situations. For example, job costing is used for situations where specifically identifiable goods are produced in batches, while direct costing is most applicable in situations where management does not want to see any overhead allocation attached to the directly identifiable costs of a product. The large number of processing methodologies presented here is indicative of the broad range of options available to the controller for processing raw data into various types of reports for management use.

INPUT: DATA COLLECTION SYSTEMS

The first step in setting up a data collection system is to determine what *types* of data to gather. You can simply collect every conceivable type of data available, but this will result in immensely detailed and cumbersome collection systems that are expensive and require a great deal of employee time to collect and record. A better approach is to determine what types of outputs are required, which can then be used to ascertain the specific data items needed to create those outputs. This allows the controller to ignore many types of data, simply because no one needs them. However, the process of determining data requirements from projected outputs must be revisited on a regular basis, for changes in the business will require changes in the required cost accounting reports, and therefore changes in the types of data collected.

The process of backtracking from a required output to a set of required data elements is best illustrated with an example. If a company is manufacturing a set of products whose components and assembly are entirely outsourced, then it is logical to create management reports that focus on the prices being charged to the company by its suppliers, rather than creating an elaborate time recording system for the small number of quality inspectors who are responsible for reviewing completed goods before they are shipped out to customers. In this case, the bulk of the data used by the costing system will come out of the accounts payable and purchasing records. Another example is a software company, where the costing focus is on the labor time charged to specific development projects and the ability of project managers to meet their deadlines, rather than on the minor cost of the software-related materials that are shipped to customers. In this case, most of the cost accounting data will come from the timekeeping and project-tracking databases. Thus, the nature of the business will drive the decision to collect certain types of data.

Once the controller knows what data to collect, there is still the issue of creating a data accumulation system. There are several factors that will influence this decision. One is *cost*; if there are many employees who will be recording information continuously, then the unit cost of the data collection device cannot be too expensive, or else its total cost will exceed the utility of the collected data. Another issue is *data accuracy*; if the data collected absolutely, positively must be correct, then a more elaborate solution, such as bar code scanning, which is designed to yield very accurate results, should be the preferred solution. However, if the level of required accuracy is lower, then perhaps manual keypunch entry or handwritten data sheets would be acceptable. Another factor is the *employees* who will use the data collection systems; if they are highly trained, then they can be relied on to use complex keypunching systems, whereas a poorly trained workforce that has no idea of what data it is collecting, or why it is being used, should be allowed to collect only data that will be heavily cross-checked for errors. Of additional concern is the *timeliness* of the data collected. If there is a need for up-to-the-minute transmission of data to managers, then the only solution will be some form of automated data gathering. However, sending only an occasional report to management may allow a slower manual data gathering approach. Another factor to consider is the *existing level of automation* within the company. For example, if there is a clear production path for all products that sends every completed item down a specific conveyor belt, then the installation of a fixed bar code scanner on that conveyor is a reasonable approach for recording data about production quantities. However, this would be a poor solution if products were being hand-carried away from a multitude of production processes to the warehouse, since many of the items created would never pass by the bar code scanner. A final consideration is the *production methodology* currently in use. If it is a lean manufacturing system, such as *just-in-time*, there will be a strong orientation away from requiring employees to conduct any data entry work, since extremely focused and efficient workflows are the key to success in this environment—which is interrupted if data entry tasks are included. In these cases, you should avoid any type of manual data entry, focusing instead on more automated approaches.

Given the above parameters, it is clear that the controller must devise a wide array of data collection tools in order to collect data in the most appropriate manner. The following bullet points describe a number of the more common data collection tools:

▪ **Punch clocks.** The punch clock is used by hourly employees to record the times when they arrive for work and leave at the end of the day. The process is a simple one: Take your time card from a storage rack, insert it into the top of the clock, which stamps the time on it, and return your card to the storage rack. The payroll staff then uses these cards to calculate payroll. The greatest advantage of this approach is that a time clock is very inexpensive. However, it requires conversion of the time card data by the payroll staff into another format before it can be used, which introduces the likelihood of computational errors. Also, it is difficult to use for recording time worked on specific jobs.

▪ **Electronic time clocks.** This clock allows employees to swipe a badge through a reader on the side or top of the clock. This results in a computer entry for the time of the scan, which is also associated with the employee code that is embedded in the card. A more advanced version uses the biometric measurement of the outlines of one's hand to determine the identity of the employee (thereby eliminating the need for an employee badge, which might otherwise be lost or used to make a scan for someone who is not on the premises). This represents a significant advance over the punch clock, because there is no need for secondary calculations that might result in an error. It also yields greater control over the time-recording process, since it gives immediate feedback to supervisors regarding missed or late scans. An additional benefit is that employees can enter job numbers as part of the scanning process, so that time is charged to specific jobs. However, the electronic time clock costs up to $2,000 each, and so is usually restricted to high-volume applications where there are many employees.

Question the Need for Labor Data Collection

In many manufacturing organizations, the direct labor staff does not vary its hours any more than does the overhead staff. They are present if there is manufacturing work to do, and they are still on site if work is slow. Thus, they are a fixed cost, not variable. Also, direct labor tends to be a small proportion of total product costs. Given these issues, the new controller should question the need for installing expensive labor tracking systems. ▪

▪ **Bar code scanners.** A bar code scanner reads bar code labels with either a fixed or rapidly rotating laser beam, and converts the bar code symbology into a character-based format that is then stored in the computer system. These scanners come in many varieties, ranging from a $100 fixed-beam scanner that looks like a pen (but which may require a number of scans to read a bar code) to a $10,000 fixed-position scanner that is bolted to a conveyor belt, and which emits 30 scans per second as bar-coded packages move past it. There are also portable scanners, which are heavily used in warehousing operations, that can store scanned information in local RAM memory for later uploading to a computer, or that contain direct radio frequency access to the company computer, and can therefore transmit the data immediately. The type of scanner purchased will depend on the level of automation required and the budget available for this purpose. Bar code scanning is highly recommended for repetitive data entry situations where the *same* data are collected many times. However, it is of less use where the data collected changes constantly, or involves a large quantity of text that would require an extremely large bar code.

■ **Terminal data entry.** A common form of data entry is to not use any new data collection devices—instead, just buy lots more computer terminals and make them available to users throughout the company. Employees can then be given direct access to the computer screens that require input from them and can enter information directly into the computer system. This avoids the middleman data entry person, as well as the risk that the data entry staff might misinterpret the data on an employee's form and type in the wrong information. The process can be facilitated by the use of error-checking protocols within the computer software, so that users will be flagged if they make entries that are clearly outside of a narrow band of expected responses. However, it can be expensive to rig all locations in a company with computer terminals and all linking wiring, so you might consider installing data collection apps on tablet computers instead.

■ **Paper-based data entry.** Despite all of the other forms of advanced data entry noted here, the most common method for collecting data is still from a paper document. This approach is inexpensive, requires no web of interlinked electronic devices throughout a facility, and is familiar to all employees as a method of data capture. However, it does not result in a fast flow of data through an organization, since it may be days or weeks before the information contained on a form is rekeyed into the computer system. Also, it is easy to lose forms, especially when they are being used throughout a facility, and there is no rigid tracking of individual forms to ensure that none are lost. Furthermore, this approach requires the services of an expensive data entry person to interpret the data on the forms (sometimes incorrectly) and type the results into the computer system. Given these problems, it is no surprise that the proportion of data gathering that uses this approach is shrinking.

Thus, there are a wide range of data entry systems available. In most instances, the controller who is designing a data collection system will need to use a mix of these options to ensure that the correct cluster of high data accuracy and low collection cost is achieved.

PROCESSING: DATA SUMMARIZATION SYSTEMS

Having covered the data collection portion of cost accounting, we now move to the various costing methodologies that are available for processing the raw data into a format that is most useful for management consumption. The primary advantages and disadvantages of the systems whose functions are noted in the following sections are:

- **Job costing.** This is primarily targeted at production situations where customized goods are produced for specific customers. It is very useful for tracking the exact cost of individual products and is the only valid technique for accumulating costs for cost-plus contractual arrangements. It can also yield accurate results about the ongoing costs of a current job, which is useful for monitoring purposes. However, this system requires a large quantity of detailed data collection and data entry, which is expensive. It also runs the risk of including some inaccurate data, which requires expensive control systems to minimize. Furthermore, there may be a significant allocation of overhead costs to each job, which may be inaccurately applied.
- **Process costing.** This is most common in situations where large quantities of exactly the same product are created. Costs are collected in bulk for entire time periods, and then allocated out to the production runs during that period. This results in a fair degree of accuracy when costs are averaged out and assigned to individual units. However, some degree of estimation is required when determining total production quantities completed, since some units may be only partially completed at the end of the production period. Consequently, there is some room for variation in final production costs. This method requires much less data collection than job costing, but the level of information accuracy is correspondingly reduced.
- **Standard costing.** This methodology is designed to set standard costs for all material and labor costs incurred by a company, against which actual results can be compared through variance analysis. This can result in excellent control over company costs, but only if the accounting staff is diligent in uncovering the reasons for variances from costing standards, and the management team is helpful in correcting the discovered problems. It is also useful for budgeting, setting prices, and closing the financial

books in a rapid manner. However, it is time-consuming to set and maintain standards; in environments where this maintenance function is not performed, standards can be so far away from actual results that variance analysis is no longer useful for management purposes. Also, a company that has adopted continuous process improvement principles will find that any standards adopted will almost immediately become obsolete, requiring constant correction. Finally, it tends to perpetuate inefficiencies if personnel use the current standard cost as a baseline for behavior; they will have no incentive to improve costs to a point that is substantially better than the preset standard, resulting in languishing efficiency levels.

▪ **Direct costing.** This is a favorite methodology for those managers who are constantly confronted with incremental costing and pricing decisions where the inclusion of overhead costs in a product's total cost will yield inaccurate information. Thus, direct costing is an ideal approach for determining the lowest possible price at which to sell incremental units. However, it yields inaccurate results when used for long-term pricing, since it takes no account of overhead costs that must be included in a company's standard prices if it is to assure itself of long-term profitability. It is also not allowed for inventory valuation purposes by GAAP, which requires the inclusion of allocated overhead costs.

▪ **Throughput accounting.** A variation on direct costing is throughput costing. This methodology holds that the only direct cost is direct materials, with even direct labor costs being thrown out when making most cost-related management decisions. The main tenet of throughput accounting is that a company must carefully manage the bottleneck operation in its production facility, so that the largest possible contribution margin is created. The main advantage of throughput accounting is that it yields the best short-term incremental profits if it is religiously followed when making production decisions.

▪ **Activity-based costing (ABC).** The ABC methodology is a much more accurate way to associate overhead costs with specific activities, which in turn can be assigned to product costs. Its main advantage is that it builds a direct correlation between the occurrences of an activity and related overhead costs, so that changes in the activity can be reliably expected to result in corresponding changes in overhead costs. This results in valuable information for the management team, which uses it not only to gain some measure of control over its overhead costs, but also to gain an understanding of which products use more activities (and therefore overhead costs) than others. The downside is that it requires a great deal of costing knowledge, time, and management commitment before a functioning ABC system becomes operational, and will henceforth require considerable upkeep to maintain. It also requires the construction of an ABC database that is separate from the general ledger, which can be an expensive proposition to both create and maintain. It is not really necessary in situations where there are few products, obvious process flows, and minimal machine setups, because a less complex cost accumulation system will still result in reasonably accurate product costs.

▪ **Target costing.** This costing methodology is the most proactive of all the methodologies, for it involves the direct intervention of the cost accounting staff in the product design process, with the express intent of creating products that meet preset cost and gross margin goals. This is opposed to the usual practice of accumulating costs after products have been designed and manufactured, so that managers will find out what a product costs after it is too late to make any changes to the design. This costing system is highly recommended to any company that designs its own products, since it can result in significant reductions in product costs before they are "locked in" when the design is completed. This technique usually requires a great deal of cost accounting staff time and can lengthen the product development process, but is well worth the effort

This brief review of the advantages and disadvantages of each costing methodology should make it clear not only that they are wildly different from each other in concept, but also that they are all designed to deal with different situations, several of which may be found within the same company. Accordingly, a controller must become accustomed to slipping in and out of a methodology when the circumstances warrant the change, and will very likely use a combination of these systems at the same time, if demanded by the circumstances.

In the following sections, we will review the workings of each of these costing methodologies.

 ## PROCESSING: JOB COSTING

Job costing involves a series of transactions that accumulate the costs of materials, labor, and overhead (of which there are two different calculations) to a specific job. For each of these costing categories, costs are accumulated through a series of transactions before they are finally charged to a specific job. In this section, we will trace the journal entries used for all of these costs.

The basic flow of journal entries required for direct materials is noted in Exhibit 5.1, which itemizes the general format of each sequential transaction. When raw materials are purchased, they are rarely charged to a particular job upon receipt. Instead, they are stored in the warehouse, so there is a debit to the raw materials inventory and a credit to accounts payable. Once production is scheduled, the raw materials are sent to the production floor, which triggers another transaction to be created by the warehouse staff—a debit to the work-in-process (WIP) inventory account and a credit to the raw materials inventory account.

EXHIBIT 5.1 Job Costing Transactions for Direct Materials

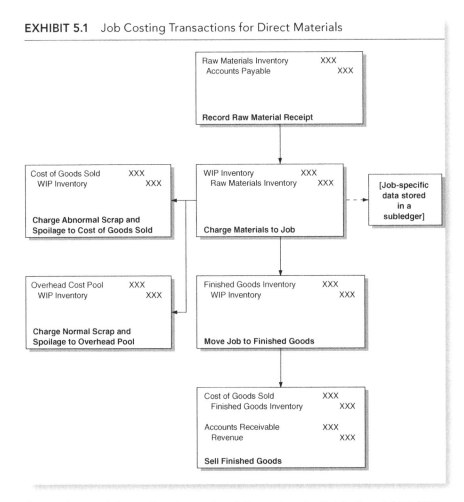

Source: Steven M. Bragg, *Cost Accounting: A Comprehensive Guide*, Copyright © 2001 John Wiley & Sons. Reprinted with permission of John Wiley & Sons, Inc.

During the production process, it is quite likely that some portion of the materials will be destroyed as part of the normal production process; if so, another entry will be required that creates a debit to the overhead cost pool and a credit to remove the cost from the WIP inventory account. This normal amount of scrap will then be allocated through the overhead cost pool back to product costs—we will deal with this issue shortly, when we talk about the cost flow for overhead costs. If there are excessive amounts of scrap, then these are charged directly to the cost of goods sold with a debit, while the WIP account is reduced with a credit.

Once the production process has been completed (which may be a few moments for simple products and months for complex ones), it is shifted back to the warehouse in the form of finished goods. To record this transaction, we use a debit to the finished goods inventory account and a credit to WIP inventory. Once the goods are sold from stock, a final entry relieves the finished goods inventory account with a credit and charges the cost to the cost of goods sold with a debit.

One of the numerous benefits of a just-in-time system is that materials are in the production process for such a short period of time that there is no point in creating transactions that move their cost in and out of WIP inventory. Instead, a single transaction shifts raw material costs from the raw materials inventory account to cost of goods sold (though there may be an extra entry to record the cost in finished goods inventory if completed products are not immediately sold). This greatly reduces the number of potential problems that can arise with the recording of transactions.

The recording of labor costs follows a slightly different path than what is typically seen for material costs. Instead of taking a direct route into the WIP inventory account, labor costs either can be charged at once to the overhead cost pool or go into WIP inventory. The charge to an overhead cost pool is done if there is no direct relationship between the incurrence of the labor cost and the creation of a product—this results in a debit to the overhead cost pool and a credit to the wages expense account. However, if there is a direct tie between the incurrence of labor costs and the production of specific products, then the debit is instead to the WIP inventory (or a separate labor account). These cost flows are shown in Exhibit 5.2.

If the wages have flowed into an overhead cost pool, these costs will be summarized at the end of the accounting period and charged to specific products based on any number of allocation methodologies. The allocation calculation will result in another transaction that shifts the overhead costs to product costs, which can occur both at the WIP and finished goods stages of production.

EXHIBIT 5.2 Job Costing: Transaction for Labor

Meanwhile, labor costs that have been charged directly to WIP inventory will then be shifted to finished goods inventory and later to the cost of goods sold in the same manner as for materials costs.

As was the case for material costs, there are a large number of labor transactions that are required to track the flow of labor costs through the production process under the job costing methodology. There is a high risk that transactional errors will arise, just because of the large number of transactions, so control systems must be created that keep errors from occurring and verify that completed transactions are correct.

The final job costing process under the job costing system is the allocation of costs to products. There are two ways to do this—either with the actual costs incurred during the production process, or else with standard costs that are later adjusted to match actual costing experience. The first of these approaches is called actual cost overhead allocation, while the latter is called normal cost overhead allocation. We will address the actual cost overhead allocation first.

Under actual costing, there are several sources of costs that will flow into an overhead cost pool. As shown in Exhibit 5.3, all production supplies that cannot be traced to a specific product will be debited to the overhead account and credited to accounts payable (the credit may also be charged to raw

Reducing the Load

Job costing is still the dominant form of costing used in most manufacturing organizations. The new controller may be overwhelmed by the sheer volume of transactions and likelihood of errors creeping into the process. Rather than trying to eliminate errors from the existing system, consider eliminating some of the data entry and journal entries associated with the system. For example, avoid assigning direct labor costs to jobs if this is a small proportion of total costs, and never track the locations of inventory items through WIP if they are being manufactured for only a few hours or days. This can eliminate a great deal of work and more than a few costing errors. ▨

materials inventory or supplies expense, if supplies were first charged to either of these accounts). As already noted, some labor costs will also be charged to the overhead account. Also, and as previously noted under the materials costing flow, normal amounts of production scrap and spoilage will be charged to overhead. Indirect wages and other indirect costs will also flow into the overhead cost pool. At the end of the accounting period, the cost pool is charged out to various products based on a variety of possible allocation calculations, which

EXHIBIT 5.3 Job Costing: Transactions for Actual Overhead Allocations

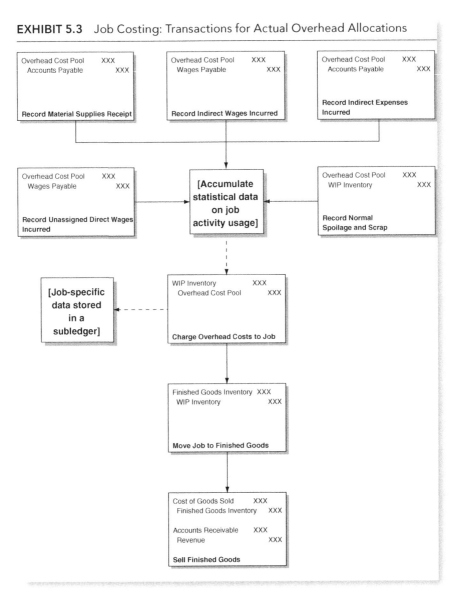

Source: Steven M. Bragg, *Cost Accounting: A Comprehensive Guide*, Copyright © 2001 John Wiley & Sons. Reprinted with permission of John Wiley & Sons, Inc.

are addressed in the activity-based costing section later in this chapter. Once overhead costs have been assigned to specific products, they follow the usual pattern of being moved to the finished goods inventory while their associated completed products are held in storage, and from there to the cost of goods sold upon sale of the product.

The allocation of costs to specific jobs can be delayed for some time under the actual cost overhead allocation method, because some costs can be compiled only at the end of the month, or perhaps not until several weeks thereafter. This is a problem for those companies that want more immediate costing information. We use normal overhead cost allocations to resolve this problem. Normal costing means that a company charges out costs in the short term using a historical average for its overhead costs, rather than actual costs. This process is shown in Exhibit 5.4. This allows costs to be charged to jobs at once. To ensure that the historical average being used for allocations does not stray too far from actual results, it is periodically compared to actual costs (which must still be accumulated), and adjusted as necessary.

When actual and normal costs are compared, there should be a small variance, which can be disposed of in several ways. One approach is to charge off the entire variance to the cost of goods sold, though this can create an unusually high or low cost of goods sold. Another approach is to spread the variance among the cost of goods sold, WIP inventory, and finished goods inventory, based on the total balances remaining in each account at the end of the reporting period. A final approach is to retroactively charge the variance to every job. These three options require an increasing amount of work to accomplish, in the order described. For that reason, the first option is the most commonly used, while allocation to individual jobs is a rarity.

The very large number of transactions required in a job costing system makes it an inefficient costing methodology from the perspective of the accounting department, which must verify that all of the transactions entered are correct. It can also call for the purchase of large quantities of data collection equipment, such as computerized time clocks and bar code scanners, which can be quite expensive. Furthermore, this system requires some participation by production personnel in the data collection process, which detracts from their primary mission of manufacturing products. However, given the need for job costing information, a company may find that there is no reasonable alternative to using this system. If so, the controller should carefully review the need for each type of data that can be potentially produced by the system, and collect

EXHIBIT 5.4 Job Costing: Transactions for Normal Cost Overhead Allocation

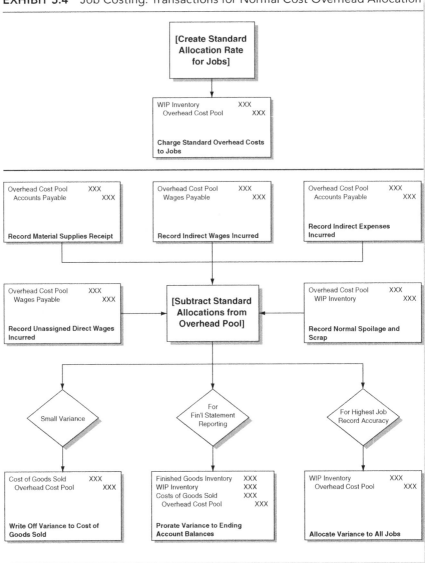

Source: Steven M. Bragg, *Cost Accounting: A Comprehensive Guide,* Copyright © 2001 John Wiley & Sons. Reprinted with permission of John Wiley & Sons, Inc.

only those that will result in valuable information—this will create a more efficient data collection environment that focuses only on key cost elements.

■ PROCESSING: PROCESS COSTING

Process costing is used in those situations when it is impossible to clearly differentiate the cost of individual units of production. For example, it is a prime candidate for use in an oil refinery, where it is impossible to track the cost of an individual gallon of diesel fuel.

The most common method for calculating process costs on a per-unit basis is to accumulate all production-related costs during the accounting period and calculate a weighted average per-unit cost based on these totals and the amount of production that was completed during the period, or which is currently still in process. An example of this calculation is shown in Exhibit 5.5.

In the exhibit, there are three blocks of calculations, each one segregated by a horizontal line. The top block contains a conversion calculation, which converts the amount of completed and WIP units into units to which

EXHIBIT 5.5 Weighted Average Costing Calculation

Units Summary	Direct Material Units	Conversion Factor	Conversion Cost Units	
Completed Units	1,000		1,000	
Ending Units in Process	350	60%	210	
Unit Totals	1,350		1,210	
Unit Cost Calculation	Direct Materials		Conversion Costs	Totals
Beginning WIP Cost	$20,000		$15,000	$35,000
Current Period Costs	$28,000		$21,500	$49,500
Total Costs	$48,000		$36,500	$84,500
Unit Totals (see above)	1,350		1,210	
Cost per Unit	$35.556		$30.165	
Unit Cost Allocation	Direct Materials		Conversion Costs	Totals
Cost of Completed Units	$35,556		$30,165	$65,721
Cost of Ending WIP Units	$12,444		$6,335	$18,779
Totals	$48,000		$36,500	$84,500

Source: Steven M. Bragg, Cost Accounting: A Comprehensive Guide, Copyright © 2001 John Wiley & Sons. Reprinted with permission of John Wiley & Sons, Inc.

materials and other costs can be allocated. The first column of numbers contains the calculation for the allocation of direct materials costs, while the final column of numbers calculates the allocation of all other production costs. For the purposes of this calculation, we assume that there are two types of costs—direct materials, which are typically added at the beginning of the production process, and all other costs, which can be added at a multitude of other points during the manufacturing sequence.

Since materials costs are assumed to occur at the earliest stage of production, the calculation of equivalent units for direct material cost allocation is quite easy—just use the number of finished goods completed (1,000) and the number of units in WIP inventory (350). However, for the purposes of allocating all other production costs, we must reduce the amount of WIP inventory by an estimate of their aggregate level of completion, which in the example is 60 percent. This results in total converted units of production of 1,210.

In the middle block of calculations, we accumulate the total cost of production and divide it by the equivalent number of units of production to determine the cost per unit. This calculation includes the costs that had been carried over in the WIP inventory from the preceding accounting reporting period, totaling $35,000. We add to this the current cost of production, which is $49,500, to yield a total cost of $84,500 that must be allocated to units of production. When divided by the slightly different units of production being used for direct material costs and all other production costs, we arrive at a direct material cost per unit of $35.556, and all other costs per unit of $30.165.

The lowermost block of calculations requires us to multiply the cost per unit (as determined in the middle block) by the total number of units (as determined in the top block). The calculation is identified with arrows. The result is $48,000 in direct material costs, of which $35,556 are charged to completed units and the remainder to WIP units. Total other production costs are $36,500, of which $30,165 are charged to completed units and the remainder to WIP. As a cross-check, we can see that the total allocated is $84,500, which matches the total amount of funds that were to be allocated, as noted on the far right side of the middle block.

This method is a simple one that requires very little data collection. However, some companies like to make the task even easier by avoiding the collection and interpretation of actual costs at the end of each accounting period. Instead, they prefer to use standard unit costs for their calculations, which allows them to calculate total costs more frequently and with no related data collection costs. This type of calculation is shown in Exhibit 5.6.

In the exhibit, the first block of calculations does not change—we still assume that a conversion factor must be applied to the ending WIP inventory for the purposes of assigning other production costs than direct materials. The difference arises in the second block, where we use only a standard cost per unit, rather than a summarization of actual costs. This cost is then carried forward into the third block of calculations, where we see that a total of $81,315 has been allocated to the ending finished goods and WIP inventory. However, this ending figure varies from the $84,500 that resulted from the preceding actual costing calculation in Exhibit 5.6. The difference of $3,185 was caused by a slight variance between the preset standard cost and

EXHIBIT 5.6 Weighted Average Cost Allocations Method Using Standard Costs

Units Summary	Direct Material Units	Conversion Factor	Conversion Cost Units	
Completed Units	1,000		1,000	
Ending Units in Process	350	60%	210	
Unit Totals	1,350		1,210	
Unit Cost Calculation	**Direct Materials**		**Conversion Costs**	
Standard Unit Cost	$32,000		$31,500	
Unit Cost Calculation	**Direct Materials**		**Conversion Costs**	**Totals**
Standard Cost of Completed Units	$32,000		$31,500	$63,500
Standard Cost of Ending WIP Units	$11,200		$6,615	$ 17,815
Standard Cost Totals	$43,200		$38,115	$ 81,315
Period Variance				
Beginning Standard WIP Cost	$20,000		$15,000	$35,000
Current Period Actual Costs	$28,000		$21,500	$49,500
Total Period Costs	$48,000		$36,500	$84,500
Standard Cost Totals	$43,200		$38,115	$ 81,315
Cost Variaiance	$ 4,800		$(1,615)	$ 3,185

Source: Steven M. Bragg, *Cost Accounting: A Comprehensive Guide*, Copyright © 2001 John Wiley & Sons. Reprinted with permission of John Wiley & Sons, Inc.

the actual cost. The presence of this variance causes us to add a fourth block of calculations at the bottom of the exhibit, in which we compare the actual costs incurred during the period to the standard costs, which shows that more costs than expected were incurred in the direct materials column, while fewer costs were incurred under the other production costs column.

The main issue for the controller is what to do with this variance. If negligible, it can be charged off to the cost of goods sold. If it is so large that expensing the difference will result in an appreciable impact on reported earnings, then a more accurate approach is to apportion the variance among the cost of goods sold, WIP inventory, and finished goods inventory.

The data collection and calculations required for a process costing system are substantially simpler than what is required for a job costing system, and so is a favorite approach for those who wish to pare their data collection costs or who produce such large volumes of similar products that there is no point in attempting to track the costs of individual products.

▓ PROCESSING: STANDARD COSTING

The first step in the creation of a standard costing system is to create a set of standard costs in a variety of different areas. The industrial engineering staff is assigned the task of creating direct labor standard costs, while the purchasing staff is most typically assigned the chore of creating standard costs for purchased goods, and the controller is called on to coordinate the development of a set of standard overhead costs. If there are subproducts created during the production process that may be valued at the end of each accounting reporting period, then the industrial engineering staff will calculate these standards. It is also possible to reduce the areas in which standard costs are used, with actual costs being accumulated in other areas. This mix of costing types can arise when there is some concern that reasonably accurate standard costs cannot be constructed, or if existing actual costing systems already produce reasonably accurate results.

Another issue to settle as soon in the standard cost development process as possible is the timing of changes to these standards. This can be done quite infrequently, perhaps once every few years, or as rapidly as once a month (which results in standard costs that are nearly indistinguishable from actual costs). The key determinant influencing the pace of change is the perceived pace at which actual costs are changing. If there are minimal changes to a manufacturing process, then there is certainly no reason to constantly review the process and set new standards. Conversely, a company that has installed an aggressive continuous improvement strategy will find that its standard costs are constantly falling behind changes in actual costs, which requires frequent revisions to standards.

The assumptions used to create standard costs must also be addressed. For example, an industrial engineer must make some assumptions about the speed of efficiency improvements being realized by the production staff (known as the learning curve) in order to determine the future standard cost that roughly matches these expected changes in efficiency. Similarly, a standard cost must be matched to the expected production equipment configuration to be used, since this has a considerable impact on the overhead costs that can be assigned to a product. Another key assumption is the volume of production, since a large assumed production run will spread its setup cost over many units, whereas a short production run will result in higher setup costs on a per-unit basis. Yet another factor is the assumed condition of the equipment to be used in the manufacturing process, since poorly maintained or old equipment will be in operation for fewer hours than would otherwise be the case. The production system being used, such as just-in-time or manufacturing resource planning, will also have a significant impact on standard costs, since different systems result in the incurrence of different types of costs in such areas as machine setup time, equipment depreciation, materials handling costs, and inventory investment costs. An issue that is particular to direct labor is the anticipated result of union negotiations, since these directly and immediately impact hourly wage rates. Given the large number of issues involved in the setting of accurate standard costs, it is no surprise that this task can require the ongoing services of an experienced group of professionals, the cost of which must be considered when making the decision to use a standard costing

A final factor to consider when creating standard costs is the level of attainability of the costs. One option is to devise an *attainable standard*, which is a cost that does not depart very much from the existing actual cost. This results in reasonable cost targets that employees know they can probably meet. Another alternative is to use *historical costs* as the basis for a standard cost. This is generally not recommended, for the resulting costs are no different from a company's existing actual cost structure, and so gives employees no incentive to attempt to reduce costs. The diametrically opposite approach is to create a set of *theoretical standards*, which are based on costs that can only be achieved if the manufacturing process runs absolutely perfectly. Since employees cannot possibly meet these cost goals for anything but very short periods of time, it tends to result in lower employee morale. Thus, of the potential range of standard costs that can be set, the best approach is to set moderate stretch goals that are achievable.

Finally, we are ready to begin using standard costs. But for what purpose do we use them? A key reason for using standards is to create benchmarks for inclusion in a manufacturing resources planning (MRP II) production system. This commonly used system multiplies a production forecast by a detailed set of product labor, materials, and capacity requirements to determine how many direct labor personnel and specific materials and how much machine capacity will be needed. This system requires extremely detailed and accurate standards to be successful. The standards needed by MRP II are for units of labor, materials, and capacity, rather than their costs. In other words, a direct labor standard for an MRP II system may be 12 minutes of labor, rather than its cost for those 12 minutes of $4.58.

Yet another use for standards is in product pricing. The company sales staff frequently asks the engineering staff to provide it with cost estimates for new product configurations, many of which are only slightly different from existing products. However, the engineering staff may take days or weeks to provide the sales personnel with this information—which may be too long to satisfy an impatient customer. By using standard costs, the sales staff can compile product costs very quickly with only a brief approval review from the engineering staff.

A very common use for standard costs is for the valuation of inventory. Many companies do not want to be bothered with the time-consuming accumulation of actual inventory costs at the end of each accounting period, and so they create standard costs for valuation purposes, which they occasionally compare to actual costs to ensure that the inventory valuation is accurate. It is not worth the effort to create standard costs for this purpose if a company's inventory levels are extremely low, or if a just-in-time manufacturing system is in use, since the amount of time that will be saved in valuing inventory is small, given the minor quantities of stock that will be kept in the warehouse. However, manufacturers with large inventory balances will find that this is still an effective way to rapidly determine the value of inventory.

Unfortunately, the use of standard costs for inventory valuation is also subject to control problems, for deliberate manipulation of standards can result in large changes in the value of inventory, which in turn impacts the reported level of company profits. For example, the standard cost for a finished goods item can include an assumption for the amount of production setup costs allocated to each item, which is heavily influenced by the assumed number of units produced in a manufacturing run. By shifting the assumed length of the production run downward, the amount of cost allocated to each unit goes up. This type of interference with standard costs can result in wildly inaccurate reported financial results.

If standard costs are used for inventory valuation, the accounting staff will periodically compare standard to actual costs to ensure that there are not excessively large differences between the two. If a company is audited at year-end, then the auditors will require a comparison to actual costs, and a write-off of the difference to the cost of goods sold (if standard costs are higher than actual costs) or an increase in the inventory balance (if actual costs are higher than standard costs). Since a significant difference between the two types of costs can result in a startling change in the reported level of income during the period when this adjustment is made, it is wise to review some of the large-cost items on a regular basis to ensure that there will be no surprises at the time of reconciliation to actual costs.

PROCESSING: DIRECT COSTING

A direct cost is a cost that is directly associated with changes in production volume. This usually restricts the definition of direct costs to direct materials and direct labor (and a strong case can be made for *not* using direct labor, since this cost tends to be present even when production volumes vary). For example, the materials used to create a product are a direct cost, whereas the machine used to convert the materials into a finished product is not a direct cost, because it is still going to be sitting on the factory floor, irrespective of any changes in production volume. The use of direct costing results in a slightly different income statement, as shown in Exhibit 5.7.

EXHIBIT 5.7   Income Statement Formatting for Direct Costing

Revenue		$1,000,000
Cost of Goods Sold		
Direct Materials	$320,000	
Direct Labor	170,000	
Total Direct Costs		$ 490,000
Gross Margin		
Operating Expenses		
Production Departmen	325,000	
General and Administrative	115,000	
Total Operating Expenses		$ 440,000
Net Profit		$ 50,000

The only difference between the income statement shown in Exhibit 5.7 and a more traditional format is that all nondirect costs have been shifted below the gross margin line and into the production department's costs. Though this seems like a subtle change, it focuses the attention of the management team on the incremental changes in the cost of goods sold that are usually masked by a large and relatively fixed amount of overhead costs.

The Simplicity of Direct Costing

When managers want cost information for a decision, the accounting staff may require multiple days to return the required information, due to the complexity of developing an overhead cost assignment. However, managers have a tendency to focus only on direct costs and are likely to throw out the overhead costs when making decisions. Consequently, the new controller can save time all around by issuing only direct costs, but be sure to warn recipients of the absence of overhead costs in the presented information and issue a general warning about the impact of ignoring the missing information. ■

By focusing solely on the direct cost of a product or activity, a controller can provide valuable information to management regarding prospective changes in costs that will arise as a result of some management action. For example, if a change to a more efficient type of processing equipment is contemplated, then the direct cost of a product may be lowered if this will result in less material usage. This may also result in less direct labor cost if the machine takes over some tasks previously performed by employees—this will cut direct costs, but may increase overhead costs if the cost of the machine is higher than that of the machine it is replacing. Yet another example is when a customer wants the lowest possible price for a product, and the company has some free capacity available for producing what the customer needs; the use of direct costing will reveal the lowest possible cost that must be covered by the price charged to the customer in order to break even. Direct costing can also be used to determine which customers are the most profitable, by subtracting the direct cost of their purchases from the prices paid, which yields the amount they are contributing toward the company's coverage of overhead costs and profit. Another very good use for direct costing is to include the concept in the budgeting system, where it is used to change budgeted variable costs to match the actual sales volumes achieved; this approach derives a much closer match between the budgeted and actual cost of goods sold, because the budget now flexes with the actual volume level experienced. For all of these reasons, direct costing is a highly recommended costing system.

However, there are a number of situations in which direct costing should *not* be used and in which it will yield incorrect information. Its single largest problem is that it completely ignores all indirect costs, which make up the bulk of all costs incurred by today's companies. This is a real problem when dealing with long-term costing and pricing decisions, since direct costing will likely yield results that do not achieve long-term profitability. For example, a direct costing system may calculate a minimum product price of $10.00 for a widget that is indeed higher than all direct costs, but which is lower than the additional overhead costs that are associated with the product line. If the company continues to use the $10.00 price for all product sales for well into the future, then the company will experience losses because overhead costs are not being covered by the price. The best way to address this problem is to build strict boundaries around the circumstances where incremental prices derived from a direct costing system are used.

Another problem with direct costing is that it assumes a steady level of unit costs for the incremental costing and pricing decisions for which it is most often used. For example, a company receives an offer from a customer to buy 5,000 units of product X at a fixed price. The cost accounting staff may determine that the proposed price will indeed yield a profit, based on the direct cost per unit, and so recommends that the deal be approved. However, because the staff has focused only on direct costs, it has missed the fact that the company is operating at near full-capacity levels, and that to process the entire 5,000-unit order will require the addition of some costly machinery, the acquisition of which will make the proposed deal a very expensive one indeed. To avoid this problem, anyone using a direct costing system must have access to company capacity information and should coordinate with the production scheduling staff to ensure that capacity levels will permit their incremental pricing and costing scenarios to be achieved.

A subtle issue that many users of direct costing systems miss is that the types of costs that fall within the direct costing definition will increase as the volume of units in a direct costing decision goes up. For example, the only direct cost involved with a single unit of production is the direct materials used to build it, whereas a larger production volume will likely involve some change in the related number of manufacturing employees needed on the production line. For example, if the direct costing decision involves an entire production line, then all of the equipment and supervisory costs tied to that production line are now also influenced by the decision to produce or not produce, and so should be included in the direct costing system. At an even larger level, the decision to use the production of an entire facility should include every cost needed to run that facility, which may include utilities, rent, and insurance—costs that are not normally included in smaller-volume production decisions. Consequently, direct costing analysis must be conducted within narrowly defined volume ranges, with careful attention to what costs are likely to vary with the volumes that are under review.

Direct costing cannot be used for inventory valuation, because it is disallowed by GAAP. The reason for this is that, under a direct costing system, all costs besides direct costs are charged to the current period. There is no provision for capitalizing overhead costs and associating them with inventory that will be sold off in future periods. This results in an imbalance between the reported level of profitability in each period and the amount of production that occurred. For example, a manufacturer of Christmas ornaments with a direct costing system may sell all of its output in one month of the year, but be forced to recognize all of its nondirect production costs in every month of the year, which will result in reported losses for 11 months of the year. Under GAAP, these nondirect costs would be capitalized into inventory and recognized only when the inventory is sold, thereby more closely matching reported revenues and expenses. Given the wide disparity between the reported results, it is no surprise that GAAP bans the use of direct costing for inventory valuation.

PROCESSING: THROUGHPUT COSTING

A costing methodology that focuses on capacity utilization is called throughput accounting. It assumes that there is always one bottleneck operation in a production process that commands the speed with which products or services can be completed. This operation becomes the defining issue in determining what products should be manufactured first, since this in turn results in differing levels of profitability.

The basic calculation used for throughput accounting is shown in Exhibit 5.8. The exhibit shows a series of electronic devices that a company can choose from for its near-term production requirements. The second column describes the amount of throughput that each of the products generates per minute in the bottleneck operation; "throughput" is the amount of margin left after all direct material costs have been subtracted from revenue. For example, the 19″ Color Television produces $81.10 of throughput, but requires ten minutes of processing time in the bottleneck operation, resulting in throughput per minute of

EXHIBIT 5.8 Throughput Accounting Method

Product	Throughput $/Minute of Constraint	Required Constraint Usage (min.)	Unit Demand/ Actual Production	Cumulative Constraint Utilization	(Cumulative Through/ Product
19" Color Television	$8.11	10	1,000/1,000	10,000	$81,100
100-Watt Stereo	7.50	8	2,800/2,800	22,400	168,000
5" LCD Television	6.21	12	500/500	6,000	37,260
50" High-Definition TV	5.00	14	3,800/1,700	23,800	119,000

Maximum Constrain Time: 62,200

Throughput total	$405,360
Operating Expenses Total	375,000
Profit	30,360
Profit Percentage	7.5%
Investment	500,000
Return on Investment	6.1%

Source: Steven M. Bragg, *Cost Accounting: A Comprehensive Guide,* Copyright © 2001 John Wiley & Sons. Reprinted with permission of John Wiley & Sons, Inc.

$8.11. The various electronic devices are sorted in the exhibit from top to bottom in order of largest throughput per minute. This ordering tells the user how much of the most profitable products can be produced before the total amount of available time in the bottleneck (which is 62,200 minutes, as noted at the top of the exhibit) is used up. The calculation for bottleneck utilization is shown in the "Unit Demand/Actual Production" column. In that column, the 19" Color Television has a current demand for 1,000 units, which requires 10,000 minutes of bottleneck time (as shown in the following column). This allocation of bottleneck time progresses downward through the various products until we come to the 50" High-Definition TV at the bottom of the list, for which there is only enough bottleneck time left to manufacture 1,700 units.

By multiplying the dollars of throughput per minute times the number of minutes of production time, we arrive at the cumulative throughput dollars resulting from the manufacture (and presumed sale) of each product, which yields a total throughput of $405,360. We then add up all other expenses, totaling $375,000, and subtract them from the total throughput, which gives us a profit of $30,360. These calculations comprise the basic throughput accounting analysis model.

Now let us reexamine the model based on a rejuggling of the priority of orders. If the cost accounting manager were to examine each of the products based on the addition of allocated overhead and direct labor costs to the direct materials that were used as the foundation for the throughput dollar calculations, she might arrive at the conclusion that, when fully burdened, the 50' High-Definition TV is actually the most profitable, while the 19" Color Television is the least profitable. Accordingly, she recommends that the order of production be changed to reflect these "realities," which gives us the new throughput report shown in Exhibit 5.9.

The result is a significant loss, rather than the increase in profits that had been expected. Why the change? The trouble is that allocated overhead costs have no bearing on throughput, because allocated costs will not change in accordance with incremental production decisions, such as which product will

EXHIBIT 5.9 Revised Throughput Analysis Based on Allocation Costs

Product	Throughput $/Minute of Constraint	Required Constraint Usage (min.)	Unit Demand/ Actual Production	Cumulative Constraint Utilization	Cumulative Through/ Product
Maximum Constrain Time: 62,200					
50" High-Definition TV	5.00	14	3,800/3,800	53,200	$266,000
100-Watt Stereo	7.50	8	2,800/1,125	9,000	67,500
5" LCD Television	6.21	12	500/0	0	0
19" Color Television	$8.11	10	1,000/0	0	0
			Throughtput total		$333,500
			Operating Expenses Total		375,000
			Profit		−41,500
			Profit Percentage		−12.4%
			Investment		500,000
			Return on Investment		−8.3%

Source: Steven M. Bragg, *Cost Accounting: A Comprehensive Guide*, Copyright © 2001 John Wiley & Sons. Reprinted with permission of John Wiley & Sons, Inc.

be manufactured first. Instead, the overhead cost pool will exist, irrespective of any modest changes in activity levels. Consequently, it makes no sense to apply allocated costs to the production scheduling decision, when the only issue that matters is how much throughput per minute a product can generate.

Capital budgeting is an area in which throughput costing analysis can be applied with excellent results. The trouble with most corporate capital budgeting systems is that they do not take into consideration the fact that the only valid investment is one that will have a positive impact on the amount of throughput that can be pushed through a bottleneck operation. Any other investment will result in greater production capacity in other areas of the company that still cannot produce any additional quantities, since the bottleneck operation controls the total amount of completed production. For example, the throughput model in Exhibit 5.10 shows the result of an investment of $28,500 in new equipment that is added later in the production process than

EXHIBIT 5.10 Revised Throughput Analysis Based on Additional Investment

			Maximum Constraint Time: 62,200		
Product	Throughput $/Minute of Constraint	Required Constraint Usage (min.)	Unit Demand/ Actual Production	Cumulative Constraint Utilization	Cumulative Throughput/ Product
19" Color Television	$8.11	10	1,000/1,000	10,000	$ 81,100
100-Watt Stereo	7.50	8	2,800/2,800	22,400	168,000
5" LCD Television	6.21	12	500/500	6,000	37,260
50" High-Definition TV	5.00	14	3,800/1,700	23,800	119,000
			Throughput Profit		$405,360
			Total Operating Expense Total		375,000
			Profit		30,360
			Profit Percentage Investment		7.5%
			Investment		528,500
			Return on Investment		5.7%

the bottleneck operation. The result is an increase in the total investment, to $528,500, and absolutely no impact on profitability, which yields a reduced return on investment of 5.7 percent.

A more profitable solution would have been to invest in anything that would increase the productivity of the bottleneck operation, which could be either a direct investment in that operation, or an investment in an upstream operation that will reduce the amount of processing required for a product by the bottleneck operation.

As another example, the cost accounting staff has conducted a lengthy activity-based costing analysis, which has determined that a much higher amount of overhead cost must be allocated to the high-definition television, which results in a loss on that product. Accordingly, the product is removed from the list of viable products, which reduces the number of products in the mix of production activity, as shown in Exhibit 5.11.

The result is a reduction in profits. The reason is that the cost accounting staff has made the incorrect assumption that, by eliminating a product, all of

EXHIBIT 5.11   Revised Throughput Analysis with One Less Product

			Maximum Constraint Time: 62,200		
Product	Throughput $/Minute of Constraint	Required Constraint Usage (min.)	Unit Demand/ Actual Production	Cumulative Constraint Utilization	Cumulative Throughput/ Product
19" Color Television	$8.11	10	1,000/1,000	10,000	$ 81,100
100-Watt Stereo	7.50	8	2,800/2,800	22,400	168,000
5" LCD Television	6.21	12	500/500	6,000	37,260
			Throughput Total		$286,360
			Operating Expense Total		375,000
			Profit		−88,640
			Profit Percentage Investment		−30.9%
			Investment		500,000
			Return on Investment		−17%

Source: Steven M. Bragg, *Cost Accounting: A Comprehensive Guide*, Copyright © 2001 John Wiley & Sons. Reprinted with permission of John Wiley & Sons, Inc.

the associated overhead cost will be eliminated, too. Though a small amount of overhead might be eliminated when the production of a single product is stopped, the bulk of it will still be incurred.

Throughput accounting does a very good job of tightly focusing attention on the priority of production in situations where there is a choice of products that can be manufactured. It can also have an impact on a number of other decisions, such as whether to grant volume discounts, outsource manufacturing, stop the creation of a product, or invest in new capital items. Given this wide range of activities, it should find a place in the mix of costing methodologies at many companies. We now shift to a discussion of ABC, whose emphasis is the complete reverse of throughput accounting—it focuses on the proper allocation of overhead

PROCESSING: ACTIVITY-BASED COSTING

An ABC system is designed to match overhead costs as closely as possible with company activities. By doing so, overhead costs can be reasonably associated with products, departments, customers, or other users of activities, which tells managers where overhead costs are being used within a company. This results in much better control over overhead costs.

There are several ways to allocate overhead costs. Some overhead costs, such as utilities, are associated with specific machines. For example, a machine may require ten cents of electricity per minute. If so, this overhead cost can be charged out to those products that are run through the machine, based on the time spent being worked upon it. Other overhead costs are associated with a specific product line and can reasonably be allocated to the activities performed within that product line.

For example, there is typically a supervisor who is assigned to a single product line. If so, the fully burdened salary of this person can be charged to such related activities as production and maintenance scheduling. Still other overhead costs may be grouped by commodity used in the production process. For example, each member of the purchasing staff may be responsible for the procurement of a specific commodity. If so, this overhead cost can be distributed to individual products based on their usage of the commodity. Clearly, there are many valid ways to allocate overhead costs to various activities, and from there to users of those costs. An ABC system creates a structured approach to the accumulation, storage, and allocation of overhead costs using many of these activity measures.

An ABC system is a difficult and complex one to create because of the wide variety of costs that must be accumulated, tracked in relation to different types of activities, and charged off. Here are the primary steps involved in creating such a system:

Step 1: Determine the scope of the system. A fully developed ABC system that encompasses all costs throughout a company is a massive undertaking that may not yield any results for several years. A better approach is to conduct a gradual rollout of the system that produces results more quickly. Accordingly, a key factor is limiting each incremental rollout of the system to a carefully defined segment of the business. The determination of scope should also include a review of the level of detailed analysis that the system is to produce, since an excessive focus on detail may result in a system that is too expensive in relation to the utility of the information produced.

Step 2: Set aside direct costs. There will be several direct costs that can be clearly and indisputably traced to specific products. These costs should be identified early in the design phase, so that they will not be erroneously added to the ABC allocation system.

Step 3: Locate costs in the general ledger. The next step is to identify each of the overhead costs in the general ledger that will be allocated by the ABC system. This can be a difficult undertaking, for the required costs may be lumped together in the ledger, and must be segregated through a new data collection system that involves the creation of a new general ledger account number. Alternatively, the split may be achieved less accurately by allocating a percentage of the cost in a single general ledger account to several overhead cost items that will then be allocated.

Step 4: Store costs in cost pools. All of the costs that have been identified within the general ledger must now be stored in a series of cost pools. Each cost pool accumulates costs that are similar to one another. For example, a building cost pool will include the costs of insurance and maintenance for a building, whereas a product line cost pool may include the marketing and supervisory costs that can be traced to a specific product line. A third type of cost pool is one that is related to a specific production batch and can include such costs as production control labor, tooling, materials handling, and quality control. The total number of cost pools used will have a direct impact on the maintenance costs of an ABC system, so the design team must balance the increased allocation accuracy associated with more cost pools with the extra labor needed to maintain them.

Step 5: Determine activity drivers. Having summarized overhead costs into a set of cost pools, we must now allocate them, which we do with an activity driver—this is a variable that reasonably explains the consumption of costs from a cost pool. For example, some accounts payable costs are closely associated with the number of checks printed and mailed, while some engineering costs vary directly with the number of design changes added to a product. Examples of other activity drivers are the number of machine setups, the number of maintenance work orders, the number of purchase orders, and the number of customer orders processed. Whichever activity driver is chosen as the basis for cost pool allocation should be easy to calculate, require minimal data collection, and have a reasonably close cause-and-effect relationship with a cost pool.

Step 6: Spread costs from secondary to primary cost pools. Some of the cost pools include costs that are, in turn, distributed to other cost pools. These costs are usually for internal company services, such as management information systems services that are provided to other departments. These secondary cost pools must be allocated to primary cost pools.

Step 7: Calculate the overhead cost per activity unit. We then divide the total number of occurrences of each activity driver into the total amount of costs in the primary cost pools for the accounting period, which results in a dollar figure per unit of activity.

Step 8: Assign activity costs to cost objects. The final step is to calculate the usage of each activity driver by a cost object (which is anything that uses activities, such as products or customers). For example, if a product requires the creation of two purchase orders (which are activity drivers) and the ABC system has determined that each purchase order requires $32.15 to create, then the amount of overhead charged to the product will be $64.30.

In brief, the ABC process involves taking costs out of the general ledger and assigning them to either secondary or primary cost pools, which are then distributed to cost objects through the use of activity drivers. The overall process is shown in Exhibit 5.12.

PROCESSING: TARGET COSTING

Most of the costing methodologies described in this chapter are primarily concerned with the interpretation of costing data after it has already been incurred. Target costing differs from them in that it describes the costs that are expected to be incurred, and how this will impact product profitability levels. By describing costs in a proactive and future-oriented manner, managers can determine how they should alter product designs before they enter the manufacturing process in order to ensure that the company earns a reasonable profit on all new products.

EXHIBIT 5.12 ABC PROCESS FLOW

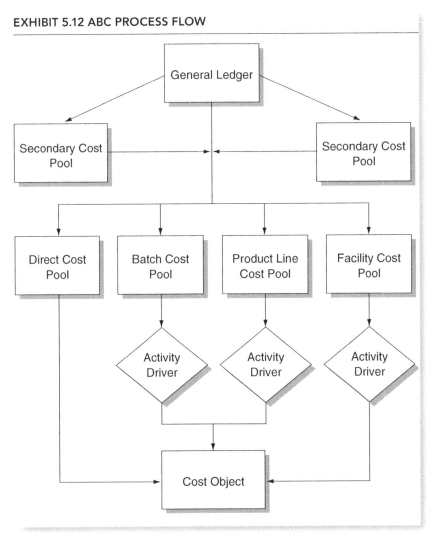

To use this methodology, the controller is assigned to a new product design team and asked to continually compile the projected cost of a product as it moves through the design process. Managers will use this information not only to make product alterations, but also to drop a product design if it cannot meet its cost targets.

There are four basic steps involved in target costing. First, the design team conducts market research to determine the price points that a company is most likely to achieve if it creates a product with a certain set of features. The research should include information about the perceived value of certain features on a product, so that the design team can add or subtract features from the design with a full knowledge of what these changes probably will do to the final price at which the product will be sold. The second step is to subtract from the prospective product price a gross margin that must be earned on the product; this can be a standard company-wide margin that must be earned on all new products, or perhaps a more specific one that management has imposed based on the perceived risk of the project. By subtracting the required margin from the expected price, we arrive at the maximum amount that the product can cost. This total cost figure drives the next step.

The design team then uses value engineering to drive down the cost of the product until it meets its overall cost target. Value engineering requires considerable attention to the elimination of production functions, a product design that is cheaper to manufacture, a planned reduction of product durability in order to cut costs, a reduced number of product features, less expensive component parts, and so on—in short, any activity that will lead to a reduced product cost. This process also requires the team to confirm costs with the suppliers of raw materials and outsourced parts, as well as the processing costs that will be incurred internally. The controller plays a key role at this stage, regularly summarizing costing information and relaying it not only to the team members, but to the managers who are reviewing the team's progress. A standard procedure at this point is to force the team to come within a set percentage of its cost target at various milestones (such as being within 12 percent of the target after three months of design work, 6 percent after four months, and on target after five months); if the team cannot meet increasingly tighter costing targets, then the project will be canceled.

Once these design steps have been completed and a product has met its targeted cost level, the target costing effort is shifted into a different activity, which is follow-on activities that will reduce costs even further after the product has entered its production phase. This final step is used to create some excess gross margin over time, which allows the company to reduce the price of the product to respond to

presumed increases in the level of competition. The sources of these cost reductions can be either through planned supplier cost reductions or through waste
reductions in the production process (known as *kaizen* costing). The concepts of
value engineering and *kaizen* costing can be used repeatedly to gradually reduce
the cost of a product over time, as shown in Exhibit 5.13. In the exhibit, we see that
the market price of a product follows a steady downward trend, which is caused by
ongoing competitive pressure as the market for the product matures. To meet this
pricing pressure with corresponding reductions in costs, the company initially creates product A and uses value engineering to design a preset cost into the product.
Once the design is released for production, *kaizen* costing is used to further reduce
costs in multiple stages until there are few additional reductions left to squeeze
out of the original design. At this point, the design team uses value engineering
to create a replacement product B that incorporates additional cost savings (likely
including the cost reduction experience gleaned from the *kaizen* costing stages
used for product A) that result in an even lower initial cost. *Kaizen* costing is then

EXHIBIT 5.13   Stages in the Cost Reduction Process

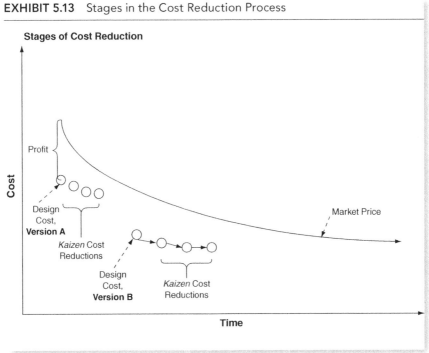

Source: Steven M. Bragg, *Cost Accounting: A Comprehensive Guide*, Copyright © 2001
John Wiley & Sons. Reprinted with permission of John Wiley & Sons, Inc.

used once again to further reduce the cost of product B, thereby keeping the cost reduction process moving in an ever-downward direction. The entire target costing process, incorporating all of the preceding steps, is shown in Exhibit 5.14.

OUTPUTS: COST VARIANCES

A costing methodology of any type is not of much use if there is no output from it that gives valuable information to the management team. One of the primary outputs that is expected is a listing of costing variances, which are actual costs that depart from expectations. There are a number of standard variance calculations that can be summarized into a report, and which we will cover in this section.

Variances fall into three categories. The first is a price variance and is the difference between the standard purchase cost of an item and the actual cost at which it was purchased, multiplied by the actual number of units purchased. It can be used to describe the variances in the general cost categories of purchased parts, direct labor, and overhead, and so is seen in three different places on cost variance reports.

The second type of variance is the efficiency variance. This is the difference between the actual quantity of resources needed to manufacture something, less the standard quantity, multiplied by its standard cost. This variance can also be broken down into three subvariances: a direct labor efficiency variance, a yield variance that relates to materials usage, and a variable overhead efficiency variance. There is no efficiency variance related to fixed overhead costs, since they are not expected to change with volume, and so have no targeted level of efficiency against which to compare.

The final variance is the volume variance. It applies to only one cost type, as opposed to the other variances; this is fixed overhead costs. Fixed overhead costs are charged to the cost of goods sold, or other parts of the income statement, as a fixed amount per accounting period, rather than as a percentage of the volume of production. Because of this difference in the method of cost allocation, a change in the actual production volume from the level that was expected when the allocation was set will result in a volume variance. It is calculated by multiplying the fixed overhead portion of the overhead rate by the number of units produced, and then subtracting this amount from the total fixed overhead cost pool.

An example of these variances and the calculations used to derive them is shown in Exhibit 5.15.

In the upper-left corner of the variance report, we see that there is a total variance of $61,725. The block of costs immediately below this shows the cost

EXHIBIT 5.14 Target Costing Process

Source: Steven M. Bragg, *Cost Accounting: A Comprehensive Guide*, Copyright © 2001 John Wiley & Sons. Reprinted with permission of John Wiley & Sons, Inc.

EXHIBIT 5.15 Cost Variance Report

	Actual	Budget	Variance
Cost of Goods Sold	265,000	203,275	(61,725)

Account Number	Account Name	Actual	Budget	Variance
4000-020	Direct Materials	102,500	76,500	(26,000)
4000-030	Direct Labor	34,000	29,450	(4,550)
4000-040	Variable Overhead	50,000	36,550	(13,450)
4000-050	Fixed Overhead	78,500	60.775	(17,725)
		265,000	203,275	61,725

Material Price Variance:
Total actual price/unit paid	10.25
Total standard price/unit paid	9.00
= Variance per unit	1.25
× Number of units consumed	10,000
= Material price variance	**12,500**

Material Yield Variance:
Total actual units consumed	10,000
Total standard units consumed	8,500
= Unit variance	1,500
× Standard price per unit	9
= Material yield variance	**13,500**

Fixed Overhead Price Variance:
Total actual price/unit paid	7.85
Total standard price/unit paid	7.15
= Variance per unit	0.70
× Number of units consumed	10,000
= Fixed overhead price variance	**7,000**

Fixed Overhead Volume Variance:
Standard overhead rate per unit	7.15
× Number of units consumed	10,000
= Total overhead charged to exp.	71,500
Actual overhead cost pool	60,775
= Volume variance	**10,725**

Labor Price Variance:
Total actual price/hour paid	8.00
Total standard price/hour paid	7.75
= Variance per hour	0.25
× Number of units consumed	4,250
= Labor price variance	**1,063**

Labor Efficiency Variance:
Total actual units consumed	4,250
Total standard units consumed	3,800
= Unit variance	450
× Standard price per unit	7.75
= Labor efficiency variance	**3,488**

Variable O/H Price Variance:
Total actual rate/unit paid	5.00
Total standard rate/unit paid	4.30
= Variance per unit	0.70
× Number of units consumed	10,000
= Variable O/H price variance	**7,000**

Variable O/H Efficiency Variance:
Total actual units consumed	10,000
Total standard units consumed	8,500
= Unit variance	1,500
× Standard price per unit	4.3
= Variable O/H efficiency variance	**6,450**

categories in which the variance arose, which sum to $61,725. Below and to the side of these variances are subsidiary variances that are linked back to the four major cost categories. For instance, the materials price variance in the upper-right corner reveals that the price paid for materials is $1.25 higher than expected, while the material yield variance located directly below it shows that 1,500 more units of materials were used for production than had been anticipated. The total variance from these two calculations is $26,000, which traces back to the total direct materials variance on the left side of the report. All of the variances trace back through the report in a similar manner. This is a good format for showing how variance calculations are derived, and how they flow through the accounting reporting system.

A company may not choose to report on all of these variances, since the detailed investigation of each one can be extremely time consuming. Thus, the variance for the direct labor price may not be reported on the grounds that management has little control over it when pricing is ruled by a formal agreement with a labor union. Similarly, the fixed overhead volume variance may not be reported because it relates more to ongoing production volumes than to management's ability to control the size of the overhead cost pool. Variances that are more commonly reported are the material price variance and all types of efficiency variances; the material price variance is used to monitor the performance of the purchasing staff, while efficiency variances are used to oversee the entire manufacturing process.

Some variances are not worthy of regular reporting, because they require an inordinate amount of data collection work in exchange for information that is of little use to management. For example, a detailed scrap variance that itemizes every item that was thrown out during a reporting period, alongside the reasons for each one, calls for a very large amount of investigative effort. The resulting report will contain information that may result in some long-term savings, but probably not enough to justify the work required to create the report.

Once the cost variance report has been completed, the accounting staff either will be asked to conduct an investigation into the causes of specific variances, or should do so on its own. If so, it is useful to know in advance what types of problems are most likely to cause variances, so that investigative work can be first targeted at these items. The most common causes of each major variance are:

- *Fixed overhead spending variance*
    - Suppliers have increased their prices for products and services that fall into this expense category. Review related supplier contracts for scheduled price increases.
    - The company has increased its usage of the products or services recorded in this category. If so, the costs may actually be variable and should be shifted to a variable overhead account.

- *Labor price variance*
    - The standard rate has not been altered to match changes in the union's labor contract.
    - The standard rate does not include extra charges, such as shift premiums, bonuses, or overtime.
    - The people actually conducting work are at different pay rates than those that were assumed to be doing the work when the labor standards were created.

- *Material price variance*
    - The actual price paid is based on a different purchasing volume than what was assumed when the price standard was originally set.
    - The standard price was erroneously copied from a similar product that has a significantly different price.
    - The purchasing staff is now buying replacement parts that have a different price than the parts that were the basis for the standard.

- *Selling price variance*
    - Products were sold with different options than the products used to set selling price standards.
    - Customers have ordered in different unit volumes than those used to determine the standard price.
    - Customers have paid prices different from the invoiced prices (which will require investigation to resolve).
    - Customers were given promotional discounts on prices paid.

- *Variable overhead spending variance*
    - The supplier has changed its per-unit pricing. Look for a contractually mandated change in the per-unit price.
    - The company is purchasing in different volumes, which alters the per-unit price paid.
    - There are misclassifications in costs between the variable overhead and other accounts.

Though there are certainly other causes for variances, these are among the most common ones, and so should be investigated first. Also, the accounting staff will find that the same causes are likely to crop up repeatedly, so it is useful to develop and continually update a list of variances caused from previous reporting periods. This becomes the accounting staff's "short list" of variance causes that can be used to track down similar problems in the future.

CHAPTER SIX

Ratio and Trend Analysis

Importance of This Chapter

Frequently, the new controller walks into a situation where there is no consistently applied ratio analysis of any kind. If so, this is a great opportunity to formulate a company-wide measurement system to use as the basis for a new set of management reports within a few days of starting work. This chapter is filled with ratios from which to make selections.

This chapter describes the analysis of a business by using ratios and trends. The most common accounting measurements are included here; these are good for analyzing the balance sheet, the income statement, and relationships between the two. In addition, there are a number of performance measurements that do not directly relate to accounting, but rather to other functional areas, such as customer service, engineering, and materials management. These additional measures are necessary, because a controller cannot do an adequate job of maintaining systems, reporting on operating results, or recommending changes without a complete understanding of all company operations and how they interact. Consequently, the controller is well advised to develop a set of ratios and trend analyses for measurements that go beyond the usual accounting measurements to encompass the operating aspects of all departments. This chapter not only shows how to calculate each ratio, but also describes why each one is useful as well as any shortcomings it may have. The chapter concludes with a discussion of how ratios interrelate, as well as their limitations. The chapter is intended to give a controller enough information to set up a complete system of ratios and trends for the continuing analysis of all company operations.

HOW TO USE RATIOS AND TRENDS

Ratios are very useful for determining the interrelationships between numbers. For example, without a ratio, a manager has no way of knowing if the amount of accounts receivable is acceptable or if there should be a major collection effort underway to bring in old accounts receivable. Similarly, only a comparison of inventory to the cost of goods sold will tell if there is an excess amount of inventory on hand. Finally, you must compare interest expense to earnings to see if there is a risk of not paying for the interest on debt, which could result in corporate liquidation. All of this information is critical, and ratios are the best possible tool for determining it.

Ratios do not have to be used solely for analyzing financial information. For example, a ratio can reveal the extent to which a company has become top-heavy by comparing the number of indirect labor people to the number of direct labor employees. Another example is a comparison of sales to salespeople to see how many sales are being obtained, on average, by each salesperson. These measures are just as important as financial ones, but their components are not all found in the financial statements.

Despite their uses, there is a problem with ratios—they give no historical perspective on a measurement. For example, a ratio may reveal the amount of inventory turnover, but this does not tell a controller how the ratio is changing over time. For this information, you must list a series of measurements on a trend line. This can be listed on a simple bar chart or a more complex three-dimensional one, or even on a primitive numeric table—the format is important only in that it must clearly show the reader any changes in the ratio. When using ratios and trend lines together, a controller has a powerful analytical tool.

A trend line does not have to contain only ratios. They are commonly used to plot revenues or specific expense line items. This information is also useful, because management can see general trends that may require correction. The most common trend line uses only revenue data, because the sales and marketing manager wants to know the trend of sales for various divisions, product lines, and products. Once armed with this information, the sales and marketing staffs can take action to either continue hot sales growth or bolster flagging growth.

An important consideration when using ratios or trend lines is that they must be used consistently. There is nothing more confusing to a management team than to receive an entirely different set of measurements every month. Some measures may be so difficult to understand that management does not have the time to interpret the newest batch of measurements, and so ignores them; this does not assist in management's control of the business!

 ## A CAVEAT

The majority of this chapter covers the measurements that give a controller a better idea of the status of company operations. The key word is *better*, for you should not rely solely on these measurements to judge company operations. It is unfortunate that many controllers manage their departments strictly "by the numbers," and make recommendations for changes elsewhere in the company based solely on that information. A good manager uses measurements only as part of the body of knowledge required to do a thorough job of effectively and efficiently running a business. Other items that a controller should know about in order to plot a strong management course in the sea of business uncertainty are:

- **Branding.** Some companies, such as CocaCola, PepsiCo, or any automobile manufacturer, spend enormous amounts of money on marketing activities to build up the public's image of their brands. This may seem like a waste of money to a typical cost-conscious controller, but it has been proven time and again that consumers will pay a significant premium for branded products. Consequently, a controller should have a sufficient knowledge of corporate branding activities before releasing a report to management that recommends deep cuts in marketing costs in order to save money.
- **Company organization.** There may be quirks in how a company is organized that have a direct impact on the measurements that a controller sees. This is especially common for a large, multi-division company, where constant reorganizations result in altered reporting relationships. For example, a controller may find that the sales department expenses for a division are rapidly surpassing the budget; a knowledge of the organizational structure might reveal that there is no one in that position due to a recent reorganization. This changes the controller's action from a stinging

memo to the general manager of the division regarding cost controls to a strong request to the human resources staff to hire a new sales manager.

- **Competitors.** The actions of competitors have a profound impact on company operations. A competing product may be priced sharply lower than the company's product, resulting in a matching price drop that is initiated by the marketing staff. Alternatively, a sudden drop in sales may simply be caused by the entrance of a new competitor, while a rapid sales increase may be caused by the demise of a competitor, sending all of its customers to the company. For example, a controller may strongly recommend a doubling of production capacity based on a sudden uptick in revenues, though a knowledge of the industry would have revealed that a close competitor has gone out of business, and the uptick should be expected to only roughly match the sales of that defunct business, which is not sufficient to warrant the investment in more production facilities.

- **Goals.** If a company has established stretch goals that will be difficult to reach, a controller should expect strains on the organization that will appear in measurements. For example, an aggressive production plan will probably result in excessive levels of overtime and extra machine repair and maintenance; knowing about the goals would keep the controller in this example from spending too much time reviewing those measures that were clearly altered by the higher levels of production.

- **Management team.** The character of the management team has a profound impact on measurements. If it is unethical, there may be problems with the period-end cutoff, because this is a prime area for manipulating the volume of sales. The problem may pervade the organization, creating difficulties due to loans to owners and managers, incorrect commission payments, or difficulties with missing assets. For example, a measurement may reveal that inventory turnover is much worse than the historical average; based only on that measurement, a controller might enter into all sorts of calculations and investigations to root out the problem, whereas the knowledge that the owners are trying to inflate inventory values to underreport the cost of goods sold will lead the controller straight to the warehouse for an in-depth audit of inventory quantities.

- **Marketplace.** The market for a company's products is rarely a completely stable one. It may be seasonal, resulting in wide revenue swings depending on the month, or it may be going through a period of rapid expansion or contraction. For example, a controller may be tracking a trend line of revenue levels and notice a sudden, sharp drop in revenues for a product line. A frantic call to the sales staff might not have been so frantic if the controller realized that the product line was lawn mowers, and that sales always drop by the middle of the summer.

- **Monopoly situations.** It is not uncommon for a company to have a small number of products in its product portfolio that have no significant competition. This minority of products typically carry high prices and correspondingly high margins, which may generate sufficient cash flow to make a significant difference to a company's bottom line. A controller must know enough about a company's competitive situation to know which products are in a monopoly situation, because these "breadwinner" products are critical. For example, a controller should carefully track price points, unit volume, and gross margins on all monopoly items in order to warn management of any price or margin erosion; controllers who do not know which products are breadwinners will probably not segregate them for measurement, possibly resulting in no one knowing about market changes that will have a major impact on company profits.

- **New market activities.** Most companies attempt to enter new markets from time to time. This is a very expensive activity, because potential new customers must be educated about the company, research and development costs must be incurred to create new products for the market, a distribution system must be created, and a variety of policies and procedures realigned to better service the new markets. Many controllers take the conservative approach and protest these activities because of the large upfront cost. However, a more knowledgeable controller will realize that new markets drive company sales, and the expenses needed to enter those markets are the necessary costs of getting into them.

- **Product pricing.** A company may base its sales strategy on having the highest or lowest product price in the marketplace. This is not something that a controller typically measures, because the most common sales-related measures track only total revenues, not the component parts, which are prices and unit volumes. However, if the strategy is to maintain the highest or lowest price, then the controller should track this information and compare it to competing prices, so that management can maintain the appropriate price points.

- **Recruiting methods.** A company that is situated in an industry in which there is only a small available pool of qualified applicants, such as an engineering or software design company, incurs tremendous recruiting costs. This may involve overseas trips to recruit foreign candidates, or perhaps paying exorbitant fees to outside recruiters to locate potential employees. In these industries, very high recruiting costs are simply a part of doing business. If a controller does not know this, the human resources staff may be on the receiving end of a series of complaints, accusing them of using the most expensive recruiting approaches, when in fact they may be doing a very cost-effective job of locating new employees.

The previous points illustrate why a controller must know an organization's strengths and weaknesses, because they have a strong impact on measurements. This knowledge can be used in another way as well, for the measurement system can be altered to take advantage of corporate strengths, and bolstered to support the weakest areas. As discussed in the Interrelationship of Ratios section later in this chapter, it is clear that the peculiarities ensconced in every company require a controller to change, add to, and delete from the existing set of measurements to arrive at a measurement system that properly tracks weaknesses while only exerting the lightest control over organizationally strong areas.

MEASURES FOR PROFITABILITY

A controller needs to accurately judge the amount of profit extracted from a company's operations, which means knowing the exact margin earned by division, product line, and product. A controller must also have a good knowledge of fixed costs and how they impact company profits at different sales levels, as well as a thorough understanding of the amount of overhead and how that relates to the cost of goods sold. This section provides the ratios and percentage calculations needed to extract this information from the income statement. The measurements are:

- **Breakeven point.** This is the sales level at which, given a predetermined gross margin rate, a company will make a profit of zero. This is important, because a company may have such a high fixed-cost structure or low gross margins that it is nearly impossible to turn a profit unless there are extraordinarily high sales. By spotting this problem, a controller can push for sales of higher-margin products or a reduction in fixed costs. To calculate breakeven, simply divide operating expenses for the reporting period by the company's historical average gross margin. For the gross margin figure, it is best to use a recent average, so that the measurement accurately reflects any recent changes.
- **Number of times interest is earned.** This is an excellent measure of the risk a company undertakes when it adds debt. If the continuing amount of

cash flow cannot cover interest payments on existing debt, then a company is in serious trouble and must take steps to reduce the level of debt immediately. The measure is also good for companies considering acquiring more debt; a poor ratio will tell them not to do so. To calculate the measurement, determine the amount of interest charged on debt for a typical period (perhaps an average of the interest payments for the last quarter). Then obtain the net income figure from the income statement and add back any non-cash expenses, such as amortization and depreciation, which yields the actual cash flow. Then divide the average interest expense by the cash flow amount to determine the number of times that interest is earned.

▪ **Operating margins by division, segment, product line.** A company must have sufficient operating margins. Otherwise, all other management decisions become superfluous, since inadequate margins do not allow a company to throw off enough cash flow to stay in business. Consequently, the controller must calculate margins in a variety of ways—by division, segment, and product line—and pass this information along to management as frequently as possible. In particular, if the controller spots a rapid drop in margins, this information must go out to management immediately, rather than waiting until the next monthly financial reporting package. Information about operating margins is too time-critical to wait. The calculation for this measurement varies somewhat depending on the type of margin being measured, but is best calculated by creating a standard report for each variation using the accounting system's report writer to extract data from the general ledger and recast it in an income statement format. This may require some changes to the chart of accounts to ensure that there is enough segmentation of information to ensure reporting accuracy.

▪ **Overhead rate.** A primary area of competition is based on price, and the only way a company can succeed in that arena is to have extremely low costs. Costs are grouped into three areas, one of which is overhead. This can be a very large amount of money, especially for those organizations with bloated organizational structures. The amount of overhead is allocated to individual products, which has a major impact on the value of work-in-process and finished goods inventory. Allocation is based on an overhead rate that is calculated by compiling overhead costs for the period and dividing by the amount of direct labor (or other activity measure) expended during the period. The resulting overhead cost per direct labor hour is then allocated to inventory based on the amount of labor hours charged to the products. This method of charging costs to products can be highly inaccurate if the overhead rate per labor hour is extremely high, because a slight change in hours charged can result in a massive change in the overhead cost of the product. Also, because many products now require very few hours of work to produce, companies are coming to the conclusion that direct labor is a poor basis for spreading overhead costs and are switching to more accurate allocation methodologies, such as activity-based costing (ABC).

▪ **Percentage return on net sales.** This is a good indicator of how well all aspects of the business are performing in order to arrive at a profit. It is best tracked on a trend line to see how the profit percentage compares to that of previous periods, and is especially useful when tracked by product line, where there should be a considerable amount of consistency in the percentage from period to period. To calculate the measurement, simply divide the profit into net sales for the same period. However, be aware that the profit percentage is subject to manipulation, because it is possible to modify accruals and noncash expenses (e.g., depreciation and amortization) to fit the profit number that management wants.

Track Profits Net of Sales Activity!

If a company has a mix of standard and custom products, the sales effort required to sell the custom work may be resulting in much worse margins than anyone suspects. This is because the typical costing system does not include the cost of sales calls. In particular, if the sales staff travels out of town to make these sales, try including the cost of their travel in the margin analysis. It is possible that the result will be negative margins. ▪

▪ **Ratio of sales returns and allowances to gross sales.** This is an excellent way to determine the quality of goods sold or of the excess amount of inventory in the distribution pipeline. A company that finds customers sending back an inordinate amount of product either has a faulty product that requires immediate corrective action, or has stuffed so much inventory into the distribution pipeline that retailers simply cannot sell it all. Tracking this information on a trend line is especially helpful, in order to see problems that may develop over several months. To calculate the measurement, divide total sales returns by gross sales; both numbers should be aggregated separately in the general ledger. The ratio can be misleading, however, because sales returns invariably relate to sales from a previous period, not the current one against which the ratio is being measured.

▪ **Sales/profits per person.** Some companies have very large staffs, and, because the payroll expense is large, they choose to use it as a major indicator of internal efficiency. When they see the sales or profits per person falling, their typical reaction is to cut staff to bring the numbers back into line with expectations. To calculate the measurement, simply accumulate the number of personnel from payroll records and divide it into either sales or profits, both of which can be obtained from the general ledger. However, the measure is easily skewed if a company uses a large number of part-time workers; if so, these people must be converted to fulltime equivalents. Also, the number can be drastically changed if a company outsources its more labor-intensive functions, essentially negating the value of the measure.

It is important to use all of the preceding measures and not just a selection, for each one tracks different information that is critical to a complete understanding of a company's costs, margins, and breakeven points. The measures are summarized in Profitability Measurements (Exhibit 6.1).

EXHIBIT 6.1 Profitability Measurements

Ratio	Derivation
Break-even point	$\dfrac{\text{Sales}}{\text{Average gross margin}}$
Number of times interest earned	$\dfrac{\text{Average interest expense}}{\text{Cash flow}}$
Operating margin	$\dfrac{\text{Revenues}}{\text{Cost of goods sold}}$
Overhead rate	$\dfrac{\text{Overhead expenses}}{\text{Direct labor}}$
Percent return on net sales	$\dfrac{\text{Net sales}}{\text{Net profit}}$
Ratio of sales returns and allowances to gross sales	$\dfrac{\text{Sales returns and allowances}}{\text{Gross sales}}$
Sales/profits per person	$\dfrac{\text{Sales}}{\text{Total full-time equivalents}}$ or $\dfrac{\text{Net profits}}{\text{Total full-time equivalents}}$

MEASURES FOR THE BALANCE SHEET

One of the most heavily measured areas is the balance sheet. When used properly, the ratios and percentages noted in this section reveal a great deal of information about a company's financial health, as well as its financial strengths and weaknesses. For example, several measures cover the size of a company's debt holdings, as well as how this bears on the firm's overall level of financial risk. Other ratios deal with the relative proportions of assets needed to create revenues and profits, which an astute controller can use to compare company performance to that of competitors as well as to that of "best practices" organizations that may lie outside the industry. Other measures can be used to determine a company's short-term liquidity (which is of particular concern to lenders), as well as the age of assets. Finally, more advanced organizations are attempting to relate their assets to market valuations to determine their success in creating value in excess of the worth of their assets; there are several ratios here to assist in these calculations. The measurements are:

- **Debt/equity ratio.** To a lender, one of the most important measures is the debt to equity ratio. This reveals the degree of leverage that management has imposed on the balance sheet by acquiring debt. If the amount of debt in relation to equity is excessively high, it may be difficult for a company to service the debt or to pay it off. When a lender sees this high ratio, it may be reluctant to issue additional debt without some other assurances from management, such as personal guarantees or additional equity investments. To calculate the measurement, simply add up all long-term and short-term debt and divide it by total equity. However, management can play with the degree of leverage by moving some debt into operating leases, which are not recorded on the balance sheet.
- **Return on assets.** This is an excellent measurement when a controller wants to know how well a company is utilizing its assets to generate revenue. If the amount of assets required in proportion to revenues is increasing, then there are inefficiencies, or at least unnecessary assets, in the organization that the controller should investigate. The components of the return on assets are shown graphically in Components of the Return on Assets (Exhibit 6.2). Note in the exhibit the large number of components that a controller can investigate in this complicated measurement; problems can occur in such diverse areas as sales or accounts receivable that have a direct impact on the measurement. To calculate it, divide total sales by total assets, the major components of which are usually cash, accounts

receivable, inventory, and fixed assets. However, this measure is not useful and can be downright misleading, when applied to a fixed asset-intensive business, such as an oil refinery, where there is a large investment that cannot be reduced, irrespective of the amount of sales generated.

▪ **Return on shareholder equity.** This is one of the most important measurements for a shareholder. When a shareholder has a choice between investing funds in a company or doing so elsewhere, it makes sense to compare this measure to alternative investments, and to choose the higher of the two, while factoring in various risk issues. To calculate it, divide net income by shareholders' equity, both of which can be found in the general

EXHIBIT 6.2 Components of the Return on Assets

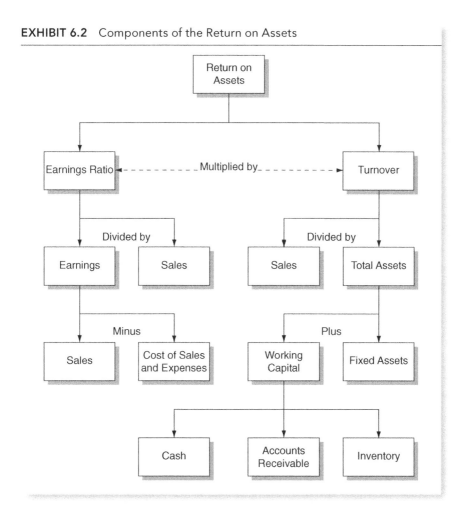

ledger. The trouble with this measure is that it does not delineate changes in risk that may go hand-in-hand with changes in net income. For example, a company can increase its return on equity by incurring debt to buy back shares; however, the increased debt makes the investment more risky, so investors should also consider the debt/equity ratio alongside this one, in order to match changes in returns to changes in risk.

- **Current ratio.** This compares the amount of short-term assets to short-term liabilities. A good ratio is one that yields enough liquidity to pay off all current assets. If the ratio does not reveal this ability, it is possible that the company has a sufficient degree of liquidity difficulty that it is in danger of going bankrupt. To calculate this measurement, divide all current assets by all current liabilities. It can be misleading if there is a disproportionately large amount of inventory in the current assets figure, because this measure is primarily designed to track liquidity, and inventory is not a very liquid asset.

- **Quick ratio.** The primary difference between this ratio and the current ratio is inventory. The reason why inventory is dropped from the quick ratio is that it is not a very liquid asset, whereas the other components of the ratio are usually easily liquidated. This ratio gives you a good idea of how quickly a company can convert its current assets into cash to pay for current liabilities, which makes it an excellent measure of short-term liquidity. To calculate the measurement, add together all cash, accounts receivable, and temporary investments, and divide by current liabilities.

- **Ratio of sales to accounts receivable.** A controller should keep a close watch over the proportion of sales to accounts receivable, since a change in the historical ratio may be indicative of worsening collection problems. To calculate the measurement, divide the amount of credit sales by the accounts receivable balance for the reporting period. The ratio should be tracked on a trend line, so that problems are more easily revealed in comparison to previous periods. The measure can be inaccurate if there is a large dollar volume of cash sales included in the sales figure; also, if the accounts receivable balance is primarily composed of a few large invoices, having even one invoice moderately overdue will severely skew the measurement.

- **Accounts payable turnover.** This ratio indicates the number of times that accounts payable were paid, or turned over, in a reporting period. It is an effective means for tracking the timeliness of payments. When tracked on a trend line, it is easy to spot when a company is entering financial difficulties, for the ratio will clearly worsen as the company delays payments. The ratio is also useful for predicting future accounts payable balances based on expected levels of purchasing. To compute the measurement, divide total purchases during the period by the ending accounts payable balance (though the average balance for the entire period is more accurate). This measure can be skewed if a company changes to or from taking early payment discounts, especially if this impacts a significant proportion of accounts payable.

▪ **Ratio of repairs and maintenance expense to fixed assets.** It is extremely useful to determine the condition of a company's fixed assets, because you can thereby determine the need for expensive replacement equipment that may significantly cut into cash or borrowing reserves. The best way to do this without making a physical inspection of the equipment is to compare the size of the repairs and maintenance expense to the amount of fixed assets. When tracked on a trend line, you can easily spot any jumps in the ratio compared to previous time periods, which indicates an aging set of fixed assets. To calculate the measurement, obtain the repairs and maintenance expense from the general ledger, and divide it by the gross fixed asset cost (i.e., before depreciation). The ratio will be much more accurate if the accounting staff splits off unrelated repair and maintenance expenses, such as for grounds upkeep, and stores this information in a different general ledger account.

▪ **Ratio of depreciation to fixed assets.** It is important to know the age of a company's fixed assets, because an excessively old asset base may soon require replacement. One of the best ways is to compare the amount of accumulated depreciation to the amount of assets; a large amount of depreciation is a good indicator of old assets. To calculate the measurement, obtain the accumulated depreciation figure from the general ledger and divide it by the total fixed asset valuation (also obtained from the general ledger). The measure can be skewed if a company uses highly accelerated depreciation methods, such as double declining balance depreciation, because this appears to show an older asset base than is really the case.

▪ **Fixed asset turnover.** This measurement shows how much of a fixed-asset investment is needed for management to achieve a specific level of sales. If the ratio increases, then the amount of assets required has gone up, which will probably also lead to a reduced return on assets (unless margins increase). To compute the measurement, divide sales by fixed assets.

- **Ratio of retained earnings to capital.** A lender or investor uses this measurement to see how many earnings have been allowed to accumulate in the company. This is an especially important factor in a privately held company, where it is common for the owners to extract as much of the retained earnings as possible in the form of distributions, leaving few assets for continuing operations; this requires constant infusions of debt to keep the company afloat, and effectively shifts much of the risk from the owners to the lenders. To compute this measurement, divide retained earnings by total stockholder's equity.

- **Economic value added (EVA).** Many controllers do not track the returns on capital that their companies are achieving. If a company's return is lower than its cost of capital, then it is making inefficient use of that capital. In fact, it may be better for investors to take their money out of such a company and invest it elsewhere. To calculate the measurement, multiply the amount of net investment (the amount of cash invested in the business, net of depreciation) in the company by the difference between the actual return on assets and the required minimum rate of return. Shrinking the amount of working capital or fixed assets, or increasing the rate of return on those assets will improve the EVA.

- **Market value added (MVA).** From the perspective of a shareholder, a company is successful if its market value in terms of the value of its shares on the open market is in excess of the amount of capital invested in the business. If its market value is less than the amount of invested capital, then management has done a poor job of generating adequate returns. To calculate the measurement, multiply the number of shares outstanding by the share price, add in the market value of preferred stock and debt, and then subtract the total amount of invested capital.

- **Working capital productivity.** It is becoming increasingly important for companies to operate their businesses on the leanest possible asset base. Not only does this improve the return on assets, but it also reduces the risk of losing assets by investing too much in a business. Much of a typical company's investment goes into working capital, which is accounts receivable plus inventory, minus accounts payable. However, the amount of dollars in working capital is not a good way to judge it, because there is no way to compare it to some other measure of activity. This is where working capital productivity is useful. To calculate it, divide the amount of working capital into annual net sales. The resulting number is most useful when tracked over time and when compared to the similar number for competitors, for it tells the amount of working capital needed to support each incremental dollar of sales.

The Impact of Working Capital

At a minimum, the new controller should track the dollar volume of working capital. This area tends to absorb excess cash due to changes in other areas, such as a looser credit policy, or an effort to stock more finished goods inventory. By refining this information to determine exactly what is causing working capital increases, the controller can keep the management team from using up more cash than necessary. ▪

These measurements are used to create an understanding of a company's level of financial risk, liquidity, age of assets, and ability to leverage assets into revenues. It is very useful to track all of this information continuously and plot it on a trend line, so that management can spot any worrisome trends and correct them as soon as possible. The measures are noted again in summary form in Balance Sheet Measurements (Exhibit 6.3).

EXHIBIT 6.3 Balance Sheet Measurements

Ratio	Derivation
Debt/equity ratio	$\dfrac{\text{Long-term debt} + \text{short-term debt}}{\text{Total equity}}$
Return on assets	$\dfrac{\text{Total sales}}{\text{Total assets}}$
Return on shareholder equity	$\dfrac{\text{Net income}}{\text{Total equity}}$
Current ratio	$\dfrac{\text{Current assets}}{\text{Current liabilities}}$
Quick ratio	$\dfrac{\text{Cash} + \text{accounts receivable} + \text{temporary investments}}{\text{Current liabilities}}$
Ratio of sales to accounts receivable	$\dfrac{\text{Sales returns and allowances}}{\text{Gross sales}}$
Accounts payable turnover	$\dfrac{\text{Net sales}}{\text{Total accounts receivable}}$
Ratio of repairs and maintenance expense to fixed assets	$\dfrac{\text{Total purchases}}{\text{Ending accounts payable balance}}$
Ratio of depreciation to fixed assets	$\dfrac{\text{Total repairs and maintenance expense}}{\text{Total fixed assets before depreciation}}$
	$\dfrac{\text{Accumulated depreciation}}{\text{Total fixed assets}}$

MEASURES FOR GROWTH

Some companies find themselves on an extremely rapid growth path. When this happens, there are financial pressures on the corporation that require different measurements to discover. For example, there will be great strains on cash flow, so there must be a close watch over the percentage change in cash flow. Other issues include changes in sales and market share; these two measures can provide contraindications by moving in opposite directions, so it is helpful to track both measures side by side. Finally, investors want to know if the growth pains are worth it, so the controller should track changes in earnings per share. The measurements are:

- **Percentage change in cash flow.** A change in cash flow is one of the first indicators of a variety of problems elsewhere in a company. For example, a decline in cash flow can be evidence of a decline in sales or gross margins, or it may be a sign of increased sales, general, and administrative (SG&A) expenses, increased fixed asset expenditures, or even of a stock buyback. Whatever the reason, this is a good first indicator of trouble. You can calculate it by adding profits to all noncash and fixed asset expenditures. It is best to track the information on a trend line in order to spot any period-to-period problems.
- **Percentage change in earnings per share (EPS).** A company may find that its sales, profits, and market share are continuing to improve, but that the EPS is not keeping pace. This can understandably cause concern by investors. The key factor causing this problem is the number of shares. An equity placement that adds to the number of outstanding shares can water down the EPS to the point where even enhanced profits will still result in a decrease in the EPS. To calculate this trend, divide net earnings by the number of outstanding shares and plot this on a trend line.
- **Percentage change in market share.** The best absolute measure of a company's performance is its market share. If the share increases, then the company is performing better than its competitors. To track it, use the market share results issued by industry trade organizations and plot the data points on a grid chart. However, a company may be gobbling up market share and still be losing sales if the overall market is shrinking, so it helps to track the *size* of the market alongside the market share trend line.
- **Percentage change in sales.** A controller should closely track the trend line for sales, not only for the company as a whole, but also for individual product lines. A continuing upward slant on a growth chart is obviously

encouraging, but sometimes the most important trend to track is the rate of growth. Any decline in the rate of growth must not only be factored into future growth projections, but may also result in a discussion with the sales force to see if management should expect a sudden dropoff in sales volume—something that impacts lots of functional areas. To create the trend line, extract the periodic sales information from the computer system, usually with the use of a report writer to extract sales by product or product line, and then plot the data points on a grid chart.

These measures are necessary for determining the amount of cash required to continue growth, the degree of growth occurring, and the extent to which investors are profiting from it. The measures are summarized in Growth Measurements (Exhibit 6.4).

MEASURES FOR CASH FLOW

A company may look great on paper—sales spiraling upward, surging profits, and a vast backlog—and still go bankrupt. Cash flow measurements can see through all of the favorable indicators to ascertain the true health of the organization. The measurements in this section focus on stripping away extraordinary cash flow items to see how continuing operations are doing, as well as the ability of a corporation to cover continuing expenses for items not appearing on the income statement, such as debt repayments and fixed-asset purchases. The measurements are:

EXHIBIT 6.4   Growth Measurements

Ratio	Derivation
Percentage change in cash flow	$\dfrac{\text{Incremental change in cash flow}}{\text{Cash flow from previous period}}$
Percentage change in EPS	$\dfrac{\text{Incremental change in EPS}}{\text{EPS from previous period}}$
Percentage change in market share	$\dfrac{\text{Incremental change in market share}}{\text{Market share from previous period}}$
Percentage change in sales	$\dfrac{\text{Incremental change in sales}}{\text{Sales from previous period}}$

- **Cash flow adequacy.** It is critical to know if the cash flow from operations is sufficient to meet all major payment commitments. These commitments do not include basic payments that are included in the income statement, such as payments for materials, utilities, or taxes; this is for non–income statement payments, such as debt payments. To calculate the measurement, divide cash flow from operations by all scheduled payments for long-term debt, asset purchases, and dividends. However, this measure is not sufficient if management is in the habit of making unscheduled payments, such as for fixed assets that are not on the annual fixed-asset purchases schedule.

- **Cash flow return on assets.** Though most companies just use the return on assets, this is a variation that may be worthwhile in some situations. Rather than dividing profits by total assets, just divide cash flow by total assets. Any difference in the two measures will be due to noncash expenses. If there is a large amount of noncash expenses, then the cash flow return on assets can be substantially higher than the simpler return on assets. This can be used to explain company performance to investors when large depreciation or amortization charges are cutting into earnings.

- **Cash flow to sales.** This is perhaps a better measure of profitability than a simple gross or net margin on sales. It reveals the total amount of cash flow attributable to each sales dollar. To compute it, divide cash flow from operations by revenues. Because the measurement strips out all noncash expenses, such as depreciation, it gives a good view of actual cash flows to be expected from operations.

- **Dividend payout ratio.** An investor who relies on company dividends wants to know the likelihood of the company's being able to continue paying out at the same rate. This measurement provides that information. By comparing the amount of cash flow to the dividend payout rate, you

Is the Owner Causing a Cash Drain?

When first starting in the controller position and if preliminary analysis shows that the company is losing money, turn to the equity portion of the general ledger and see if the company owner is paying himself large distributions. If so, and this is happening despite putting the company through difficult cash-flow problems, the new controller should seriously consider working somewhere else. Laboring under constant cash flow problems caused by the boss is a no-win situation. ■

can easily track the proportion of cash that goes to dividends; if the ratio worsens over time, it is likely that the dividend will be cut. To calculate the measurement, divide the total amount of dividends by the total cash from operations. It is best to track this information on a trend line to spot changes over time.

▪ **Long-term debt repayment.** A controller must be able to judge a company's ability to repay debt, so that recommendations can be made to alter operations in favor of reducing debt, if the chief financial officer (CFO) decides that to be a prudent strategy. Many companies that are not fiscally sound can convince themselves otherwise, simply by continuing to pile on the debt. A controller can tell if a company is truly solvent by tracking debt levels over the course of a year to see if there are periods when short-term debt is completely paid off. If not, a company frequently rolls over short-term debt into long-term debt with a fixed repayment schedule; this too can be a sign of fiscal trouble if the controller finds that the excessive amount of debt is leading to an unfavorable debt/equity ratio or if the number of times interest is earned is dropping. If a controller just wants to see if a company is capable of paying off continuing long-term debt payments, which are composed of both interest and principal, divide the total amount of long-term debt payments by cash from operations. If the ratio is unfavorable, it is probably time to extend the terms of the debt, so that the periodic payments are smaller

▪ **Operating cash flow.** There are many factors that can impact cash flow, and many of them are extraneous ones that rarely repeat. Though you would think that these extraneous factors will eventually go away, there always seem to be a few that interfere with the determination of cash flow from basic operations. This measurement is based on only operating elements, excluding all other factors. This gives a controller the best information about the true status of cash flows. To compute the measurement, add noncash expenses to profits, and then adjust for changes in working capital (accounts receivable, accounts payable, and inventory). Just as important, the measure excludes any changes caused by investment income, fixed-asset sales, or extraordinary items such as income from legal or insurance settlements.

Compiling cash flow measurements should be at or near the top of the controller's "to do" list when the true health of a company needs to be obtained. If a controller does not regularly review this information, there is a risk that the company will find itself in a difficult cash position simply because the controller did not exercise enough foresight to accumulate the necessary information in advance. The measures are summarized in Cash Flow Measurements (Exhibit 6.5).

 ## MEASURES FOR NONFINANCIAL PERFORMANCE

This section deals with measures that a controller is not so accustomed to measuring—nonfinancial performance. These measures can cover an extraordinarily wide range of activities, from engineering to sales and marketing. Many companies are now realizing that nonfinancial performance in these other areas is just as important to corporate success as the purely financial measures that they are more accustomed to perusing. This section divides nonfinancial performance measurements into the traditional departmental functions (e.g., accounting, production, etc.), and describes a variety of measurements for each area that are extremely helpful for determining their efficiency, effectiveness, speed, and level of experience, all of which are direct contributors to corporate success.

Accounting

This section covers the performance measurements that a controller should use to manage the accounting department. The most heavily reviewed item is the

EXHIBIT 6.5 Cash Flow Measurements

Ratio	Derivation
Cash flow adequacy	$\dfrac{\text{Cash flow from operations}}{\text{All scheduled payments for long-term debt, asset purchases, and dividends}}$
Cash flow return on assets	$\dfrac{\text{Cash flow}}{\text{Total assets}}$
Cash flow to sales	$\dfrac{\text{Cash flow from operations}}{\text{Total revenue}}$
Dividend payout ratio	$\dfrac{\text{Total dividend payments}}{\text{Cash flow from operations}}$
Long-term debt repayment	$\dfrac{\text{Total long-term debt payments for the period}}{\text{Cash flow from operations for the period}}$
Operating cash flow	Profits + noncash expenses ± changes in working capital

average collection period for accounts receivable, because inattention to this area can lead to severe cash flow problems. It is also common to closely review the percentage of accounts payable discounts taken, so that the accounting department is not inadvertently responsible for extra expenses that could have been avoided. In addition, it is increasingly common to track the number of days required to release financial statements, with some companies even tying a controller's bonus to this measure. Finally, an increasingly common set of measures is to track the efficiency of the accounting staff, much as the production staff has historically been tracked, by determining the number of errors committed and transactions completed per person.

- **Average collection period.** This is one of the best ways to determine the quality of accounts receivable. It shows the number of days that the average account receivable has gone unpaid. If the number of days resulting from the calculation is close to the number of days before which invoices are due (e.g., payable in 30 days), then it is unlikely that there are very many old accounts receivable, which highlights the ability of the accounting staff not only to issue error-free bills that are promptly paid, but also to rapidly collect overdue invoices. Conversely, an excessive number of collection days points to probable issues on the same topics. To calculate the measurement, divide average annualized receivables by average daily credit sales.
- **Percentage of accounts receivable.** One of the primary measurements on which the controller is judged is the ability of the accounting staff to collect accounts receivable on time. If this does not happen, a company ends up with an excessive investment in accounts receivable, which is a poor use of funds. Also, older accounts receivable are at a greater risk of not being collected. To calculate this measure, print out an aged accounts receivable report, which should list at the bottom the total receivable amount in 30-day time buckets. Add up the summary totals for those time buckets considered to be overdue (e.g., everything over 60 days old), and divide it by the total of all accounts receivable.
- **Ratio of purchase discounts to total purchases.** A company can save a fair amount of money by taking advantage of early payment discounts. Only a small percentage of suppliers offer early payment discount options, but if a company takes advantage of them all, the savings can add up to a tidy sum. The amount saved as a percentage of all purchases does not change much over time, so tracking the percentage of discounts taken is an easy way for the controller to discover if the accounts payable staff is missing out on some discounts. To calculate it, track the purchase discounts in

a separate general ledger account, and divide this monthly figure by total purchases. Then track the resulting percentage on a trend line.

▪ **Time to produce financial statements.** In today's competitive environment, it is no longer acceptable to wait a month to receive the results of the previous month's performance. Most managers need financial information as fast as possible, so that they can rapidly spot problems and correct them. The calculation is an easy one; just add up the days from the end of the month to the point when financial statements are issued.

▪ **Transaction error rate.** One of the most time-consuming activities in the accounting area is fixing errors. If something is wrong, the best person to find the error and fix it is a senior staff person or manager, and this type of person is usually already in short supply and certainly overworked. Consequently, there tends to be a long backlog of problems that the accounting department has in its queue, which may involve wait time by other departments, suppliers, or customers. Clearly, the controller must pay close attention to the transaction error rate, since it has such a major impact on workflows in the accounting area. This is not a measure that can be easily tracked by an automated system. Instead, the best approach is to review the transaction journals at the end of each month and add up the number of special debits and credits that were entered in the system—each one usually represents the correction of a problem. Then divide the number of errors by the total number of transactions, which also comes from the transaction logs. The main issue with this measure is that it only tracks items that have been corrected, not those that are still pending (which may be far larger than the number being corrected).

▪ **Transactions processed per person.** Above all others, the accounting department is driven by the need to process large quantities of transactions, such as billings and payments to suppliers. Because of the large volume, this calls for extremely high levels of efficiency. By tracking the number of transactions processed per person, the controller can benchmark internal performance against that of other organizations to see if there are grounds for revamping processes to increase efficiency. The calculation varies somewhat by type of transaction, but it essentially requires that the controller accumulate data on the number of transactions processed during a specific time period, and the effort required to process them.

All controllers must be efficient in producing financial statements, collecting accounts receivable, taking purchase discounts, and processing transactions, and these measurements are the primary control point over those activities. The measures are summarized in Accounting Measurements (Exhibit 6.6).

Customer Service Measurements

If there is a separate customer service department (or even if not), the measurements noted in this section are useful for determining the degree of customer satisfaction. Customer turnover shows the extent to which a company can retain its existing customer base, while two other measures note the types and quantities of complaints received, as well as the company's speed in responding to them. The measurements are:

▪ **Customer turnover.** A company expends a vast amount of resources to acquire new customers. It is much more inexpensive to retain the ones it already has than to find new ones, but this is sometimes lost on aggressive sales managers who celebrate acquiring new customers; the loss of an old one tends to pass unnoticed. The controller can point out this problem by reviewing the billing records to see which customers have not done business with the company for a long time. To calculate it, compare the billing database to the list of customers to whom the company has sold products or services in the past year and determine how many have not been invoiced in the last quarter (or some other time period). Divide the number of noncurrent customers by the total number of customers to determine turnover.

EXHIBIT 6.6   Accounting Measurements

Ratio	Derivation
Average collection period	$\dfrac{\text{Average annualized accounts receivable}}{\text{Average daily credit sales}}$
Overdue accounts receivable	$\dfrac{\text{Total of overdue accounts receivable}}{\text{Total accounts receivable}}$
Ratio of purchase discounts to total purchases	$\dfrac{\text{Total purchase discounts taken}}{\text{Total purchases}}$
Time to produce financial statements	(Financial statement issue date) − (First day of the month)
Transaction error rate	$\dfrac{\text{Number of errors}}{\text{Total number of transactions}}$
Transactions processed per person	$\dfrac{\text{Number of transactions completed}}{\text{Number of full-time equivalents required to complete transactions}}$

▪ **Number of customer complaints.** Any well-run company should know exactly how many customer complaints have been received, as well as the issues to which they pertain and how they were resolved. This information should be contained in a customer complaints database that is accessible to as many employees as possible. Only by tracking this information and taking corrective action as necessary can a company fix those problems that irritate customers enough to lead them to contact the company. To calculate the number of complaints, access the complaints database and summarize the number of complaints by time period. It is even more effective to summarize the complaints by *type* of complaint, which tells management what areas need the most corrective action.

▪ **Response time to customer complaints.** If a customer complains and then does not receive a response within a reasonable time period, that customer is probably gone for good. By closely tracking the time it takes to respond to customer problems, management can alter the response system, which results in more satisfied customers who will continue to buy from the company. To calculate it, create a complaints database in which all contacts are logged; then subtract the response date from the initial contact date. An even better measure is to track the time it takes to completely resolve each complaint, rather than just the time to make an initial contact.

These measures are summarized in Customer Service Measurements (Exhibit 6.7).

Distribution Measurements

Many companies seem to think that their jobs are complete once they have manufactured products; however, there is an art to delivering products to cus-

EXHIBIT 6.7 Customer Service Measurements

Ratio	Derivation
Customer turnover	$\dfrac{\text{(Total customer list)} - \text{(Invoiced customers)}}{\text{Total customer list}}$
Number of customer complaints	Summarize complaints from complaints database for specified date range
Response time to customer complaints	(Response date) − (Initial contact date) or (Final resolution date) − (Initial contact date)

tomers as quickly and with as little damage as possible. This section covers the primary measurements to use when evaluating this key function. The first measure covers the time needed to deliver products to customers, while the second explores the proportion of deliveries that meet expectations. The final measure is useful for discovering the amount of damage to products during transit. The measurements are:

- **Average delivery time.** The distribution function is responsible for picking products, packaging them, and delivering them to the customer. If the customer is in a hurry to receive the product, the time needed to get the product into the mail is critical. To calculate this measurement, note in the company's computer system the date and time when an order is sent to the shipping area, and compare this to the date and time when the order was listed in the shipping log as having been shipped. This is an easy calculation if the ordering and shipping functions are linked in the computer system, but otherwise very difficult. It rarely makes sense to track the time required to actually deliver the product to the customer, because the customer may specify a slow delivery method that will skew the measurement.

- **Percentage of on-time deliveries.** It is very important that the company deliver products on the date requested by the customer. Many customers are now using just-in-time (JIT) manufacturing systems, and so they want deliveries on a specific date, which means that they cannot be delivered early or late. To calculate this measurement, there must be a requested delivery date entered into the computer system for each customer purchase order; otherwise, it is impossible to determine when an order is supposed to ship. Next, there must be a shipment date recorded, against which the controller can match the required date. The computer system can then subtract the delivery date from the required date and summarize the difference for all deliveries. However, there must also be an adjustment to the calculation for the estimated shipment time to the customer. It is very useful to add a detailed listing of all "problem" shipments to this measurement, so that management can see where problems have occurred and correct them.

- **Percentage of products damaged in transit.** Most companies do not deliver their own products to customers; a third-party carrier does it for them. The company must know if the carrier is damaging any of the delivered products, because this is not exactly good customer service, so that it can take steps to switch to a new carrier. This is a difficult measure to calculate unless customers tell the company about the damage; consequently, the best measurement point is customer complaints, which should be logged into a complaints database. The controller can then select only those complaints pertaining to damaged products, and divide this number by the total number of products shipped.

If these measures are not tracked regularly, management will have no way of knowing the performance of its distribution function. The measures are summarized in Distribution Measurements (Exhibit 6.8).

Engineering Measurements

The engineering department has a direct impact on product costs, as well as the efficiency of other departments, such as materials management and production. The measurements in this area are necessary to ensure that the key engineering functions are running properly, thereby improving the efficiency of other downstream operations. The bill of materials (BOM) accuracy measurement is mandatory for ensuring that the correct quantities and types of parts are available for production. There are also several measurements, which can be used together or separately to determine the engineering department's speed in completing new product designs as rapidly as possible. A parts usage measure is crucial for determining the engineering staff's ability to use existing parts in new products, greatly easing the work of the materials management staff, which must procure and store new parts. Finally, another measure determines the ability of the engineering staff to meet target costs; this skill is crucial for ensuring that a company prices its products at a price point that gives it a profitable share of the market. The measurements are:

- ▪ **BOM accuracy.** The engineering department has a major impact on the efficiency of the materials management department, in that it must specify in advance the materials needed to produce products. Without this information, the materials management personnel are reduced to

EXHIBIT 6.8 Distribution Measurements

Ratio	Derivation
Average delivery time	(Delivery date) − (Date order was sent to shipping area)
Percentage of on-time deliveries	(Required date) − (Actual delivery date)
Percentage of products damaged in transit	$\dfrac{\text{Damage-related complaints in complaints database}}{\text{Total complaints in complaints database}}$

guessing about the contents of new products, which commonly results in purchases of items that are never used, which contributes to an excessively large inventory. The materials list is commonly known as a BOM. To calculate its accuracy, review a BOM with the engineering, warehousing, and production staffs to ensure that all parts are actually needed. Each mistake, either in terms of quantities or item codes, is an error. Divide the number of accurate parts by the total list of parts needed to derive the accuracy percentage.

Is there a Bill of Materials?

A major concern for every controller of a manufacturing company is the accuracy of inventory records. If they are inaccurate, this greatly impedes all efforts to create accurate financial statements. An excellent clue to the accuracy of the inventory is the existence and frequency of updates to BOMs. If none are maintained, this is excellent evidence of minimal management attention to a key area of operations. ▪

- **Number of patent applications filed.** Leading-edge research gives a company a good basis for building products that no one else can match. A good sign of this research is the number of patent applications filed during the period. It is easily tracked by the legal staff, which usually assists in creating and filing the necessary documents. However, filing a patent application and translating this into new products that generate sales requires lots of other activities, so patent activity is not a sure sign of future success.
- **Percentage of sales from new products.** The previous measurement showing the number of new products is not as important as the percentage of sales being derived from them, since this is a more sure measure of corporate health. To calculate it, summarize the sales from new products (it is helpful to arrange the chart of accounts in advance to track this information) and divide by total sales.
- **Percentage of new parts used on products.** The engineering staff should always strive to reduce the number of new parts in each product design to the absolute minimum, because not doing so entails buying from additional suppliers, as well as stocking extra parts in the warehouse, which requires an additional investment. To track it, compare the BOM for each new product to the existing list of parts in inventory to see which items are new. Then divide the number of new parts by the total number of parts used in the product.

- **Percentage of new products introduced in the period.** A key measure of a company's ability to thrive in the marketplace is the percentage of its products that are new. An old product line generally leads to declining sales, so the reverse is also true—constantly replenishing the product line leads to more revenues. To calculate the measurement, add up the number of new products introduced during the period and divide by the number of products available at the beginning of the period. This measure can be significantly skewed by how you define a new product; if a minor product enhancement is defined as a new product, the company is only fooling itself into believing that it is creating new products.

- **Percentage of products reaching market before competition.** It is not very useful to a company to release fabulous products to the market long after the competition when there is no one left to buy them. Instead, a company must tightly focus on bringing products to market as soon as possible, even if they are not quite as perfect as the designers would like. A good way to measure this is to manually track the product release date, and then keep abreast of release dates by competitors to see when they release similar or competing products. However, the measurement is quite judgmental, because it is sometimes difficult to determine if a competitor's product is similar to what a company has already released.

- **Percentage of released designs matching target costs.** A new product will not be very profitable if the costs designed into it are so high that the company either cannot obtain a profit when selling at a competitive price, or must sell at an exorbitant price in order to obtain a profit. Instead, the controller should verify that product designs are being released that have costs matching expectations (the target cost). To calculate the measurement, summarize all actual costs for a product and divide them by the original target cost, which should be noted in the engineering documentation. It may also be useful to track the percentage by which released designs are missing their targets, so that management can work on gradually dropping costs down to target levels.

- **Time from design inception to production.** The engineering staff must be able to produce new product designs as rapidly as possible in order to beat the speed with which competitors are introducing products. This is an ever-declining time period, so it is best to track the design time on a trend line, working toward extremely short design periods. To calculate it manually, note the design start and end dates and subtract the former from the latter to derive the total number of design days. The design time will vary greatly by product, of course, since they may vary greatly in complexity, so it is best to track this information separately for each product line.

Many companies treat their engineering departments as something of a "black hole"—they feed money into it, and new products come out from time to time, though no one knows their exact configurations, nor when they will be released. A better approach is to use the measurements in this section to determine the speed with which new products are being created, the efficient use of old parts in new products, and the level of detail that the department is providing the materials management personnel in terms of the parts needed to build each product. The measurements can also be used to determine the impact on sales of new product introductions. Finally, the department must be responsible for hitting prearranged target costs; there is a measurement here for determining that information. In short, this section provides the tools to attain a high level of control over the engineering department. The measures are summarized in Engineering Measurements (Exhibit 6.9).

Human Resources

The human resources department fulfills a wide variety of tasks, some of which must be completed properly if a company is to avoid government fines, promptly fill new positions, and avoid excessive levels of overhead. The measure that

EXHIBIT 6.9 Engineering Measurements

Ratio	Derivation
BOM accuracy	$\dfrac{\text{Number of accurate parts per BOM}}{\text{Total list of parts on BOM}}$
Number of patent applications filed	Number of applications logged in as having been sent during the period
Percentage of new products introduced in the period	$\dfrac{\text{Number of new products introduced in the period}}{\text{Number of products available at the beginning of the period}}$
Percentage of sales from new products	$\dfrac{\text{Revenues from new products}}{\text{Total revenues}}$
Percentage of new parts used on products	$\dfrac{\text{Number of new parts in BOM}}{\text{Total number of products released}}$
Percentage of products reaching market before competition	$\dfrac{\text{Number of products released before competition}}{\text{Total number of products released}}$
Percentage of released designs matching target costs	$\dfrac{\text{Summary of actual product costs}}{\text{Summary of target costs}}$
Time from design inception to production	(Completed design and signoff date) – (Design start date)

is central to the needs of a growing firm that has an insatiable need for new employees is the time needed to fill requested positions. Other firms with lesser hiring needs may concentrate on fulfilling government requirements, such as the percentage of minorities on the payroll. There are several other measures covering the trend of fringe benefits or indirect labor to direct labor, which are useful for determining the trend of employee-related costs. For a more progressive company that wants to have a highly trained staff, there is also a measurement for tracking the percentage of employees with certifications. Some combination of these measurements will fulfill the requirements of most human resources departments. The measurements are:

- **Average time to fill requested positions.** One of the human resources department's most important tasks is to assist in finding good candidates for requested positions throughout the company. In a rapidly growing company, where continued growth is almost entirely dependent on finding additional staff, this is the department's most critical function. To calculate it, create a log book in which the date of all new position requests are received by the human resources staff, as well as the date on which offer letters are accepted by recruits; the difference between the two dates is the average time to fill requested positions.

- **Average yearly wage per employee.** It is of moderate use to management to know the average annual pay of its employees, since this gives it some idea of the company's pay levels as compared to the industry. For example, if the employee turnover rate is high and the average pay rate is low, this may be an indication that the company must start offering higher pay rates in order to retain staff. To calculate it, use a report writer to create a standard report listing everyone's pay rate; this usually requires two lists, one for the hourly staff and one for the paid staff. Then summarize each list. Multiply the total on the hourly employee list by the total number of standard hours worked in a year (usually 2,080), and multiply the total on the salaried employee list by the total number of pay periods. Then add the two lists together and divide by the total number of employees. This calculation may be slightly skewed if there are many part-time employees, since this will translate into a very low annual pay rate.

- **Employee turnover rate.** By far the most important measurement in the human resources area is employee turnover. It is exceedingly expensive to recruit and train new employees, so management must tightly focus on retaining all current staff. To calculate it, add up the number of people who have left the company, and divide by the number of employees at the beginning of the measurement period. It may be useful to subdivide this measurement so that the most critical departments, such as engineering, are tracked separately.

▪ **Indirect to direct personnel ratio.** Management may want to know if a company is becoming top-heavy with an excessive number of people in the overhead areas, such as administration, accounting, or engineering. Changes in this proportion are most clear when tracked over time (perhaps annually). To calculate it, summarize the number of personnel in overhead positions (the easiest way is to use the payroll system to list personnel by department) and divide that number by the total in direct labor positions (i.e., the production department). Another way to measure this is to use payroll dollars instead of headcount, which gives a more accurate picture of a company's proportional investment in indirect labor.

▪ **Minorities percentage.** Depending on the size of a company, there may be federal government reporting requirements for the percentages of various types of minorities in a company. If so, the best way to track this information is to record a minority code in the payroll or human resources computer systems for each person, so that a simple computer query can extract the information needed for various government reports.

▪ **Percentage of employees with certifications.** A company with many certified employees is a company with a great knowledge base that will contribute toward constant system improvements. Certifications fall into nearly every functional area, from certified management accountants to certified engineers. This information can be recorded in the human resources database with a code, and can be extracted with a simple query. To calculate it, divide the total number of people with certifications by the total number of employees. This measurement can be subdivided into departments, so that management can determine skill levels by functional area.

▪ **Ratio of fringe benefits to direct labor.** The human resources staff is responsible for the cost (though not necessarily the types) of fringe benefits offered to the staff, which is principally comprised of medical insurance. Senior management sometimes looks at the ratio of fringe benefits to direct labor to see if too much is being spent on fringe benefits, and may cut back in this area if they perceive that to be the case. To calculate it, summarize the fringe benefit cost per person and divide it by the direct labor cost, which is usually obtained through the payroll system.

▪ **Trend of headcount.** Some managers like to review the number of people in each department, preferably on a trend line, to spot unusual changes in headcount. This is most informative when tied to various activity measures (usually revenues), so that there is a direct relationship between an activity and headcount. Headcount is easily extracted from the payroll database, though you must be careful to translate any part-time staff to full-time equivalents to ensure comparability across time periods.

There are many measurements available to track the performance of the human resources staff, or of the employees for whom they are responsible. Not all of these measurements should be used at one time, however. For example, a rapidly growing company will focus primarily on the department's ability to rapidly recruit new people and will want to know about employee turnover, but a more staid organization may be more interested in obeying rules and regulations, and so will focus on minority percentages. For this area, the controller must fit the measurements to the circumstances. The measures are summarized in Human Resource Measurements (Exhibit 6.10).

EXHIBIT 6.10 Human Resources Measurements

Ratio	Derivation
Average time to fill requested positions	(Date offer letter is accepted by recruit) – (Date of receipt of position request)
Average yearly wage per employee	$\dfrac{\text{(Summary of all hourly wages} \times \text{number of annual working hours)} + \text{Summary of all salaries)}}{\text{Number of employees}}$
Employee turnover rate	$\dfrac{\text{Number of employee departures}}{\text{Number of employees at beginning of period}}$
Indirect to direct personnel ratio	$\dfrac{\text{Number of personnel in overhead positions}}{\text{Number of personnel in direct labor positions}}$ or $\dfrac{\text{Total payroll of overhead positions}}{\text{Total payroll of direct labor positions}}$
Minorities percentage	Summarize by minority code in payroll or human resources systems
Percentage of employees with certifications	$\dfrac{\text{Number of employees with certifications}}{\text{Total number of employees}}$
Ratio of fringe benefits to direct labor	$\dfrac{\text{Total fringe benefit expense}}{\text{Total direct labor expense}}$
Trend of headcount	(Total full-time employees) + (Total full-time equivalents for part-time employees)

Materials Management Measurements

Materials management area can be one of the most streamlined operations in a company. Measurements are needed to verify the extent of the department's efficiency. For example, inventory accuracy is needed to ensure that a material requirements planning (MRP) system operates properly. Also, an inventory turnover measurement is needed to verify the outcome of MRP and JIT systems. In addition, there are several measures for determining the department's success in shrinking the number of suppliers, as well as of switching to more efficient electronic commerce systems. It is also important to track the percentage of on-time parts delivery, since this impacts the ability of the production department to complete new products on time. The measurements are:

▪ **Inventory accuracy.** The inventory database must accurately reflect the quantities, part numbers, and locations of all inventory in stock. If not, the materials management staff cannot be sure about what materials are in stock, and will probably purchase extra materials to cover this level of uncertainty, which increases the inventory investment as well as the potential level of obsolescence. To measure it, print out a listing of the inventory and its locations and audit a significant sample from the listing. Divide the number of test items with correct information by the total number sampled to obtain the accuracy percentage.

▪ **Inventory turnover.** Inventory turnover tells management the proportion of inventory in stock (as raw materials, work-in-process (WIP), and finished goods) as compared to the cost of goods sold. A high proportion of inventory indicates that there is an excessive investment in working capital that is a good target for reduction. To calculate it, add up the cost of all inventory and divide by the annualized cost of goods sold. This calculation can be skewed if there is a large amount of finished goods on hand (which can fluctuate widely if sales are highly seasonal)

▪ **Number of suppliers used by commodity code.** The materials management staff can become overwhelmed if it is managing too many suppliers. It is better to utilize the services of a smaller number of suppliers, so that a company has enough time to implement supplier rating systems, electronic data transfers, and mutual product designs with a limited group of business partners. An excessive number of suppliers in each commodity code is a clear indicator that some shrinkage of the supplier base is in order. To calculate it, use the accounts payable database to create a list of all suppliers from whom the company has made purchases in the last year, and sort the list by commodity code.

- **Obsolete inventory percentage.** An excessive amount of obsolete inventory is an indicator of too much inventory on hand (since not all of it is being used), an inadequate materials management system (since it is not using up in-house parts), or of the unwillingness of management to dispose of old parts. In any of these cases, a controller needs to emphasize that eliminating the root causes of obsolescence are a primary method for reducing materials costs. To calculate it, use the materials management system to extract all inventory records for which there has been no inventory movement for a long time (which can vary from a few months to years, depending on the industry); when the costs of these inventory items are divided by the total inventory cost, this yields a rough measure of total obsolescence. The measure can be skewed by items that are old, but which can be sold—a review by management will easily uncover these items.

- **Percentage of on-time part deliveries.** The most important function for the materials management staff is to ensure that materials arrive on time, so that the production process is not held up. This requires tight control over the arrival of needed materials. To calculate this measurement, create a report in the computer system that compares the requested arrival date on all company purchase orders to the dates on which parts were actually received (which should be entered by the receiving staff).

- **Total number of components.** Many companies are overwhelmed with an excessive number of parts, many of which have not been used in a very long time, but which the materials management staff must still track. If there is an excessive amount, the best management action is to undertake a detailed review of parts usage to see what can be eliminated from stock. To calculate this measurement, run an inventory listing for all items currently in stock, and add up all the line items. It is also helpful to compare the number of parts to sales, since the number of parts will probably increase with revenues. It is also useful to create a "where used" report that shows the products for which each part is used; if a part is in stock but is not used on any current products, then it is a prime candidate for elimination.

The amalgam of measurements in this section will serve the controller in determining departmental performance for almost any performance improvement project. The measures are summarized in Materials Management Measurements (Exhibit 6.11).

EXHIBIT 6.11   Materials Management Measurements

Ratio	Derivation
Inventory accuracy	$\dfrac{\text{Number of accurate test items}}{\text{Number of items sampled}}$
Number of suppliers used by commodity code	Sort accounts payable list of suppliers by commodity code
Obsolete inventory percentage	$\dfrac{\text{Cost of inventory items with no recent usage}}{\text{Total inventory cost}}$
Percentage of on-time part delivery	(Actual arrival date) − (Requested arrival date)
Percentage of suppliers using EDI	$\dfrac{\text{Number of suppliers with EDI linkages}}{\text{Total number of suppliers}}$
Total number of components	Summary of all inventory line items

Production Measurements

The production department has been greatly impacted by JIT production methods, and to a large extent the measurements in this section are needed to identify its success. A key JIT concept is reducing equipment setup times, so there is a measurement for that. Also, there is a measure for tracking the proportion of successfully completed products; under JIT, this should be very nearly 100 percent. The turnover of WIP inventory should also increase under a JIT system, so there is a supporting measurement here for that. There are also more traditional measures that are not used in JIT, such as the percentage of scrap, and labor productivity. The measurements are:

- **Average equipment setup time.** In a JIT manufacturing environment, it is critical to only produce what is immediately needed. However, most companies still make long production runs, even though this generates more products than are needed. They do this because the production equipment takes so long to set up that it is only cost-effective to make long production runs. The solution, then, is to reduce the length of the equipment setup times. This is tracked separately for each piece of equipment, and is usually done by either the production or process engineering staffs. The calculation is the time (in hours, minutes, or seconds) required to switch a machine over from one type of production to another.
- **Percentage of acceptable products completed.** Management should know what proportion of every production run results in good products that are acceptable for sale. This is absolutely critical in an industry such as

chip wafer manufacturing, where yield rates may be as low as 20 percent. To calculate the measurement, create a system for collecting and counting all unacceptable products from a production run, and then divide this amount by the total of all products created in the run (either acceptable or not). It may only be necessary to aggregate this information for a single monthly measurement, but it is more common to run the measurement by product line, since yield may vary dramatically by type of product.

▪ **Percentage of scrap.** A good way to determine if the production department is making efficient use of materials is to track the amount of scrap generated by the manufacturing process. An excessive scrap amount is an indicator of a variety of items, such as improper machine setup (which requires extra material to test it), employee theft of materials, and faulty products that are detected during the production process and thrown away. Due to the large number of underlying problems, this measure should be considered only a symptom of the real problem, with much additional work required to discover the underlying issues. There are several ways to calculate the measurement. The most inaccurate is to throw all scrap into scrap bins, and then periodically weigh the bins to estimate the cost of what is inside. A more accurate approach is to use an MRP system to determine the material cost that should be required for scheduled production, and then compare this to the actual cost to determine the difference. It can be especially difficult to determine the cost of products that were scrapped after some amount of labor and overhead had already been applied to them.

▪ **Unit output per employee hour.** A company that operates along traditional lines, using long production runs, wants to know about the ability of its employees to churn out products at the highest possible speed. This measurement is no longer used in a JIT environment, where the emphasis is on only producing what is needed, rather than producing at the fastest possible rate. Also, focusing on this measure tends to increase the production error rate, since employees will complete products irrespective of problems, because they are being judged on their speed, not their accuracy. Nonetheless, if a controller still wants to calculate this measurement, the best approach is to aggregate all personnel in an assembly line or on a specific job, add up the hours worked from payroll records, and divide this amount by the number of products completed during the same time period. This number will be inaccurate if the payroll hours include a holiday for which employees are being paid. The number will also be incorrect if the output is based on direct labor dollars (instead of hours), because the dollar amount can be considerably increased by overtime or shift differentials.

■ **WIP turnover.** A company that is focusing on improving its JIT manufacturing systems uses the WIP turnover rate as one of its primary measures of success. This is because a properly functioning JIT system requires very little inventory in the manufacturing process, so the WIP turnover rate should be very high. To calculate the measurement, divide the period-end WIP figure by the cost of goods sold for the year. This measure should be tracked on a trend line.

Traditional production systems focus on improving the speed of output, while newer systems tend to focus on product error rates and the amount of WIP. This section has the measurements a controller needs to track the performance of either type of system. The measures are summarized in Production Measurements (Exhibit 6.12).

Sales and Marketing Measurements

The sales department represents the controller's leading edge of information about conditions in the marketplace. Measurements for this area must be constructed that yield as much market information as possible. One is market share, which reveals a company's share of the market "pie." Another key factor is a company's ability to convince customers to sole source their purchases through it. Also, several other departments depend on the sales staff to keep a steady flow of orders coming into the company; a backlog measurement is a prime advance indicator of potential trouble. Finally, there are several sales

EXHIBIT 6.12 Production Measurements

Ratio	Derivation
Average equipment setup time	(Start time for new production run) – (Stop time for last production run)
Percentage of acceptable products completed	$\dfrac{\text{Number of rejected products}}{\text{Number of products in production run}}$
Percentage of scrap	$\dfrac{(\text{Actual cost of goods sold}) - (\text{Standard cost of goods sold})}{\text{Standard cost of goods sold}}$
Unit output per employee hour	$\dfrac{\text{Aggregate output per production area}}{\text{Total hours worked in production area}}$
WIP turnover	$\dfrac{\text{Total WIP}}{\text{Annual cost of goods sold}}$

trend lines to watch that indicate problems with the rate of sales growth (or decline) that are of use when planning for new products or upgrades to existing products. These measurements follow:

- **Market share.** Sometimes an upward trend in sales volume disguises a decline in market share. For example, upward sales growth in the computer industry means little, when everyone's sales are growing; only growth that exceeds the growth of competitors matters, because this allows a company to exercise economies of scale, thereby lowering costs and reaping greater profits than competitors. Market share is a difficult item to measure; the best calculation is to fund an industry trade group that releases an annual or quarterly market share survey. If there is no trade group, the marketing staff must conduct its own research, which will probably be moderately inaccurate; nonetheless, either method will reveal changes in market share over time that management should act on as necessary.
- **Number of major accounts for which the company is the preferred supplier.** The ultimate goal of any sales department is to make the company the sole supplier to the best customers. This allows it to incrementally raise prices enough to reap good margins, while at the same time avoiding an excessive number of sales contacts, which merely increase overhead costs. To calculate it, the sales staff must contact suppliers to determine company sourcing status; the total number of these customers must then be divided by the list of active major customers. This is a difficult measurement to construct, for there may be some debate regarding what constitutes a major account; the best approach is to set a hard limit on sales volume from each customer during the previous year—if a customer exceeds that level, it is designated a major account.
- **Ratio of backlog to sales.** The sales department must support the production department in having enough sales on hand to avoid a significant slippage in the flow of production, which may result in major layoffs in the production area. A good control point is to constantly compare the dollar volume of backlog to a short-term record of sales to see if there are sudden changes in the backlog that require immediate action by the sales force. To calculate it, summarize the dollar value of all orders not yet in production (which is usually available on the production backlog report), and divide it into a rolling average of the last three months' sales.
- **Sales trend by product line.** The sales and engineering staffs need to know when the trend of product sales is beginning to slow or decline, so that they can either run promotions to increase sales or renew sales with

replacement products. To do this, there should be a trend line, preferably in graphic form, for each product line. To calculate it, accumulate product sales under different sales codes or general ledger accounts, and transfer the monthly sales information to a graphical display. It is dangerous to report this information on an excessively summarized level, since it may hide a multitude of sales variations for separate products or product lines that are being grouped into a single trend line.

A controller should track all of the measurements in this section, because each one shows a different aspect of the sales and marketing functions, and all of them are important. You should track market share, as well as the trend of sales by product line, while it is always prudent to determine the size of the backlog. Finally, the sales staff should always strive to achieve sole-source status with suppliers, and the controller should remind them of this responsibility by tracking that information and reporting it back to them. All of these measures are key to controlling the sales and marketing department. The measures are summarized in Sales and Marketing Measurements (Exhibit 6.13).

Cycle Time

There is one measurement that cuts across all departmental boundaries. That is cycle time, which is used to determine the time taken to complete a transaction.

EXHIBIT 6.13 Sales and Marketing Measurements

Ratio	Derivation
Market share	$\dfrac{\text{Dollar volume of company shipments}}{\text{Dollar volume of industry shipments}}$
Number of major accounts for which the company is the preferred supplier	$\dfrac{\text{Number of major sole-source customers}}{\text{Number of major customers}}$
Ratio of backlog to sales	$\dfrac{\text{Dollar volume of all orders not yet in production}}{\text{Average of sales for last three months}}$
Sales trend by product line	Summary of sales by product code
	or
	$\dfrac{(\text{Summary of current period sales by product code}) - (\text{Summary of previous period sales by product code})}{\text{Summary of previous period sales by product code}}$

Because many transactions cut across departmental boundaries, the measurement is placed here, rather than under the previous department headings. This is also done to emphasize the importance of the measurement. Poor cycle time leads to very slow customer service, which is bad for customer retention and therefore revenues.

Major processes, such as order fulfillment, run through multiple departments, and so are not actively tracked by individual departments (they just blame problems on the other departments that are also involved in the process). However, these are frequently the cause of major inefficiencies in a company, and so the controller should periodically review the time required to process transactions through them, so that management has a clear understanding of the time interval (or "cycle time") needed. The calculation will vary depending on the process, but the basic method is to create a set of standard transactions and run them through a process, taking note of the beginning and ending dates (or times). The average transaction length becomes the official cycle time for the process.

In short, a controller should continually track cycle times to enhance a company's level of performance and competitiveness. The measure for cycle times is summarized in Cycle Time Measurement (Exhibit 6.14).

INTERRELATIONSHIP OF RATIOS

Focusing on a problem ratio and resolving the underlying issues can create problems with other related ratios. For example, a company's debt covenant may specify a current ratio of 2:1. If the ratio is 1.5:1, the controller can borrow money and retain the cash to improve the current ratio. However, the controller's action also worsened the company's ratio of long-term debt to shareholder's equity. The controller must be aware of changes to other ratios that may result from fixing seemingly unrelated measurements. A number of impacts on related ratios are noted in Impact on Related Ratios (Exhibit 6.15).

EXHIBIT 6.14 Cycle Time Measurement

Ratio	Derivation
Cycle time	(Process end time) – (Process start time)

EXHIBIT 6.15 Impact on Related Ratios

A Change in This Ratio	Impacts These Ratios
Current ratio	Management improves the ratio by borrowing money and retaining *the cash: the ratio of long-term debt to shared-holder's equity* worsens because debt has increased.
Ratio of long-term debt to shareholder's equity	Management improves the ratio by liquidating short-term investments to pay down the long-term debt; the *current ratio* worsens because investments have been reduced.
Ratio of net sales to receivables	Management improves the ratio by factoring receivables: the *ratio of net profits* to net sales worsens because there is a service charge associated with factoring the receivables.
Turnover of inventories	Management improves the ratio by selling off inventories; the *ratio of gross profit to net sales* worsens because management must pay premium prices to buy raw materials on short notice and ship it to the company by express freight.
Ratio of net sales to working capital	Management improves the ratio by extending payables; *the ratio of gross profit to net sales* worsens because suppliers will not ship additional raw materials, so management must pay premium prices to buy raw materials on short notice and ship it to the company by express freight.
Ratio of repairs and maintenance to fixed assets	Management improves the ratio by cutting the amount of maintenance work on equipment; the *ratio of net income to net sales* worsens because production capacity drops when equipment breaks down.
Number of times fixed charges are earned	Management improves the ratio by using cash on hand to pay down debt; the *current ratio* worsens because the cash is used.
Ratio of gross profit to net sales	Management improves the ratio by increasing prices; the *ratio of net income to net sales* worsens because fewer people buy the product at the higher price.
Ratio of operating expenses to net sales	Management improves the ratio by reducing the accounting department's payroll; the *ratio of gross profit to net sales* worsens because there is no cost accountant to review increased product costs.
Ratio of net income to net sales	Management improves the ratio by selling manufacturing equipment and recording a gain on the sale; *the ratio of gross profit to net sales* worsens because production capacity is reduced, and production must be given to subcontractors at a higher cost.

SETTING UP A SYSTEM OF RATIOS AND TREND ANALYSES

There are enough measurements in this chapter to keep even the most analytical controller happy. However, there are so many that issuing all of them will drown the management team in a flood of data that it has no time to read. The controller must select only a portion of all measures for perusal by management. The controller must know how to pick the correct measures and how to present them in a clear and understandable format.

The first step is to match the measurement system to company objectives. Some management teams are driven by strong revenue growth, because they have a tight focus on grabbing as much market share as possible; this is common in a new industry. For this situation, there should be a preponderance of measures that closely track all changes in revenue streams. Other companies are in slow-growth industries where the focus is on gaining a slight edge in profitability over the competition. In this case, the bulk of the measures should track gross and net margins and the key components thereof. Another common occurrence, especially in high technology industries, is for corporate success to be largely driven by the organization's ability to acquire and retain the best employees. In this case, the most important measurements may not even be financial—they are human resources related, such as employee turnover percentages and the time needed to fill open positions. Consequently, company objectives play a strong role in a controller's choice of measures to report.

Another important consideration for creating a measurement system is the strengths and weaknesses of a company's controls. For example, if there are many divisions, all of which handle a large amount of cash, it is reasonable for a controller to create many cash-related measurements that track cash receipts and disbursements, as well as the company's ability to collect the cash from all divisions and properly invest it. Another example is inventory systems; if there is a strong JIT manufacturing system in place, then there is little need to expend an excessive amount of company resources on measuring the small amount of inventory needed to maintain it. However, a befuddled manufacturing system may call for a considerable amount of inventory measuring—perhaps weekly or even daily—as well as constant tracking of obsolete inventories. If there are strong controls already in place, such as a billing system that creates perfect customer billings, then there is little need to measure it. However, strong controls frequently become strong because employees know that they are being measured; completely removing the measurement tells employees that the control is no longer important, so they do not expend the same effort to keep the control strong. Consequently, it is less necessary to measure strong control points than weak ones, but these measurements should not be completely eliminated; instead, they should be conducted less frequently.

A key consideration that is all too frequently ignored is the time needed to collect information that forms the basis for a measurement. If the data collection systems needed to calculate a measurement are not in place, a controller should seriously consider abandoning the measurement unless it is absolutely critical or it is only needed for a single measurement, not to be repeated. For example, if a controller receives a request for sales broken down by product but finds that the accounting system will not easily divulge this information, the only option in the short term may be to go through all invoices issued for the month and manually summarize the information. Clearly, this is not a viable option for the long term. If the controller cannot find a more automated approach to collecting the information, it is time to discuss the cost of collecting the data with the person requesting the information to see if it is really needed. Too often, a controller simply goes on wasting time month after month, issuing measurements that require vast amounts of manual labor, when the information was only needed once.

Another approach is for a controller to track all possible measurements, but to only report those results to management that do not meet expectations. For example, the accounting staff can track every conceivable measurement related to the engineering department, but only reveal those measurement results that show problems. Though this approach will tightly focus management attention on problem areas, there are several reasons for not using it. One is that, even though only high-variance measures are being reported, some of these measures may be in areas so unimportant that management is simply being distracted from more important tasks. Another reason is that this approach puts a large burden on the accounting staff. Many measures must be manually calculated, and doing this for a very large number of measures is not a good use of staff time. Finally, management can become confused when it is presented with a different set of measurements every reporting period; some measures may be unfamiliar, so the controller must retrain management to understand the new measures. This not only wastes the controller's time, but it also interferes with the orderly conduct of management work. Consequently, tracking all measures and reporting by exception is probably too labor intensive and complicated to be an effective measurement presentation approach for most companies.

An example of how to determine what ratios to track follows: Leforto Electronics designs circuits for other manufacturing companies. It has no inventories, and most of the staff is in the engineering department. The company is growing at a very rapid rate through increasing sales to a small number of key accounts. In this case, the controller can safely avoid measurements for inventory. Because engineers are generally hard to come by, there should be a measurement to track employee turnover, as well as one to track the time needed to acquire new recruits. Given the small number of customers, a customer turnover statistic may be of some importance. Also, since the company does nothing but design circuits, it is reasonable that profitability is closely tied to the speed with which the engineers complete their design work, so a measurement should track the percentage of design jobs completed on time. Finally, given the small number of customers, it is possible that there are a few large invoices to customers, which makes cash receipts very "lumpy." Given this issue, there is a strong need to monitor the age of accounts receivable, as well as short-term cash forecasts. This is a simple example, but it is evident that the measurement systems needed for Leforto Electronics will vary considerably from companies in other industries, where the underlying operating conditions might make all of Leforto's measurements useless, while calling for a completely different set of measures.

A good example of a company that must use an entirely different set of measurements is a manufacturing company. This one we shall call Manfred Manufacturing. This company builds a large number of products, which requires a large number of component parts. It sells them to a large number of distributors, most of whom buy in small quantities; some are old friends of the owners. The industry is a mature one, so profit margins are low. The direct labor content of most products is high. In this case, there is no need to track engineering variances at all. Instead, there must be a strong emphasis on inventory tracking as well as obsolescence, since inventory probably constitutes a large part of the balance sheet. In addition, there must be careful margin tracking for all products and product lines in order to find and correct the prices of products with low margins. Also, because some customers are friends of the owners, it seems likely that their credit standing is being ignored, so close tracking of overdue accounts receivable is critical. Finally, because of the large labor component in product costs, the controller should adopt measurements for tracking labor efficiency as well as hours charged to specific jobs. In comparing these two examples, it is evident that a controller must take into account such disparate items as a company's industry, number of customers, preponderance of certain departments, and even owner friendships when devising a good set of performance measurements.

CHAPTER SEVEN

Internal Control Systems

Importance of This Chapter

The regulatory environment places a considerable emphasis on controls, if only to reduce fraud and improve the accuracy of financial reporting. This chapter includes many examples of internal controls and fraud situations, and so serves as the starting point for a detailed corporate controls examination.

Historically, the reason a company places emphasis on its internal control systems is to keep fraud from occurring. Although reducing fraud losses is still a valid concern, more companies now emphasize internal controls because they monitor the consistency with which transactions are completed. This change in emphasis has been brought about by the realization that a company can generate a significant competitive advantage by improving the quality and speed of delivery of its products by tightly monitoring its systems. Thus, internal controls are used not only to combat fraud but also to monitor the consistency and completion speed of transactions.

Besides objectives, this chapter also notes how responsibility is assigned for various controls. This is not a simple issue, because controls spread across many departments, making it difficult to pin down the reason for a control failure. In addition, the chapter contains an elementary set of control points that are useful for controlling the most basic company functions. Though by no means complete, they give the reader a rough overview of the types of controls that a controller should consider installing. In addition, controls may eventually outlive their usefulness due to changes in the business. Accordingly, guidelines are provided on how to spot and eliminate these controls. Fraud is then discussed: the types of fraud you encounter, how to detect it, and how to prevent it. Most controllers will encounter a case of fraud at some time in their careers, though it may be as minor as petty cash pilferage, so these sections serve as a good reference point for how to identify, prevent, and deal with such problems. Finally, the chapter notes the main points of the Foreign Corrupt Practices Act, which is a federal law that directly impacts a company's internal control systems. In short, this chapter provides an overview of controls—why they are used, how to create them, and when to eliminate them.

OBJECTIVES

It is not sufficient to scatter a large number of controls throughout a company's transaction processing systems, because this random approach may result in an insufficient number of controls over key risk factors, while adding an excessive number of controls in areas where there are few risks. The upshot of a control system that is poorly planned is a high-risk transaction environment that is nonetheless burdened with an excessive number of controls. This section discusses the primary control objectives that a controller should consider in order to implement only those controls that are most important for a specific set of transactions. The main control objectives are:

- **Authorization.** Was the transaction authorized by management? This could be evidenced in a general way by establishing related policies, contract authorization limits, investment limits, and standard price lists; or specific authorization may be needed in a given situation.
- **Reconciliation**. Periodic reconciliations of physical assets to records, or control accounts, should be made. This can include bank reconciliations, securities inventories, physical inventories of raw materials, and comparison of work-in-process and finished goods to control accounts.
- **Recording**. Transactions should be recorded, not only in the proper account, but also at the proper time (i.e., proper cutoff) and with the proper description. No fictitious transactions should be recorded, and erroneous material and incomplete descriptions should be avoided.

- **Safeguarding**. Physical assets should not be under the physical custody of those responsible for related recordkeeping functions. Access to the assets should be restricted to designated individuals.
- **Valuation**. Provision should be made for assurances that assets are properly valued in accordance with generally accepted accounting principles (GAAP) and that the adjustments are valid.

These five control objectives relate to the prevention of errors and the detection of any errors or irregularities in transactions. They must be considered when the evaluation of an internal control system is made.

RESPONSIBILITY FOR INTERNAL CONTROLS

Although the controller has a major involvement in the design and maintenance of internal controls, he or she is not the only one responsible for internal controls. This is an especially important factor to consider because of the Foreign Corrupt Practices Act (Foreign Corrupt Practices Act), which can entail jail terms for senior company management if there are inadequate control systems. In addition to this factor, there are many control systems that extend beyond the reach of a typical controller's jurisdiction; therefore, other people within a company must take a hand in creating and maintaining those systems. This section discusses the various positions within a company that are responsible for internal controls, as well as the extent of that responsibility. They are noted as follows, in descending order by position:

- *Board of Directors.* This group is ultimately responsible for a company's control systems, as it is responsible for total company performance. Unfortunately, it operates at such a high level that it cannot adequately monitor, or even have a knowledge of, all key control systems. It can alleviate this problem by forming an audit committee to which the internal audit department reports; this allows the Board to closely monitor all reviews of the control system, which allows it to mandate changes that are deemed necessary by the internal audit staff.
- *Senior management.* Although the Board of Directors is theoretically responsible for the adequacy of controls, it is senior management that actually has this responsibility from a practical perspective. This is because senior management is "closer to the action," with a much more detailed knowledge of operating conditions. Accordingly, the senior management team must

ensure that there is an efficient and effective system of internal controls that results in accurate financial information, as well as the safeguarding of assets. Senior management must:

- Assume responsibility to shareholders for the accuracy of financial reporting.
- Create and maintain a properly documented internal control system.
- Create and maintain the proper environment to enforce the necessary controls. This may require the use of policies, procedures, and statements of ethical standards to enforce.
- Identify the risks inherent in the business and the potential for errors and irregularities in various parts of the transaction processing systems.

- *Financial management.* Though other members of management have responsibility for the adequacy of controls, this burden falls heaviest on the members of the financial management team, for they are presumed to have the highest degree of training and experience in this area. Also, the majority of control points are typically installed in areas that are under the direct control of the financial managers. Consequently, from a practical perspective, these employees have the bulk of the real responsibility for controls. The financial management team must:

  - Know the technical requirements of a sound financial control system and how to create such a system based on the nuances of the existing business.
  - Verify that a sufficient number of controls are installed and that they operate in a satisfactory manner.
  - Enforce conformance to all controls, as noted in policies and procedures.
  - Assume direct responsibility for the accuracy of the information contained in periodic financial statements and accompanying notes.

- *Internal audit staff.* This group has a major impact on the presence of adequate control systems. It is responsible for reviewing the existence and effectiveness of control systems in a variety of areas, and reports to management on the adequacy of those controls, as well as any deficiencies. However, the audit program followed by this group is usually approved by the internal audit committee, which is a subset of the Board of Directors. If this program is inadequate, the internal audit staff will not conduct a sufficient number of reviews to ensure the adequacy of internal control systems. Also, this group is not empowered to change any control systems; instead, it only reports on problems. This limits the effectiveness of the internal audit staff in forcing necessary changes to control systems.

■ *Independent auditor.* This position is listed as the lowest of the management positions, although in reality it is located here simply because it is the only position in the list that falls outside of the corporate hierarchy. As part of an outside auditor's audit of a company's financial statements, it is customary to determine the strength of the underlying control systems that support those statements. If weaknesses in the control systems are discovered, the auditor is in a unique position to report this information to senior management as well as the Board of Directors as part of a management report that frequently accompanies the audited financial statements. The reported weaknesses can also be accompanied by recommendations to improve the situation. However, a controls review is considered only to be part of the audit work for a full audit, and not for a review or compilation; these two lesser forms of financial review are increasingly common for many companies, so in these cases, the external auditor has minimal impact on the state of a company's control systems.

Read Your Audit Reports!

A good source of information about control weaknesses is prior management reports issued by the external auditors. The new controller should peruse all of these reports that have been issued for the past few years to see what problems the auditors uncovered, and which ones have not yet been resolved. ■

Responsibility for the adequacy of a control system is spread throughout a company, with theoretical responsibility residing in the Board of Directors and practical responsibility sitting squarely on the shoulders of the financial and senior managers. This group is assisted by the internal and external auditors, who can recommend changes to existing controls but do not have the authority to make any changes.

EXAMPLES OF INTERNAL CONTROLS

This section provides a "laundry list" of controls that are commonly used. Controllers can pick from this list when creating control systems for their companies. However, do not be misled into believing that the only crucial controls are noted below. On the contrary, there are many controls that are industry-specific that will not be found anywhere in this book. To gather information about these special controls, it is useful to consult with an auditing firm that has experience in a specific industry, or obtain advice from an industrial trade group with similar expertise. Conversely, it is not necessary to implement every control listed in this section, because this would introduce a great deal of inefficient control redundancy. The best use of this section is as a reference for carefully selecting controls that can be shaped and altered to fit a company's specific needs. The controls are grouped by balance sheet and income statement category. They are:

- *Cash*
  - Compare check register to actual check number sequence.
  - Control check stock.
  - Control signature plates.
  - Perform bank reconciliations.
  - Review uncashed checks.
- *Investments*
  - Impose investment limits.
  - Require authorizations to shift funds among accounts.
  - Verify that investments do not exceed federally insured limits.
- *Accounts receivable*
  - Require approval of credit memos for bad debts.
  - Require constant review of old accounts receivable.
- *Inventory*
  - Conduct inventory audits.
  - Require approval to sign out inventory beyond amounts on pick list.
  - Restrict warehouse access to designated personnel.
- *Employee advances*
  - Continually review all outstanding advances.
  - Require approval of all advance payments to employees.
- *Fixed assets*
  - Ensure that fixed-asset purchases have appropriate prior authorization.
  - Verify that correct depreciation calculations are being made.
  - Verify that fixed-asset disposals are properly authorized.
  - Verify that fixed assets are being utilized.
- *Accounts payable*
  - Compare payments made to the receiving log.

▪ *Notes payable*

  ▪ Require approval of the terms of all new borrowing agreements.
  ▪ Require supervisory approval of all borrowings and repayments.

▪ *Revenues*

  ▪ Compare all billings to the shipping log.
  ▪ Require approval of unusual customer payment terms.

▪ *Cost of goods sold*

  ▪ Compare the cost of all completed jobs to budgeted costs.
  ▪ Pick from stock based on bills of material.
  ▪ Purchase based on blanket purchase orders and related releases.
  ▪ Reject all purchases that are not preapproved.
  ▪ Require approval of all overtime expenditures.

▪ *Travel and entertainment expenses*

  ▪ Audit expense reports at random.
  ▪ Issue strict policies concerning allowable expenses.
  ▪ Require supervisory approval of all expense reports.

▪ *Payroll expenses*

  ▪ Require approval of all overtime hours worked by hourly personnel.
  ▪ Require approval of all pay changes.

▪ *Occupancy expenses*

  ▪ Compare the cost of employee furnishings to company policy.
  ▪ Compare the square footage per person to company policy.

▪ *General*

  ▪ Audit credit card statements.
  ▪ Impose a total monthly dollar limit on credit card purchases.
  ▪ Impose single transaction limits on credit card purchases.
  ▪ Impose supplier exclusions on credit card purchases.
  ▪ Require supervisory approval of credit card statements.

▪ *Other: Contracts*

  ▪ Require monitoring of changes in contract costs.
  ▪ Require monitoring of when contracts are due for renewal.
  ▪ Require specific authorizations for various levels of monetary commitment.

The controls noted in this section are among the most common ones used, irrespective of the type of industry. Although a controller may select the majority of his or her controls from this list, it is important to consider special controls that are indigenous to specific industries and do not appear on this list.

 ## WHEN TO ELIMINATE CONTROLS

Most controllers are good at imposing new controls, but few give any thought to eliminating them. This is a useful exercise, because fewer controls translate into less work by the staff and (sometimes) quicker transaction processing times. This section discusses how to set up an orderly system for reviewing controls at regular intervals and eliminating those that are no longer necessary.

In order to review the need for controls, you must first know what they are. Many controllers have no idea of the types of controls a company uses, because they have inherited an informal mass (or mess) of controls from the previous controller, and never trouble themselves to understand the system. Accordingly, the first step is to conduct a broad-ranging series of interviews with employees to understand the flow of transactions throughout the company, and then convert this information into a set of easily understandable flowcharts. A quarterly control review can be scheduled in which the controller scans the existing controls to see if any controls have become unnecessary; this happens when changes in business conditions, such as new operating procedures, outsourcing, or reengineering, render existing controls obsolete. Any additions to or deletions from a company's control systems must be reflected in the flowcharts, so they must be updated regularly, even if the formal control review takes place only quarterly. Using flowcharts and a scheduled control review allows a controller to eliminate unnecessary controls.

Although flowcharts are an excellent method for tracking control points, a controller can take the concept too far. It can take an enormous amount of time to convert every conceivable process into a flowchart, and more time to ensure that it stays correct. To avoid too large a time investment, those systems that have no significant financial impact, such as the scheduling for janitorial services, should be ignored and concentration should be on key transactions, such as order fulfillment.

Once key controls have been documented, the controller should determine how much it costs to have them in place. This step is important, for a controller is responsible for installing controls that are *cost effective*, not ones that require so much effort that company operations are severely burdened by them. To determine control costs, observe controls in action to see how much labor and material costs are required to maintain them. This is a very inexact science, and a controller may be forced to rely on nothing more than the opinions of the employees who use the controls. Still, even estimates of costs are better than no information at all.

A controller should also categorize each control as being a major or secondary control. Most control systems have multiple controls that focus on solving a control problem, with a few controls being extremely important and others being relatively unimportant. For example, a primary control over inventory is installing a fence around the warehouse to eliminate pilferage, while a secondary control is bonding the warehouse staff so that a company can obtain reimbursement if an employee is caught stealing inventory. By categorizing controls in this manner, a controller can see which controls are necessary and which can be deleted.

The final step in determining which controls can be eliminated is to add control costs (as previously determined) to the chart that categorizes controls as being major or secondary. This allows a controller to quickly skim through the list of controls and see whether there are any secondary control points that are very expensive. If so, these are prime candidates for elimination. Before deleting these controls, first make a determination of the risk of not having them. Even an expensive secondary control point may have some value if it provides control over a potential asset loss that is so large that the control is still worth having. Risks that fall into this category include loss of investment accounts due to embezzlement or the loss of entire facilities due to fire damage. For these situations, which are admittedly few in number, it may still be worthwhile to retain controls that would otherwise be eliminated.

A simpler, though less effective, way to review controls is to constantly review the need for control reports. All companies rely on a large number of reports that list transactions; when regularly reviewed, these reports act as controls over a large number of activities. A controller can determine whether these reports are needed by tracing them to report recipients and quizzing them regarding the need for the reports. This can result in a major reduction in the number of reports used, which leads to major time savings if the reports are being manually prepared.

A more common method of reducing the number of controls is to conduct an intensive review of controls whenever there are significant changes to the business, such as reengineering projects, outsourcing of major functions, or downsizing. When these events occur, the controller should be heavily involved in examining proposed system changes, which will likely result in the elimination of large numbers of controls. It is common to enroll the internal audit staff in these reviews, because it is largely concerned with the adequacy of existing controls. However, although there will almost certainly be some reduction in the number of controls as a result of these changes, there may be a need for an entirely new set of controls that are just as, if not more, expensive than the controls being eliminated.

Involve Yourself in Best Practices Implementations

Unfortunately, the presence of control points can make any process less efficient, since it may require labor to complete them. Consequently, best practices projects tend to focus on their elimination on the grounds that efficiency can thereby be improved. In order to avoid hard feelings when the new controller recommends against a new best practice because of control weaknesses, it is useful to monitor the progress of best practices teams to see what recommendations they are likely to make. ▪

When a controller decides to eliminate a control, it is best to review the decision with anyone who may be using the control for other reasons. This is a major concern when the control point is a report that contains valuable information. For example, a control report that lists all fixed assets may also be used by an accounts payable person to determine the value of assets to be reported to the government for the calculation of property taxes. When these types of controls are eliminated, there may be so much extra work required by other parts of the company to "fill the gap" of the information that is no longer available that the cost of stopping the control may exceed the cost of leaving it in place. Thus, checking with potential users is key prior to stopping a control point.

Finally, it is common to order the elimination of a control point, only to find that the controller's order is ignored by the staff. This happens when employees are so overwhelmed with work that there is a strong predilection toward keeping systems the way they are, rather than working through the details of system changes. It is also common when control changes are not properly thought out; the staff realizes that there are unresolved issues and balk at making changes until these issues have been resolved. In the first case, the controller should request the assistance of the internal audit staff, which can conduct periodic reviews of processes to see if changes have actually been implemented. In the second case, the controller is well advised to listen to staff objections and work through changes with them, which usually results in altered systems that are more clearly understood and which have greater staff acceptance.

In short, a controller can eliminate unnecessary controls by conducting a periodic review of existing controls, itemizing why they are used, and including the cost of each one as well as the changes in risks if they are eliminated. A detailed review of this information will usually reveal a number of control points that are too expensive for the level of incremental control they provide. It is important to review proposed control eliminations with other employees to ensure that there are no undocumented uses for the controls that may justify their continued existence; this review may also uncover objections to changing the system, which the controller should deal with prior to making alterations. By following these steps, a controller can keep the number of controls to a minimum, while still ensuring that a company's major control objectives are met.

TYPES OF FRAUD

All controllers must be aware of the primary types of fraud. By knowing them, a controller can design effective control systems for their prevention. This knowledge is also useful for those controllers who are interested in increasing transactional efficiency by reducing some control points—only by knowing how employees can take advantage of a reduced set of controls to commit fraud can you judge which controls can be safely eliminated.

All types of fraud involve the theft of company assets. However, within the broad category of "assets" lie a large number of subcategories, such as fixed assets, employee advances, and cash. The type of fraudulent activity needed to take each of these subcategories of assets away from a company differs for each category, and is described in the following list by subcategory:

- **Expense account abuse**. Employees run extra expenses through their expense reports that are not allowed by company policy, or use false receipts to charge extra expenses that did not actually occur. Employees may also charge expenses that are higher than allowed by company policy. For example, employees may take first-class plane trips, charge through exorbitant meals, and expect reimbursement for non-business expenses, such as gifts or clothes.
- **Nonpayment of employee advances**. Employees who have requested an advance payment of their paychecks or an advance to cover trip expenses will not pay back the company for these expenses. This tends to be a passive activity, for they do not actively try to bilk money from the company—they just do nothing to pay back what they have already been paid.

Store Employee Advances in an Asset Account

It is difficult to collect an employee advance almost every time one is paid out, making this one of the most common forms of fraud. To create an automatic monthly reminder, be sure to record each advance in an asset account, and then insert an account reconciliation reminder for that account in the monthly closing checklist; by doing so, someone has to review outstanding advances every month. ▦

- **Purchases for personal use**. Employees can take advantage of the authorization systems built into the purchasing system to order items for their personal use. This is most common when a company has high approval limits, so that employees can order items with no fear of review by their supervisors. This is also common when companies exercise little control over company credit cards, so that employees can charge through purchases that are not in any way related to company business.
- **Supplier kickbacks**. Employees in the purchasing function can arrange with suppliers to buy their products and services at inflated costs in exchange for direct payments back to the employees. Depending on the quantities purchased, the amount of these kickbacks can be enormous.
- **Theft of cash and investments**. The primary target of many employees who commit fraud is cash. This can be done in a variety of ways. One is to steal a blank check and make it out to the employee. Another is to gain control of bank account authorization codes and wire large amounts of funds to an employee-controlled bank account. Yet another approach is to steal cash. However, from a practical perspective, this tends to be the most difficult area in which to steal a large amount, for most companies tend to focus their controls on this asset area.
- **Theft of fixed assets**. Fixed assets that are not bolted down, are small in size, and have a high resale value are subject to theft. This is especially true if the assets are rarely used or stored in out-of-the-way locations, so that no one will notice a theft for some time. This type of fraud is especially common in companies in which there is minimal tracking of assets. Conversely, large and heavy equipment that requires immense effort to move is practically immune to theft.
- **Theft of inventory or supplies**. Employees can remove supplies and inventory from the company, either for personal use or for resale. Supplies are especially easy to remove, because they are not tracked as carefully

as inventory items and are not normally stored in a restricted area. This is an especially large problem if inventory items have a high street value, are small enough to be easily concealed, and are not rigorously tracked. Large and inexpensive inventory items are much less likely to be stolen.

These asset areas correspond roughly to the asset section of the balance sheet. The most commonly recognized fraud areas involve cash and investments, but it is actually much easier for an employee to steal assets in other areas, such as inventory, because the greatest concentration of controls cover the cash area, with weaker controls elsewhere.

PREVENTING FRAUD

For some firms, the cost of fraud is so crippling that at a minimum it takes a large bite out of profits, and in some cases takes down the entire company. Even if the amount being stolen is small, most controllers feel as though fraudulent activities are a personal affront, for it means that someone has found a way to circumvent the control systems that were personally installed by them. Accordingly, this section is designed to give a controller a list of warning signs for how to spot fraudulent activities, and what to do about it.

There are two sets of fraud indicators. The first is at a high level: How management acts and its way of running the company are either direct indicators of fraud by management or indicate a general pattern of behavior that, if duplicated lower down in the company, will create an environment in which fraud will flourish unchecked. The high-level indicators are frequently missed, because the controller is so wrapped up in managing at this level that the signs are too close to see. It is best to ask the company auditors for their opinions regarding fraud indicators at this level, for they can provide a more balanced, outside view of the situation. The high-level fraud indicators are:

- **Management creates an overly complex organizational structure**. If there are so many interlocked organizations that it is difficult to track transactions through the myriad of entities, it is possible that senior management has purposely created this level of complexity in order to hide fraudulent transactions.
- **Management has an excessive emphasis on meeting profit goals**. If the management team cares for nothing but meeting profit goals, this channels everyone's activities in that direction. This may seem innocuous,

but if the goals are extremely hard to reach, there is a considerable temptation for employees to fabricate profits by any number of means in order to meet their goals. This is particularly a problem when large bonuses are awarded when profit goals are met.

▪ **Management has an aggressive attitude toward financial reporting**. The management team may use the loosest possible interpretations of the accounting rules in order to recognize revenue and income. When this is present, it is possible that management is also engaged in other activities that are beyond the accounting rules. Surprisingly, controllers do not always see this, because they may have been in the accounting department so long that they accept the loose accounting interpretations as normal.

▪ **Management is unwilling to pay for good controls**. A management team with an undue focus on profits may not want to pay for the more expensive control points that will prevent large-scale fraud. Employees will eventually determine where there are no controls or weak ones, and some will be tempted to exploit the situation.

▪ **Management is dominated by one person**. If there is a strong owner or chief executive officer (CEO) running the company who brooks no discussion of decisions made, there is a strong risk of fraud, probably by that person. The risk is especially high in this situation, because the CEO has absolute authority to do anything—no controls will be effective.

▪ **Management prefers excessive decentralization**. The management team may have a preference for minimal control from the headquarters facility. This is a laudable approach in many situations, but there should be a sufficient level of oversight to at least ensure that adequate control systems are in place at all subsidiaries.

▪ **Management turnover is high**. When there is a large amount of churning among the management ranks, it may indicate that there are ongoing activities that are questionable, and that the departing people have chosen to leave rather than be associated with the company.

▪ **Customers or suppliers are suing the company**. There may be lawsuits pending related to not paying suppliers or not providing complete services to customers, and which may be caused by fraud on the part of senior management. These lawsuits frequently escape the attention of the controller, because they are handled through the legal department.

▪ **Management is forcing a rapid pace of growth**. If a company is going through a period of rapid growth, it is extremely difficult to maintain control systems. Also, because so many people are being hired during this period, it is difficult to conduct an adequate level of screening of incoming employees, so there is a greater likelihood of hiring someone who has committed fraud in the past.

■ **Management is acquiring a large number of companies**. When management acquires a series of companies within a short period of time, it is possible that it will buy into a company where fraud is present. This is because a newly acquired company may have poor control systems that allow this to happen. The real problem is that, because of the pace of acquisition, the controller may not have sufficient time to create and monitor controls at each newly acquired company, which means that there is an environment in which fraud can continue to flourish.

Show Management the Error of Their Ways

As noted above, the management team can be indirectly responsible for a weak control system. When this happens, collect all information about fraud losses into a summary document and present it to the management team, noting what types of controls could have been imposed that cost less than the resulting losses. ■

There are a number of warning signals to look for at an employee level that may be indicators of fraud. These indicators require no special control system; a controller simply needs to be aware of them in order to identify situations in which there is a stronger likelihood of a possibly fraudulent situation. If a number of the following factors are present, a controller is justified in conducting an especially careful audit to determine whether there are fraudulent activities occurring. The warning signs are:

■ **401k withdrawals**. An employee is more likely to commit fraud if short on cash. One sign of this is repeated withdrawals from a 401k plan or reductions in the amount of paycheck withdrawals that go to the plan. Another sign of this is a long history of asking for advances on paychecks.
■ **Bad debt write-offs**. There appears to be a large proportion of bad debt write-offs occurring. There may not be any increasing trend line indicating this, since fraudulent write-offs may have been going on for a long time, so an alternative way to tell is to compare the rate to industry standards.
■ **Inventory discrepancies**. If there are constant discrepancies between expected inventory records and actual counts, this is a sign of possible

inventory theft; this also applies to manufacturing tools, which are especially easy to sell.

▪ **Invoicing discrepancies**. A common type of fraud is to intercept incoming checks and hide the theft by constantly modifying customer invoices with adjustments of various kinds to make them match a smaller amount of customer payment. A large number of invoice adjustments is a sign of this problem.

▪ **Lack of supervision**. Some employees, for whatever reason, have not been subjected to close management for a long time, which gives them an opportunity to devise fraudulent activities in the absence of any oversight.

▪ **Large personal expenditures**. Some employees spend their fraudulently acquired funds in a very public manner; seeing an employee arrive in a new and expensive car is an indicator of this, especially when combined with a change of home address, which may indicate the purchase of a more expensive home.

▪ **No competitive bidding**. A number of contracts are being awarded without any competitive bidding, which indicates that suppliers may be paying purchasing personnel to do this. However, this is increasingly difficult to prove, because just-in-time manufacturing principles dictate that sole sourcing is a better purchasing technique than using competitive bidding.

▪ **No payment from the sale of assets**. When a controller notices that there are fewer assets, either from sale documents or a fixed asset audit, it is useful to see if cash was received as part of the transaction. If there does not appear to be any compensation for transferring the asset to the recipient, the controller should suspect that funds were pocketed and investigate further.

▪ **No vacations**. Key staff people somehow never manage to take any vacation time for years on end, which may indicate that they are afraid of having their activities detected in their absence.

▪ **Supplier addresses match employee addresses**. A virtually certain indicator of fraud is when an employee sends in invoices from a fictitious company and has the payments sent to his or her home address. Though it can be difficult to compare the list of employee addresses to the same information for suppliers, it may be worth the effort if a controller suspects that there are problems with supplier payments.

Though these indicators of fraudulent activities are legitimate, a controller must realize that there are also real reasons for many of the same activities, so it is easy to receive a false impression that someone is committing fraud. For example, an employee may not have taken vacation during the past year, but this may be due to a workload so severe that there really was no way to take it. To avoid false indicators, it is better to rely on a combination of factors. For example, if a billing clerk suddenly arrives in a new sports car, and this is coincident with a number of billing irregularities, then there are excellent grounds for conducting an investigation.

While noting that several indicators in combination represent a reasonable warning of the presence of fraud, it is even more likely that the vast majority of fraud cases leave no warning signs at all. Many perpetrators conduct their activities on such a low level, taking assets worth very small amounts, that it is very nearly impossible for anyone to spot them. In these cases, the controls that would be necessary to prevent or find fraud would be so onerous that the cost of the controls would very likely exceed the cost of the fraud. For example, employees may be using the company postage machine to send out personal mail. The control over this might require installing a lock on the machine as well as direct supervision when it is in use. Doing this may be more expensive than the cost of any lost postage. In short, many fraud cases involve losses on such a small scale that it is not worth the effort of installing controls to ensure that it does not happen.

Other fraud cases *do* involve potentially large losses. A controller should prevent these situations from occurring, since they can have a large impact on company cash flow and profits. The best way to determine the extent of potential fraud is to review all areas of the company and estimate the largest amount of fraud that can possibly occur in each function. To use the previous example, the upper limit on losses through a postage machine is the amount of postage stored in it, which rarely exceeds $1,000 and is usually considerably less. However, the potential for inventory theft in a large warehouse area may run into millions of dollars. Another example is sending wire transfers; if a person can send one for all available company funds to a numbered Swiss bank account, this can bankrupt a company. Of the three examples, it is clear which areas require a broader range of controls. Accordingly, a controller should first evaluate all functional areas to determine the degree of potential loss and hone in on those areas in which the company can lose large sums.

When a controller reviews a business to locate potentially high-risk fraud situations, there is a great likelihood that the review will miss some potential situations if the controller does not have a strong knowledge of the business. For example, if a manufacturing company hires a controller from one of the service industries, that controller will not have a good knowledge of internal controls over manufactured goods, and of how materials can be removed from the system without detection. In this situation, a controller can flowchart the main processes of the company, which also yields an excellent knowledge of operations. However, many controllers, especially new ones, do not have time for such an in-depth review. In these cases, the controller can bring in the company auditors, who have presumably audited many similar companies, and who have considerable knowledge of control systems. The auditors can conduct the review and make a number of recommended system changes in a short period of time. In short, assessing the existing control environment requires a good knowledge of systems, which may call for outside assistance in conducting the review Aside from the use of control systems to combat fraud, there are other ways to detect it, such as notification by fellow employees. In many cases, other employees are well aware of fraud situations and make the (false) assumption that management knows about it too and has chosen to take no action. The best way to clear up this level of employee uncertainty as well as to be on the receiving end of information about fraud problems is simple accessibility. It is very helpful if a controller or someone on the controller's staff is a gregarious type who mixes constantly with other people in the company. By making themselves available, the accounting staff puts itself in a better position to be trusted by other employees, which results in information about improprieties. Notification by employees is an important second source of information about fraud.

There are many warning signs that indicate the presence of fraud. A controller is well advised to review this information from time to time to determine whether there are conditions at a company that make it easy for fraud to occur. In addition, there should be a periodic review of control systems to monitor the risk and amount of loss at various points in the company. If there have been changes in these factors since the last review, consider altering the controls. Finally, it is important to keep lines of communication open between the accounting staff and the rest of the company, for hints from employees run a close second as a good method for spotting fraud cases. By using general indicators and good control points, and by being receptive to employees, a controller will have a much better chance of finding fraud in the company.

HOW TO DEAL WITH A FRAUD SITUATION

A controller faces difficult choices when confronted with a fraud situation—should the company go public and push for criminal charges against the perpetrator, or is it better to reach a private resolution? Some companies even accept payment back from the problem employee and then *retain* that person! This section discusses the factors in favor of and against each option.

The following list notes the primary options available to a company when resolving a fraud situation. The first point is the most drastic resolution, with succeeding options declining in severity. For each item, there is a discussion of the likely results of each action, as well as any moral considerations.

- **Bring criminal charges**. This option sends the clearest message to employees—the company will not tolerate fraud under any circumstances. Therefore, it tends to have a positive impact on reducing subsequent fraud. Also, from a moral standpoint, it is the correct action to take, because there is now a public record that a person has committed an illegal act, which gives adequate notice to other companies that may hire the individual. However, publicly held companies tend not to take this route, because a public display of the corporate incompetence that originally allowed the fraud to take place does not give the company a positive public image, and may even lead to the firing of top management by the Board of Directors. Consequently, and unfortunately, many companies tend to shy away from this option.
- **Demand restitution and fire the employee**. This option is the most common one. A company is certainly justified in demanding restitution, and should always fire anyone committing fraud, as this avoids the chance of any recurrence of the situation. Also, because there are no legal proceedings, stockholders will not find out about the fraud situation, which upholds the reputation of the company as well as senior management. However, this does not create a public record that the wrongdoer has committed fraud, so other companies that hire this person will have no way of knowing that they are hiring a "bad apple." Thus, this option is not as morally acceptable as the first option.
- **Dismiss employee for cause**. Many companies take this approach if there is no reasonable chance of recovering missing funds or other assets. This approach also avoids any legal controversy that may result in adverse publicity. However, it creates no public record of wrongdoing, so the perpetrator is free to commit fraud again elsewhere.
- **Permit employee to resign**. This approach is sometimes allowed for employees who have committed fraud but who occupy such high-profile positions that their firings would excite comment by the business community. The same option may be extended to employees who have worked for a company for such a long time that management feels it has some obligation to allow a quiet departure. However, from a moral perspective, this is one of the worst options; another company will have no reason to suspect that

there was a criminal situation at a previous company, because there is no record of a firing. By selecting this option, a company allows a perpetrator to continue fraudulent acts at other organizations.

▪ **Demand restitution and permit the employee to stay**. Though this option allows a company to recoup its losses, it runs the substantial risk of having the perpetrator commit fraud yet again. Also, other employees will see that there was no drastic action taken, so they will either be encouraged to commit fraud themselves, or will at least have a minimal incentive for reporting future cases of fraud to management. Despite these drawbacks, companies continue to select this option for two reasons—either the person committing fraud is a member of the family that owns the company, or management feels that it has a better chance of getting its money back by having direct control over the payroll deductions that will gradually return the cash.

▪ **Do nothing**. Companies pick this option primarily because the person committing fraud is a co-owner of the business, which makes it difficult to take any action. This has a demoralizing effect on other employees who see illegal activities taking place without any fear of retribution, and frequently leads to excessive levels of employee turnover, as people find other companies with more upright moral standards.

The range of actions that management can take to combat fraud is very broad. The best approach is to take a stern stand against all cases of fraud, which has the multiple benefits of setting a good example for other employees to see, giving a company some chance of reacquiring lost assets, and of leaving a public record of criminal activity, which gives other companies due notice of a prospective employee's character. The other options for dealing with fraud will result in increasing levels of difficulty, such as no return of lost assets, reduced employee morale, possible increases in employee turnover, and additional fraud cases at other companies as employees emigrate to new companies and commit crimes again. In short, management should react strongly to any cases of fraud, including prosecution to the fullest extent of the law.

FOREIGN CORRUPT PRACTICES ACT

The Foreign Corrupt Practices Act requires a publicly traded company (it does not apply to privately held companies) to keep in reasonable detail "books, records, and accounts" that accurately and fairly reflect its transactions and disposition of assets, and maintain an adequate system of internal controls. The control system must have the following attributes:

- Transactions must occur under the authorization of management.
- Transactions must be properly recorded.
- There must be reasonable controls over access to assets.
- There must be periodic reconciliations of recorded to actual assets, with an investigation of any differences.

This Act is particularly applicable to multinational organizations, so the controllers of these organizations must be aware of it and its ramifications for enhanced control systems. To be in compliance with the Act be particularly mindful of the adequacy of company control systems, as well as of subtle changes in financial results that may indicate the presence of control problems.

CHAPTER EIGHT

The Fast Close*

Importance of This Chapter

One of the most common challenges for the controller is to close the month-end books and issue financial statements as fast as possible. The resulting statements are being demanded by corporate management, outside investors, and the Securities and Exchange Commission (for public companies) on the shortest possible timelines. However, the closing process has traditionally been a slow one, with most companies requiring several weeks to close their books and issue financial statements. Companies with more organized closing systems can reduce this process to perhaps one week, while those companies with the best closing processes can reduce the entire interval to just a few days. The wide disparity in closing times shows that this is a rich area of opportunity for the controller.

* Adapted with permission from Chapter 18 of Steven M. Bragg. Controller's Function, 4th Edition (Hoboken, NJ: Wiley, 2011).

This chapter walks you through the process of closing the books and creating financial statements faster.

DIFFERENT TYPES OF FAST CLOSE

Several variations on the fast close concept have appeared, causing some confusion about the nature of each one. The *fast close* is simply an acceleration of the standard closing process, resulting in approximately the same financial reporting package being issued (possibly somewhat stripped down). The focus of this approach is a careful examination of the closing process to strip out wait times, consolidate tasks, eliminate unnecessary functions, add transaction best practices, and selectively apply automation where necessary. It is a task in which an industrial engineer trained in efficiency improvements would feel quite at home.

The *soft close* is less labor-intensive than a regular close, because it does not generate as much information. It is designed solely for internal corporate use, so its end product is only those management reports needed to run operations. With this reduced reporting goal in mind, the accounting staff can eliminate the use of overhead allocations. It may also be possible to stop some accruals and ignore the elimination of intercompany transactions, depending on the level of reporting detail desired. The soft close is most commonly seen in companies that only issue quarterly or annual reports to outside entities, leaving all other months available for the soft close.

The *virtual close* involves the use of a largely automated accounting system, one that can produce required financial information at any time, on demand. This approach is rarely used, and only in the largest companies that can afford to install an enterprise resource planning (ERP) system that automatically consolidates and reports financial information. Also, the underlying transactions that feed into the ERP system must be essentially error-free, so an accurate virtual close is really the result of a hefty software investment as well as years of continual process improvements. The financial reports resulting from a virtual close tend to be stripped-down versions of generally accepted accounting principles (GAAP)–compliant reports, since this approach avoids the need for such manual tasks as overhead allocation, accrual transactions, and the establishment of various reserves.

If achieved, a virtual close can be useful in fast-moving industries where financial results must be monitored on a frequent basis in order to make rapid-fire changes to a company's tactical or strategic direction, or at least to identify problem areas for fast management attention.

 ## HOW TO ACHIEVE A FAST CLOSE

Reducing the time required to close the books is something that an industrial engineer can relate to—it is all about examining the existing process and finding ways to strip out unnecessary activities and perfect the completion of what is left. Since these activities have very little to do with the GAAP in which every accountant is trained, it should be no surprise that many controllers have no idea how to achieve a fast close. This chapter reveals how to do so.

Document the Existing Closing Process

The first step in achieving a fast close is the complete documentation of every step in the closing process. This should address all functional areas of the close, including payroll, invoicing, payables, inventory, cash, and the general ledger. Some companies in specialized industries may require additional closing tasks. The primary focus of this documentation should be a complete itemization of the nature of each task, who completes it, the time required to complete it, and any queue times that appear when a task is shifted to a different person within the process. An example of the resulting documentation for the payables process is shown in Exhibit 8.1. The analysis in the exhibit shows a common state of affairs—lengthy queue times, a multitude of processing tasks, and high transaction error rates in some areas, all of which result in a payables closing process of four days.

When the documentation of all the closing processes is combined, it will reveal that most closing activities can be completed within one week of month-end. However, some activities cannot be started until other closing tasks are finished, which greatly increases the duration of the close. For example, if there are multiple company divisions, the additional tasks of currency conversion, mapping subsidiary entries to the corporate chart of accounts, and eliminating intercompany transactions will not begin until the subsidiaries have closed their books and forwarded their results to the corporate office. Also, even if a company only has a single location, it must prepare preliminary financial statements, review them for mistakes, create adjusting entries, add descriptive footnotes, and issue the resulting statements. These added tasks can easily

EXHIBIT 8.1 Payables Closing Analysis

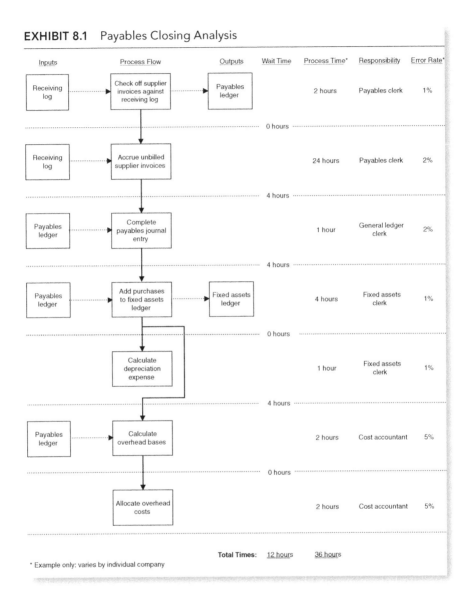

Inputs	Process Flow	Outputs	Wait Time	Process Time*	Responsibility	Error Rate*
Receiving log	Check off supplier invoices against receiving log	Payables ledger		2 hours	Payables clerk	1%
			0 hours			
Receiving log	Accrue unbilled supplier invoices			24 hours	Payables clerk	2%
			4 hours			
Payables ledger	Complete payables journal entry			1 hour	General ledger clerk	2%
			4 hours			
Payables ledger	Add purchases to fixed assets ledger	Fixed assets ledger		4 hours	Fixed assets clerk	1%
			0 hours			
	Calculate depreciation expense			1 hour	Fixed assets clerk	1%
			4 hours			
Payables ledger	Calculate overhead bases			2 hours	Cost accountant	5%
			0 hours			
	Allocate overhead costs			2 hours	Cost accountant	5%

Total Times: 12 hours 36 hours

* Example only: varies by individual company

extend the closing work into an additional week, as revealed by the closing time line shown in Exhibit 8.2.

The closing time line in the exhibit breaks down the most common closing tasks into four-hour increments. Some closing tasks may appear to

EXHIBIT 8.2 Combined Closing Time Line

Payroll Activities	Complete all time records	Accrue wages, vacation time	Complete billable hours	Complete payroll journal entry						
Invoicing Activities		Bill recurring invoices		Bill for prior month deliveries, services	Bill for rebillable expenses	Accrue unbilled revenue	Accrue commissions, bad debts			
Payable Activities				Accrue unbilled supplier invoices	Complete A/P journal entry	Update fixed assets, calculate depreciation	Calculate overhead bases	Allocate overhead costs		
Inventory Activities		Ensure inventory cutoff		Count and value inventory	Determine LCM*	Determine obsolete reserve	Complete inventory journal entry			
Cash Activities		Review uncashed checks		Complete bank reconciliations						
Final Closing Activities								Convert currency, map to chart of accounts, eliminate intercompany transactions	Create preliminary financial statements, analyze adjust results, and complete internal financial statements	
	Day One	Day Two	Day Three	Day Four	Day Five	Day Six	Day Seven	Day Eight	Day Nine	Day Ten	Day Eleven

* LCM = Lower of cost or market

183

require an excessive amount of time, such as the three days needed to complete a bank reconciliation. These long durations are typically caused by long queue times—for example, the bank reconciliation may only require an hour to complete, but the company must wait several days for the bank to deliver its bank statement, which causes the long task duration. Thus, the bulk of the eleven days of closing time in the exhibit is caused by queue time, rather than actual work.

Alter the Timing of Closing Activities

The easiest and least expensive way to enhance the speed of the close is to shift work outside of the period traditionally reserved for closing activities. In most situations, controllers have grown accustomed to beginning their closing activities after the reporting period has been completed and plowing through a fixed set of closing activities until the financial statements are completed many days later. A better approach is to review the closing activities to determine which ones can be shifted into the previous month, or delayed until after the close is completed. A number of items to consider completing before the core closing period are:

- ■ **Bank reconciliation.** Most banks offer online access to transaction information that is accurate through the preceding business day. If so, get into the habit of updating the bank reconciliation every day, so there is no need to wait until month-end to receive a hard copy of the bank statement. Alternatively, request the bank to alter the period of the bank statement, so it closes several days prior to the company's reporting period. This means that the statement will arrive in time for reconciliation prior to the commencement of closing activities.
- ■ **Overhead allocations.** The allocation of overhead costs is usually based on some activity measure, such as machine hours or labor hours. Since the activity measure is typically tracked outside of the accounting system, there is a tendency for it to be one of the last items available for closing calculations. To avoid this problem, consider using either the activity statistics from the preceding month for overhead allocations, or a rolling average of several preceding months.
- ■ **Recurring invoices.** Some companies earn revenue from highly predictable billings, usually for some type of maintenance or subscription service. If this is the case, and the amount of each billing is already known well in advance of the invoicing date, consider shifting the billing activity into

the week before the close. To avoid having the revenue be recorded in the wrong month, be sure to set the invoice date forward to the date when the company customarily issues the invoices.

- **Bad debt reserve.** The reserve for bad debts is no more than an estimate of what bad debts are expected to be in the near future. That being the case, it is unlikely that updating the contents of the reserve a day or two prior to the end of the reporting period will have a significant incorrect impact on the size of the reserve.

- **Interest expense.** To complete an early accrual of the interest expense for the reporting period, the controller needs a good idea of whether debt levels are expected to change during the last few days of the reporting period, which is usually easy if there is an adequate cash forecasting system in place. Even if the anticipated debt level is incorrect, the amount of incorrectly accrued interest expense only covers one or two days, and so it is sufficiently insignificant to have only a minor impact on the financial statements.

- **Unpaid wages.** If a company has mostly salaried employees, the unpaid wages accrual will only apply to a few employees, so estimates can safely be used to arrive at an approximate unpaid wage expense before the reporting period has closed. However, if there are many hourly employees, this may be quite a large accrual, where more accuracy is needed. If so, an early accrual is still possible if headcount levels are steady and employees work the same number of hours each day. A third alternative is to install a real-time timekeeping system, such as a computerized time clock, so that actual employee time worked is available with a delay of no more than one day. This allows the controller to estimate the wage accrual for the last day of the reporting period—all other information used to create the accrual uses actual hours worked.

- **Vacation time.** The accrual for vacation liability is one that some controllers do not update frequently, on the grounds that headcount levels are stable, so the liability is easily estimated. However, in cases where headcount levels fluctuate, the size of the liability may also change to a considerable extent, and so may have a noticeable impact on financial results. If this is the case, update the vacation accrual as soon as the last payroll register of the reporting period has been completed. This document contains all the information needed to update the accrual and is usually available several days prior to the end of the reporting period.

- **Account reconciliations.** It is absolutely necessary to keep track of the contents of the larger asset and liability accounts to ensure that costs are not inadvertently parked on the balance sheet instead of being charged to expense in the correct period. Though there is a risk that such items may be added to the balance sheet in the last day or two of the reporting period, it is usually a reasonable risk to complete account reconciliations a day or two early and simply adjust the accounts in the next reporting period for any late entries.

■ **Depreciation.** Controllers usually wait until all accounts payable have been received before updating the fixed assets register and *then* calculating depreciation—which places it near the end of the closing process. However, it is possible to update the fixed assets register several days early and record the resulting depreciation before the core closing period. The main risk is that new fixed assets will be acquired in the last days of the reporting period, which means that their related depreciation expense will not be recorded. However, the additional depreciation (not normally a large amount) can be added to the next reporting period as a one-time adjustment, with the correction being made at some point outside of the other closing activities.

■ **Commissions.** If a company incurs a substantial commission expense, then the commission calculation is a key part of the closing activities, typically positioned right after final invoices are issued. To reduce the amount of calculation effort in the midst of the core closing activities, consider performing an early calculation of all other commissions that were earned on invoices issued earlier in the reporting period. This should leave only a few commission calculations for the smaller number of invoices issued at the end of the period. Also, the controller may be in the habit of waiting for the sales staff to review the commission calculations to ensure that the commission accrual is correct. However, this additional wait may not be necessary if the total amount of the commission will not change—only the salesperson being paid. Thus, waiting extra time for a commission calculation review may not be necessary.

■ **Financial statement error review.** The controller is usually under a great deal of pressure at the very end of the closing process to conduct a fast review of the financial statements, correct any obvious errors, and then immediately release the financials. This approach tends to ignore small errors and leaves little time to investigate the reasons for larger ones, so the causes of errors continue to exist. A better approach is to review the financials just before the end of the reporting period, when most of the underlying transactions have already been completed. This gives more time to create permanent fixes, and leaves only a few late transactions to review again once the financial statements have been created during the core closing period.

It is also possible to defer items until *after* the core closing period. Some areas in which a deferral makes sense are:

- **Rebillable expenses.** A major problem area for service-related companies is accumulating rebillable expenses from its employees (which can take days) in order to include these charges in the monthly billing to their customers. Waiting for these expenses can unduly delay the closing process. A better approach is to create an invoice at once that excludes the rebillable expenses, thereby allowing one to close the books. At this point, the company has the option of immediately issuing the invoices (for better cash flow) or of waiting for the employee expense reports to arrive and then retroactively adding them to the original invoices.
- **Invoice mailing.** The purpose of the close is to issue financial statements, not invoices. However, the mind-set of many controllers is that they must first create invoices for the reporting period, then mail them, and then go back to the preparation of financial statements. Instead, create the invoices and then put them to one side until the financial statements have been released. Cash flow will suffer, but if a fast close is more important, then this is the correct approach.
- **Error investigation.** If errors in the financial statements are spotted, a detailed analysis of their causes in the midst of the close is a bad use of the accounting staff's time. Instead, make a list of the errors and then conduct a thorough investigation after the financials are issued. There is far less pressure once the close is completed, so a more thorough error analysis can be completed afterwards.

Revise the Financial Statement Contents

Sometimes the cause of a lengthy close is the nature of the financial statements being issued. There may be several variations of the reports, or they may include too much data of various types to make it possible to accumulate all the necessary information in a reasonably short period of time.

The controller may be issuing redundant financial statements. For example, one version goes to the manufacturing vice president and contains information that is not included in the version going to the sales vice president, and so on. If there are a multitude of reports to issue, the controller will have a very difficult time releasing them without adding several days to the close. A better approach is to convince the report recipients that a single set of statements will suffice for all of them. If anyone insists on the inclusion of additional data, then ask if this data can be issued separately after the primary financial statements have already been released.

Another problem with financial statements is the frequent inclusion of cost accounting and performance analysis metrics in the statements. This information usually includes some operational data that must be separately accumulated and manually reviewed, so it requires considerable extra time to collect and insert into the financials. A much better approach is to create a separate reporting package for this additional information that is released on a different schedule, so it does not interfere with the release of the primary financial statements. A likely outcome is that the additional information will be released more frequently, perhaps on a weekly schedule, so managers will receive more timely information as a result of this change.

Optimize the Use of Journal Entries

Manual adjustments to the financial statements are made through journal entries. Since they are manually created, they require additional time to complete, and are subject to error. Therefore, reducing the number of journal entries and adding some elements of automation to any remaining entries will speed the closing process.

If the controller is excessively detail-oriented, she may have fallen into the habit of creating journal entries for extremely minor items that have no significant impact on the financial statements. For example, she could be creating an unpaid wages accrual when the number of hourly laborers is a tiny fraction of the total workforce, or spreading the cost of personal property taxes across the entire year when the total amount of the expense does not justify the extra effort. These smaller entries could have been started when the related dollar amounts were larger, and then no one ever decided to cancel the entries once the need for them declined. The obvious solution is to review every journal entry made in the past month and see if any can be permanently eliminated without damaging the accuracy of the financial statements.

The controller should complete the same journal entries for every reporting period, so there is more consistency in the numbers presented. However, a more common state of affairs is for some journal entries to be inadvertently skipped in some reporting periods or even entered twice, resulting in clearly inaccurate financials that must be investigated and fixed—thereby lengthening the close. A better approach is to create a standard checklist of journal entries that includes a checkbox or space for initials to indicate the completion of each entry, as well as a reference number to show where the standard journal entry template is stored in the accounting software. This more methodical approach will ensure that the entries are used every time.

The best way to handle journal entries is to convert as many as possible to recurring entries, so that a single entry at the beginning of the year will be automatically generated by the accounting software for all subsequent periods of the year. If entries are not sufficiently similar over multiple periods to be worth placing in a recurring entry, then at least standardize the entry by creating a journal entry template in the accounting software. By using the same entry format in every reporting period for the same journal entry, the controller avoids the errors that can arise when an entry is individually created in each period, probably resulting in some errors that require subsequent investigation and correction.

In larger companies, a number of people may be authorized to make journal entries. If so, there is a strong chance that employees may independently create the same entry, resulting in duplication that must be corrected—which slows down the close. In order to improve the quality of journal entries, consider limiting general ledger access to the smallest possible number of people, who can more easily track which entries have been made. Though this may appear to create a bottleneck that could lengthen the close, it avoids more time lost to error correction.

If a company has several subsidiaries, it may suffer from a wide array of local charts of accounts that must be manually mapped to the corporate chart of accounts as part of the closing process. This mapping approach can be automated with either customized software or through a mapping module that is available in high-end accounting software packages. An alternative that requires no automation is to force all subsidiaries to use the same chart of accounts, so no mapping is required. This approach will be time-consuming, so you can ensure that the data capture needs of each subsidiary are met, and may result in a rather large chart of accounts. However, the payoff is in a much easier consolidation process that will reduce the length of the close.

Centralize Accounting Activities

A major cause of closing problems in multilocation companies is differences in the way accounting transactions are processed in each location. This causes differences in local transactional training, makes it difficult to apply accounting best practices across the organization, and causes delays in the completion and forwarding of closing information to corporate headquarters. Also, if the headquarters staff detects problems with the forwarded information, it must send a request back to the subsidiary for an update and wait for a reply—which takes more time.

There are several ways to address the problem of decentralized accounting. One approach is to keep accounting staff in all locations, but to issue a centrally promulgated series of accounting policies and procedures to those locations. If properly enforced, this gives the corporate controller assurance that all transactions are dealt with in the same manner in all locations. It has the additional benefit of allowing one to compare the closing performance of each location; since they are all using the same systems, they should be able to close at about the same time.

An alternative approach is to centralize all accounting operations in one location. This approach certainly reduces the total accounting headcount, since the accounting managers required at each outside location are no longer needed. This also allows the company to concentrate all of its efforts on improving the efficiency of a single accounting operation, which usually results in a much faster rate of best practices adoption, and therefore a faster closing speed. Another speed improvement results from the centralization of all error investigation and correction, thereby eliminating the extra queue built into a more diffused accounting environment where update requests are sent to outlying locations. This approach works best if the company has invested in an ERP system that is linked to all company locations; with such a system in place, the central accounting staff can more easily pull in operational information from outlying locations for a variety of purposes, which also contributes to a faster close. On the downside, consolidating accounting operations can run into considerable resistance from division managers, who like to keep an accounting staff close at hand.

Even if a company only has one location, it can still adopt the centralization approach to the faster close by concentrating closing activities with fewer people. By doing so, there is no need to hand off closing activities from one person to another, thereby eliminating queue times. Also, with fewer people involved, there is less chance that closing transactions will be misinterpreted, so there will be fewer errors to investigate and correct. Further, if some accounting staff are not involved in the close, this makes it easier to apportion all nonclosing actions to them, leaving the employees working on the close to devote virtually all of their efforts to this activity. The bottom line is that any level of increased centralization will improve the speed of the close.

Specific Improvements to Functional Areas

There are a number of best practices impacting specific functional areas that have the ancillary effect of improving the speed of the close. The following list outlines best practices by functional area that have this impact:

- **Inventory.** Without a doubt, the finest closing-related inventory best practice is to create an extremely accurate inventory tracking system. Doing so involves proper labeling of all inventory items and rack locations, consolidating parts, assigning accurate part numbers, loading the resulting information into an inventory tracking database, and cycle counting the inventory repeatedly. By doing so, you can eventually gain complete comfort in the accuracy of the inventory without having to perform a physical count—and this saves an enormous amount of closing effort. Another best practice is shifting as much inventory as possible to the shop floor, where it is charged to expense in the current period. This reduces the amount of time-consuming inventory valuation work by the closing staff. Finally, there should be a long-range effort to shrink the total amount of inventory, thereby reducing the level of importance of this asset and the associated amount of closing activities. Inventory reduction activities can include:

  - Reduce the length of supplier lead times.
  - Shift raw materials ownership to suppliers.
  - Drop ship inventory direct from suppliers to customers.
  - Schedule smaller production batches.
  - Produce to order rather than to stock.
  - Reduce machine setup times.
  - Reduce the number of products and product options.
  - Monitor and adjust safety stock levels on a frequent basis.
  - Monitor and disposition obsolete inventory on a frequent basis.

- **Billing.** The creation of period-end invoices can occupy the largest part of the closing process in many companies. There are several ways to reduce the level of this invoicing activity. One is to shift the billing of recurring invoices into the preceding week; this is quite possible if the invoices are generated regularly and are always in the same amount. Another approach is to give the accounting staff direct access to shipping information by linking their computers to the those of the shipping department; this eliminates the wait time for shipping documents to be manually sent from the shipping to the accounting department. Yet another option is to eliminate invoices entirely by integrating electronic billings with the company's computer systems; when a shipment occurs, the computer system sends an electronic invoice with no manual input from the accounting staff. Finally, consider referencing supporting documentation for an invoice with the words "billing as per the attached document," rather than laboriously transferring the information from the supporting documentation onto the invoice.

▪ **Payroll.** The expense related to salaries and wages may comprise a company's largest expense category, and so can occupy a considerable proportion of the closing process. There are several ways to streamline activities associated with this area. One is to simplify the commission structure. Commissions are usually calculated after the final invoices are generated for the month, and so they are one of the last transactions to be compiled before the preliminary financial statements are issued. Thus, implementing a highly simplified commission structure can reduce the size of a bottleneck closing operation. Also, do not wait for the inevitable adjustments to the commissions by the sales staff to be received before closing the books—though the person receiving a commission may change, the total amount of the initial commission calculation is probably correct, so book the commission without further adjustment. It is also useful to implement both computerized time clocks (for in-house hourly staff) and Web-based timekeeping (for traveling or widely dispersed employees). By doing so, the accumulation of timekeeping information becomes much simpler, both for the generation of an unpaid wages accrual and for use in billing employee time to customers. An easy improvement is to place a cap on the amount of unused vacation time that employees are allowed to carry forward into the next year. By doing so, the vacation accrual becomes extremely simple, requiring only the recording of the maximum possible vacation carry forward as the ongoing accrual, rather than the detailed analysis that is normally required.

▪ **Payables.** Many controllers get into the habit of waiting up to a week after the period-end for supplier billings to arrive in the mail before they will even consider closing the books. With some up-front effort, it is possible to create a reasonably accurate accrual of supplier invoices that have not yet been received, thereby eliminating this extensive waiting period. There are two ways to eliminate the wait. One approach is to require that virtually all purchases above a minimum level be pre-authorized with a purchase order. By doing so, the computer system can automatically compare the authorized purchase orders to received supplier invoices and received goods, yielding a list of authorized purchase orders for which there has been a receipt but for which no supplier invoice has arrived. The resulting report can be used as the basis for an unbilled payables accrual on the beginning of the first day of the closing process. An alternative approach for those companies not using purchase orders is to manually track the arrival dates and amounts of supplier invoices, so the controller can estimate the size of accruals for selected larger expenses. Though not as accurate as the purchase order approach, this alternative can be effective for smaller companies with lower purchasing volume.

A lesser concern in the payables area is the processing of supplier invoices that *do* arrive, but whose arrival is inconveniently at the end of the reporting period, when there is little time to properly process them. One way to reduce the volume of these invoices is to create a procurement card program within the company, whereby employees are encouraged to use credit cards for smaller purchases. Another approach is to use negative assurance to obtain payment approval—simply send an invoice copy to the invoice approver, and proceed with payment by assuming that they approve unless they say otherwise. Finally, a more advanced system requiring considerable custom programming is to have the receiving staff check off received items in the computer system for which a purchase order has already been created, with the computer system automatically scheduling payment without any operator intervention—this approach essentially eliminates all accounts payable labor, but is difficult to create and install.

■ **Cash processing.** Though the processing of cash is part of the closing process, it occupies a relatively small place in the closing proceedings. As noted earlier, it is possible to use daily online bank reconciliations to avoid the period-end bank reconciliation. Also, to avoid spending time processing cash receipts at the end of the reporting period that could be used for other closing activities, consider using a lockbox where check images can be accessed online. By doing so, you can be assured that the lockbox operator is depositing cash receipts as rapidly as possible, while the logging of cash receipts into the computer system can be delayed until after the close is completed, using the online check images.

Though a considerable amount of time is required to implement some of the preceding best practices, their eventual implementation can lead to startling improvements in the duration of the closing process. In particular, the use of an inventory tracking system, electronic billings, computerized time clocks, and a payables accrual can lop multiple days off the duration of the close.

Incorporate Automation into the Closing Process

Few of the preceding suggestions require the use of advanced computer systems, since much of the closing process really revolves around scheduling, error reduction, and the content of the deliverable. Nonetheless, the following technologies are useful for squeezing some additional time from the closing process:

- **Workflow management system (WMS).** A WMS was originally designed to speed the flow of very large document volumes among large numbers of employees and allocate work to those with the shortest backlog. This would appear to be at odds with the concept of the ideal closing team, which has very few members. However, it can be used to enforce the flow of closing activities in a specific order, which may support closing procedures that are being regularly tweaked to create better performance. It also tracks who worked on each activity and how long they needed to complete a task, which is useful for examining the performance of the closing team. It is also useful if the closing team is dispersed over several offices, since it can coordinate their activities.
- **Consolidation software.** If there are multiple divisions to consolidate, then consolidation software is an alternative to a centralized accounting system. Consolidation software combines financial data from multiple entities, even if reported in different currencies, while also using accounting rules to account for the percentage of equity ownership. This software is very expensive, usually requires custom programming to link to the corporate accounting system, and is clearly designed only for large corporations. Consolidation is an integral part of the Oracle and SAP ERP systems.
- **Data warehouse.** If there are many accounting databases throughout a company, one way to organize the data for easier financial querying and reporting is to construct a data warehouse. This is a central database that regularly extracts and consolidates data from a company's various computer systems. With it, the corporate staff can conduct drill-down analyses of the accounting data to find errors (depending on how much data has been uploaded into the data warehouse), thereby reducing that portion of the closing process related to error investigation. However,

data warehouses are very expensive and time-consuming to construct, requiring custom interfaces to every local database from which data is to be copied, and also require a great deal of ongoing maintenance to ensure that local system changes, deletions, and additions are reflected in the data warehouse.

- **ERP system.** An ERP system is a highly complex, interlocking set of databases and computer programs that are used to run essentially all company operations. It is very expensive, difficult to install, and requires altered company procedures to match those required by the ERP system. However, it also allows the closing staff to directly access accounting information anywhere in the company and includes work-flow management as well as consolidation modules.

With the exception of consolidation software, improving the speed of the close is almost never a sufficient reason to install any of the above systems. It is generally better to use nonautomation techniques to shrink the duration of the close to the greatest extent possible, and then see if the cost of the additional automation is worth the remaining reduction in the closing interval. Once all of the nonautomation closing improvements are implemented, a controller may find the remaining closing interval to be so short that the considerable additional cost of automation is not worth the investment.

 ## ENHANCED CLOSING PROCESS

If a controller follows the advice in the preceding sections, the result should be similar to the improved closing time line shown in Exhibit 8.3.

The exhibit reveals that at least some portion of almost every closing activity can be shifted into the days prior to the core closing period. Cash-related activities should be completely removed from the core closing period. The sole major remaining functional area requiring considerable effort during the core close is the issuance of customer invoices, after which the only remaining closing task of substance is the assembly of the final financial statements. All other closing tasks in the core period relate to the review of information already entered prior to the end of the reporting period, or else the compilation of financial information for the final day or two before the period closed.

EXHIBIT 8.3 Enhanced Closing Process

* LCM = Lower of cost or market

CHAPTER NINE

Internal Audit Function

Importance of This Chapter

The new controller may initially ignore any internal audit staff that her company may have. However, as this chapter points out, internal auditors can be an excellent resource for examining a variety of problems within a company. By understanding how this function works, the controller can use it as a resource to accomplish a number of key goals that she might not otherwise have sufficient staff to accomplish.

A key factor in the internal audit function is the manager to whom the function reports, since an incorrect reporting relationship can lead to skewed audit programs that avoid the areas supervised by that manager. Another issue is the objectives that the internal audit function should follow; too narrow a set of objectives may avoid reviews of key areas that are in serious need of help, while an excessively broad range of objectives will water down the department's ability to complete a reasonable set of target programs in a timely manner. A wide range of suggested activities for the internal audit staff are listed in this chapter, which are of use when determining a set of audit programs for the upcoming period. Finally, key factors are noted to consider when creating and maintaining a management system that provides an effective degree of control over the internal auditing staff. Thus, this chapter consists of an overview of the internal audit function, why it exists, what it does, and how to manage it.

 ## REPORTING RELATIONSHIPS

Many companies adopt a reporting relationship between the accounting and internal auditing functions that leads to strained relations between the two functions. This section analyzes the problem and suggests a solution.

Many companies have the head of the internal audit department report to either the controller or (more commonly) the chief financial officer (CFO). They do so on the grounds that the bulk of the work performed by the internal audit staff addresses accounting and finance issues, so it makes sense to cluster the departments together. In addition, the internal audit staff is usually trained in accounting and is probably looking toward a promotion into the accounting and finance staffs once they have completed a tour of duty in the internal audit area. By keeping the two departments "under one roof," the accounting and finance staffs get a close look at the internal audit staff and can use this knowledge to promote them into the most appropriate positions. Thus there are valid reasons for having the internal audit staff report to the manager of the accounting or finance functions.

Unfortunately, this relationship does not work very well, because the job of the internal audit staff is largely to review and report on the operations of the accounting and finance staffs. Because these reports tend to focus on problems, they do not cast the management of the accounting and finance departments in an overly favorable light. Consequently, if the internal audit staff reports to this area, it is common for the controller or CFO to design audit programs that focus on relatively innocuous areas, or else to focus on other parts of the company, while ignoring the accounting and finance areas. These outcomes tend to focus minimal internal audit attention on key accounting and finance processes, which is the precise area in which the auditors should be spending most of their time.

If the internal audit staff is to conduct unencumbered reviews of the accounting and finance areas, it is necessary to shift the reporting relationship away from them. This allows the internal audit staff to avoid any problems caused by managers who do not want to have deleterious results shown to senior management. However, moving management of the function to a different area of the company raises similar problems, for anyone to whom the function reports will also not want the group to conduct any internal audits on areas that may reflect poorly on the manager. Consequently, the internal audit function should only report to positions at the top of the organization, where the manager is responsible for the entire company, and thus has no reason to avoid poor results in specific areas. This position can be the chief executive officer (CEO), but if this person is engaged in questionable activities, he or she may try to quash *all* internal audit activities. The best alternative is the board of directors, which is responsible for no company functions and is only concerned with maintaining the most efficient and effective operations, as well as appropriate levels of control over assets. The board can direct the internal audit staff by forming an audit committee. This committee can approve suggested audit programs, besides its usual function of selecting and overseeing the activities of the external auditors. This solution gives unfiltered information to the board, while also allowing it to target those areas of the company that it feels may be in most need of a review.

Since this section has recommended that the internal audit staff not report to the controller, you might ask why this chapter is even included in this book— after all, if it is not managed by the controller, why discuss it? The reason is that the controller can still have a considerable amount of control over the annual list of audits that the department conducts. This happens for two reasons. First, the controller is the senior accounting officer in the company, and as such is in the best position to spot problem areas and request audits that will highlight problems. Second, whether there is a direct reporting relationship or not, the manager of the internal audit staff will recognize that the controller is more senior in the corporate hierarchy, and so it is a good idea to at least listen to any recommendations for future audits. For these reasons, the controller still has a considerable amount of influence over the activities of the internal audit staff, no matter who is the manager of the function.

In short, it is inappropriate for the internal audit staff to report directly to the controller or CFO, because they can skew audit programs to show the accounting and finance areas in the best possible light. It is better to assign the audit staff to the audit committee of the board of directors, which is a much more impartial management group.

COMPOSITION OF THE AUDIT COMMITTEE

The audit committee should be a standing committee of the board of directors and should be comprised primarily of nonofficer directors. These directors should not be involved in the management of the company, nor have previously been its officers. These restrictions are intended to create the most independent overview environment possible for the committee.

The committee is generally comprised of between three and five members, not all of whom must have an accounting, auditing, or finance background. It can be more useful to have some directors with a solid operational knowledge of the industry in which the company operates; these people can spot potential control weaknesses, based on their knowledge of how transactions flow in an industry-specific environment. Nonetheless, at least one committee member should have considerable training or experience in the accounting and finance arena. The committee should be expected to meet on at least a quarterly basis.

The CFO is rarely a member of this committee. Instead, sometimes she will be asked to attend its meetings in order to advise committee members on specific issues, or to answer questions about problems that the committee has uncovered through its review activities. The CFO should certainly maintain a strong line of communication with committee members, in order to inform them of possible accounting rule changes or prospective policy changes that may impact the reporting of financial information. The CFO should also educate committee members about key financial topics, such as corporate lines of business, accounting policies, legal obligations, regulatory filings, and industry accounting practices.

The director of the internal audit function usually reports to the CFO, but can report instead to the audit committee. The most common reporting relationship is for the internal audit director to be supervised by the CFO, but to have unimpeded access to the audit committee at any time; this reporting system is designed to give committee members direct access to the results of internal audits, while at the same time giving the internal audit director the ability to go around the CFO if that person appears to be obstructing the dissemination of internal audit results.

In short, the audit committee's structure is intended to be as independent of the management team as possible, while still giving it direct access to key accounting and audit personnel within the management team.

Ask to Attend

The controller is not normally invited to meetings of the audit committee, since the CFO represents the accounting department. However, the committee discusses a number of topics relevant to the controller's job and is also attended by several company directors. In order to keep abreast of audit problems and meet several directors, it is worth asking to attend as an observer. ■

ROLE OF THE AUDIT COMMITTEE

The goal of the audit committee is to assist the board of directors by providing oversight of the financial reporting process and related controls. The committee is not empowered to make any decisions—rather, it recommends actions to the full board, which may then vote on its recommendations. The exact range of tasks granted to the audit committee will vary, but are generally confined to the following issues:

- *Tasks related to company management:*
    - *Review expenses incurred by the management team.* Used to spot any excessive use of corporate funds by managers.
    - *Review business transactions between the company and the management team.* Used to ensure that managers are not enriching themselves at the expense of the company, as well as not holding their personal interests above those of the company.
- *Tasks related to external auditors:*
    - *Recommend the hiring of external auditors.* Used to ensure that a truly independent auditor is hired, rather than one having connections with the company in some way that may influence its review of the company's financial statements. The audit committee should also base this recommendation on the auditor's expertise in the industry, the quality of its services, the extent to which it performs other services for the company, and the amount of its quoted fees for the audit.
    - *Review auditor recommendations.* Used to ensure that control issues spotted by the auditors are properly dealt with by the management team, resulting in a stronger control environment.
    - *Review disputes between the external auditors and management.* Used to determine if the management team is attempting to force the auditors to agree with an alternative accounting treatment for transactions.
    - *Review the use of external auditors for other services.* Used to determine if the external auditor has obtained such a significant amount of extra business with the company that it may be less inclined to issue an unfavorable audit opinion, due to the risk of losing the additional business.
- *Tasks related to internal audits:*
    - *Review the replacement of the internal audit director.* Used to verify that the internal auditor director is being replaced for reasonable cause, rather than because the CFO wants to install a more malleable director.

▪ *Review the internal audit staff's objectives, work plans, training, and reports.* Used to verify that the internal audit staff is appropriately targeted at those areas of the company at greatest risk of control problems, and that the audit staff is appropriately trained to handle the audits. A detailed review of the annual work plan will reveal if the internal audit director has allocated a sufficient amount of time to each audit, or has sufficient staff available to complete all goals.

▪ *Review the cooperation received by the internal auditors.* Used to spot possible areas of fraudulent activities, since minimal cooperation is a signal that an auditee may be hiding information from audit teams.

▪ *Review disaster recovery plans.* Used to ensure that adequate recovery plans have been created and tested for the most likely disaster scenarios.

▪ *Tasks related to financial systems:*

  ▪ *Investigate fraud and other forms of financial misconduct.* Used as the grounds for a direct investigation of any situation possibly involving deliberately inaccurate financial reporting or the misuse of company assets.

  ▪ *Review corporate policies for compliance with laws and ethics.* Used to ensure that all corporate policies, irrespective of their relationship to financial systems, are constructed in accordance with local regulations, and meet the restrictions of the corporate statement of ethical activities.

  ▪ *Verify that financial reports address all information requirements of lenders.* Used to ensure that lender-required financial information is reported to them at the appropriate times and in the correct formats, so there is minimal risk of losing vital credit lines as a result of missing information.

  ▪ *Review all reports to shareholders, including special reports, for consistency of information.* Used to verify that all reports present a consistent picture of corporate financial health to investors. This is of particular concern for special reports, which tend to include different types of measures (such as EBITDA instead of the net income figure found on financial statements) and bullish statements by management that do not always match the tenor of information presented in the standard set of financial reports.

Of special interest is the audit committee's emphasis on the *review* of a wide range of financial activities—with the exception of one item: The audit committee is empowered to *investigate* fraud and other forms of financial misconduct, rather than review the results of such an investigation by someone else. The reason for this direct action is that employees are probably involved in the fraudulent activities, which may possibly involve members of management, so the audit committee can obtain an unbiased review of the situation only by doing so itself.

Thus, in all cases besides the investigation of financial misconduct, the audit committee's role is to examine the results of a variety of audits and other investigations to ensure that the company's system of financial reporting fairly represents actual operating results.

INTERNAL AUDIT OBJECTIVES

It is important to determine the correct set of objectives for the internal audit staff. These objectives are used as the framework for constructing audit programs, as well as for determining the most appropriate skill set for the staff, plus the number of people needed to staff the department. Devising the correct set of objectives has a direct bearing on both the structure and work of the department. This section describes a typical set of objectives, as well as some changes to the list that are appropriate under certain circumstances.

There is a broad range of internal audit objectives that a company can adopt. The exact number and type of objectives can vary greatly, depending on the anticipated size and skill of the audit staff, as well as the perceived need for audit reviews (which is frequently based on the past history of the company) by the management team that creates or approves the list of objectives. For example, a company may have had a great deal of trouble convincing its staff to follow a specific set of procedures, and so it will place great emphasis on an objective that hones in on the consistent use of policies and procedures. Another company may have had trouble with fraud or harassment in the past, and so one of its key objectives will be to ensure that the company's code of ethics is being followed. Yet another company may have been burned by inconsistent financial reporting, which calls for an objective that tracks this issue. The most common minimum objectives for the internal audit department will address the need to safeguard assets and create accurate financial statements. These objectives are strictly financial in nature, and can be handled by an audit staff with a traditional financial background and minimum training in company procedures. These are also useful objectives when the audit staff is so small that there is no room to pursue a wide-ranging set of objectives. These objectives are:

- That control systems will adequately safeguard company assets
- That company financial statements follow generally accepted accounting principles (GAAP) or international financial reporting standards (IFRS) and are accurate

These objectives can be widened to include reviews of operating policies and procedures. This is a common objective if there are perceived problems in this area. Also, problems in operations tend to have an impact on the accuracy of the financial statements, so many companies take the view that this objective goes "hand in hand" with the earlier objective for financial statements and therefore must be included. However, this requires a broader range of skills and a much larger work plan, so this objective tends to result in a larger and more experienced audit staff. This objective is:

- That the company is following operating policies and procedures

Given the degree to which computer systems are integrated into a company's most crucial operations, it is also common to specify an objective that addresses this area. By doing so, a company must add a highly skilled group of computer system auditors to the internal audit staff. Any review work involving computer systems requires a considerable degree of knowledge, primarily of systems design and testing. Some more detailed reviews may even require a knowledge of programming languages, though it is customary to contract out this more specialized audit work, since it is difficult to find and retain personnel with such unique skill sets. This objective is:

- That computer systems are accurately processing data

It is common for companies to also require reviews of ethical standards by the internal audit group. This requirement is frequently a result of a highly public scandal that has damaged the company's reputation or of a large lawsuit settlement that could have been avoided if there had been higher ethical standards (e.g., kickbacks, sexual harassment, etc.). Since this type of audit tends to fall outside of the experience of a typical internal auditor, it is customary to bring in a consultant to advise on how to construct and follow through on ethics audits (with the primary focus being on audits of scheduled ethics training of employees). This objective is:

- That the company is following an approved set of ethical guidelines

There should be an objective that requires the internal audit staff to support the activities of the external auditors. This objective is necessary because the fees charged by the outside auditors can be reduced by supplementing their work with that of the internal auditors. There is a limit to how much work the inside auditors can perform, because an excessive degree of assistance by them would interfere with the independence and objectivity of the external auditor's work. Nonetheless, the outside auditors may rely on them for a significant volume of work. This objective is:

▪ That the department adequately supports the activities of external auditors

The previous objectives have addressed key areas of a company that must be reviewed. In addition, there should be an objective that requires the internal audit manager to prepare an annual internal audit plan for reviewing the previous objectives. This is important, because it forces the manager to address such issues as the importance of various audits, the degree to which some objectives are being addressed at the expense of others, and the adequacy of the department's staffing and expense budget. This objective is:

▪ That it creates an annual audit plan that addresses all of these objectives

The final objective relates to the output from the work of the internal audit department. While the previous objectives have established a direction for the audits to be conducted or the management of that work, there is no provision for what the department is supposed to do with the results of all this work. Accordingly, the final objective requires the department to create reports that detail all findings and make recommendations to resolve problems. In addition, the objective should require that the reports be distributed to those levels of management that can use the information to resolve the problems. This final objective closes the loop on all activities required of the internal audit department. This objective is:

▪ That it provides written reports of its findings to those levels of management needing the information in order to correct faulty systems

The bulk of these objectives relate to the types of audit work to be conducted by the department, with the key areas including the safeguarding of assets, accuracy of financial statements, and reviews of operations and computer systems. Many of these objectives are discussed again in the next section, where we derive internal audit activities based on each of the objectives.

INTERNAL AUDIT ACTIVITIES

This section is based on the objectives that were described in the previous section. Though there are a few activities noted here, the reader should not rely on this list to create a comprehensive set of activities for an internal audit department. The reason is that there will certainly be additional activities that are unique to each company; also, there may be a number of activities that are specific to particular industries. A manager who is compiling activities for this department should talk to consultants, external auditors, and trade associations that have considerable experience in specific industries to obtain input on additional activities for the department. This will yield a more comprehensive set of tasks for the internal audit department.

Recruit from the Internal Audit Staff

Internal auditors do not necessarily have to be CPAs or even have earned a degree in accounting, since they are called upon to conduct audits in a variety of areas well away from the controller's department. However, as evidenced by a number of the following bullet points, many of them have considerable accounting experience. If so, use an internal audit of the accounting department as an excuse to evaluate them and extend job offers for an internal transfer to the department if they appear likely to be a good addition. ▪

The eight internal audit objectives noted below are all followed by a variety of related audit activities.

1. **Objective: That control systems will adequately safeguard company assets**
   - Cash: Verify that there are adequate controls over petty cash.
   - Fixed assets: Verify that there is a sufficient degree of control over borrowed assets. Verify that there is a sufficient degree of control over the acquisition and disposal of assets.
   - Inventory: Verify that there are sufficient safeguards against the loss of inventory. Verify that there is a sufficient degree of control over consigned inventory.
   - Supplies: Verify that there is a sufficient degree of control over the purchase, storage, and use of supplies.

2. **Objective: That company financial statements follow GAAP or IFRS and are accurate**
   - Cost of goods sold: Verify that product bills of material are accurate. Verify that the cost of goods sold is correctly computed. Verify that there is a proper cutoff of receipts and shipments at the end of the reporting period.
   - Expenses: Verify that all expense accruals are correctly calculated. Verify that all prepaid expenses are expensed in the correct periods. Verify that expenses are incurred only up to budgeted levels. Verify that paychecks are only calculated and paid for current employees. Verify that payroll amounts are correctly calculated. Verify that the assumed resale values of fixed assets are reasonable, based on a current review of asset values. Verify that the authorization for incurring expenses is appropriate. Verify that the time period over which depreciation is taken is reasonable, based on industry standards and historical usage.
   - Revenue: Verify that billings are only made for services and product sales that are actually completed. Verify that invoices are recorded in the correct periods and amounts.

3. **Objective: That the company is following operating policies and procedures**
   - Determine labor productivity.
   - Investigate and determine the cause of transactional errors.
   - Review the appropriateness of expenses for new construction.
   - Review the fixed-asset purchasing goals after the fact to see if goals were met.
   - Review the obsolescence of existing equipment.
   - Verify the appropriateness of pay levels based on experience and education.
   - Verify from a sample of expense reports that only those approved types of travel expenses are being reimbursed.
   - Verify that bank reconciliations are regularly performed and reviewed.
   - Verify that financial statements are published within specified due dates.
   - Verify that machine run rates are within expected levels.
   - Verify that product quality levels match minimum standards.
   - Verify that production scrap rates are within expected levels.
   - Verify that shipments are made on scheduled ship dates.
   - Verify the accuracy and timeliness of all key transactions.

4. **Objective: That computer systems are accurately processing data**
    - Verify from a sample of transactions that the computer system is correctly calculating accounting transactions.
    - Verify that data from an acquired company are accurately entered into the existing computer system.
    - Verify that new systems under development are designed with an appropriate number of control points to ensure proper processing of transactions.
    - Verify that there are a sufficient number of safeguards built into the system to ensure a rapid recovery from catastrophic computer damage.
    - Verify that there is sufficient testing of systems and data during a conversion of computer systems to a replacement system.

5. **Objective: That the company is following an approved set of ethical guidelines**
    - Follow up on reported ethics cases and determine the extent to which formal ethics training programs would have avoided the situations.
    - Verify from training records that each employee has received at least the minimum number of ethics training hours per year.
    - Verify that the training materials used to teach ethics to employees contain information that matches and supports the principles described in the company's official ethics policy.

6. **Objective: That the department adequately supports the activities of external auditors**
    - Verify that the internal audit staff completed the tasks assigned to it by the external auditors.
    - Verify that the tasks assigned to the internal audit staff to support the external auditors were completed to the satisfaction of the external auditors.
    - Review the entire external audit program and make recommendations to increase the share of work completed by the internal audit staff, in order to reduce fees charged by the external auditors.

7. **Objective: That the department creates an annual audit plan that addresses all of these objectives**
    - Verify that a broad range of managers are consulted regarding the contents of the annual audit plan.
    - Verify that the annual audit plan contains some reviews for the previous audit objectives related to control over assets, ethics, operations, financial accuracy, and operations.

※ Verify that the key control problems pointed out by the external auditors are being addressed by the annual audit plan.

8. **Objective: That the department provides written reports of its findings to those levels of management needing the information in order to correct faulty systems**

※ Verify that feedback is solicited from auditees regarding the findings and recommendations made in audit reports.

※ Verify the degree to which recommendations have been implemented, subsequent to the release of audit reports.

This section presented a wide-ranging list of internal audit activities that are closely tied to the audit objectives described in the last section. However, this is not a comprehensive list, so other industry-specific sources should be consulted in order to compile a more complete listing of activities.

 ## MANAGING THE INTERNAL AUDIT FUNCTION

The internal audit department is not a line function, so there are no regular outputs to examine, nor are there any direct cost savings or added revenues attributable to it. This lack of clear results makes it somewhat more difficult to manage the function. This section describes the main steps that a manager should complete in order to create a management system for the internal audit function, as well as a means for determining the status of activities and controlling it based on that information.

The first step in managing the department is to create and disseminate a clear set of responsibilities for the internal audit staff. This gives the department definitive guidelines to follow, as well as direction in its daily activities. A typical responsibility statement should include:

* That control systems will adequately safeguard company assets
* That company financial statements follow GAAP or IFRS and are accurate
* That the company is following operating policies and procedures
* That the company is following an approved set of ethical guidelines
* That computer systems are accurately processing data
* That the department adequately supports the activities of external auditors
* That it creates an annual audit plan that addresses all of these objectives
* That it provides written reports of its findings to those levels of management needing the information in order to correct faulty systems

Once these objectives are in place, the manager can focus on the primary output—the annual audit plan—as the easiest means for managing the department. The annual plan is usually a brief document that lists every audit to be completed during the year, as well as a brief description of the objectives of each audit. For example, it might include the following audit:

Review the method for recording additions, changes, and deletions of fixed assets to and from the accounting records for the Anderson-ville facility. The audit will verify that the correct capitalization limit is being observed, that there are documented and justified reasons for making alterations to the fixed asset records subsequent to additions, that deletions are recorded properly, and that the sale amounts of assets are reasonable.

Get on the List!

A well-managed annual audit plan will leave room for a few unplanned audits, but do not rely on trying to jam extra audits into the plan once it has been finalized. Instead, correspond regularly with the internal audit manager about the status and priority of various audit requests during the annual budgeting process to ensure that key accounting reviews will be included. ◼

Though this audit description gives you a good idea of what will happen during an audit, it does not yield a sufficient degree of additional information, such as the number of hours budgeted for the work, who will be assigned to the project, or when it will take place, for a manager to achieve tight control over the department. This requires a more detailed audit budget for the year, such as the one shown in Exhibit 9.1. The primary information contained in this budget are the budgeted hours scheduled for each job and the estimated range of dates during which work will be completed.

Once armed with the internal audit budget, a manager can exercise a much greater degree of control over the internal audit department. The budget information allows a manager to use the following controls:

- Compare budget to actual hours worked.
- Compare budget to actual project start dates.
- Compare budget to actual project completion dates.
- Compare budget to actual staffing requirements.

Division	Project	Hours	Start Date	End Date	Personnel
Denver	Fixed assets	240	01/01/XX	02/15/XX	Smith/Jones
Denver	Billings	280	01/01/XX	02/21/XX	Barnaby/Granger
Boston	Fixed assets	240	02/16/XX	03/31/XX	Smith/Jones
Chicago	Fixed assets	240	04/01/XX	05/15/XX	Smith/Jones
Chicago	Billings	280	02/22/XX	03/07/XX	Barnaby/Granger
Atlanta	Fixed assets	240	05/16/XX	06/30/XX	Smith/Jones
Atlanta	Billings	280	03/08/XX	04/21/XX	Barnaby/Granger

EXHIBIT 9.1   Sample Internal Audit Budget

In addition to these quantitative control points, there are a variety of other controls that a manager can use. These extra controls tend to supplement the quantitative controls and can be "mixed and matched" to derive a set of controls that are best suited for specific situations. The extra controls are:

- Compare the written objectives of the department to its actual activities.
- Ensure that the internal audit staff coordinates its work to support that of the external auditors.
- Ensure that there is an up-to-date policies and procedures manual that clearly shows how audit work is to be conducted.
- Review audit reports for activities conducted, findings noted, and recommendations given.
- Review comments from departments that were the subject of audits.
- Review the mix of scheduled reviews to see if there is a lack of attention to specific areas, such as reviews of accounting, computer, or operational controls.
- Review work papers to ensure that audits were completed in as thorough a manner as possible.
- Verify that audit recommendations are being acted on.
- Verify that auditors have a sufficient educational background to conduct specific types of audits.
- Verify that the audit committee is satisfied with departmental performance and follow up on any shortcomings.
- Verify that the department is reviewing the controls being built into new computer systems.

- Verify that the department is sufficiently large to accomplish all planned goals.
- Verify that there are scheduled reviews of the company's ethical standards.
- Verify that there have been no restrictions of departmental activities due to intransigence by auditees and bring up exceptions with the audit committee for action.

It is important to have prior knowledge of the activities of and conditions in the internal audit department before selecting from the previous list of management controls, because this information has a direct bearing on which controls are selected. How do you gather this information? There are a variety of information sources that can be consulted, including:

- **The depth and accuracy of audit planning.** An internal audit is a project, and as such must be adequately planned and then managed against that plan to ensure that audits are completed on time.
- **The image of the department.** The department manager and any staff members who are in direct contact with other departments must present a positive and professional image, especially when conducting reviews, discussing recommendations, or presenting findings.
- **The opinion of the outside auditors.** The external auditors are accustomed to working with the internal audit staff from time to time and can usually provide an opinion regarding the quality of the department's work.
- **The quality of personnel practices.** The members of the internal audit staff should have a high level of training, possess adequate knowledge of the areas being audited, have clear career paths that are well documented, and be conversant in the use of any new technologies that assist them in conducting their jobs.
- **The reaction of departments that have been reviewed.** Any auditees should have a positive view of the internal audit department (unless it discovered massive problems!), since auditors should conduct their reviews in a professional manner and keep auditees well informed of their progress and recommendations.
- **The reaction of senior management and the board of directors.** These managers should feel that the internal audit group has provided meaningful insights on company operations, as well as made solid improvement recommendations.
- **The types of recommendations in previous audit reports.** If there are a large proportion of less important recommendations, this is a sign that the internal audit staff is either not well acquainted with the systems it is

reviewing, or that the quality of work conducted is so low that no significant recommendations are likely to be found.

Only by reviewing this information can a manager determine the particular strengths and weaknesses of an internal audit department, which can then be used to select the specific control methods necessary to manage the department. In general, a successful internal audit manager should utilize all of the quantitative measures noted in this section and supplement them with a selection of qualitative controls (also noted in this section) that are tailored to the specific circumstances of the department. Only by doing so can a manager create a management system that is both efficient and effective, which will result in a high-performance internal audit department without an excessively burdensome management system.

Fund Additional Audits

If the internal auditors' schedule is completely booked for many months in advance and there is no way for the controller to schedule a key audit, consider shifting budgeted funds from the accounting budget to that of the internal audit department. Offering to pay for an audit can give an audit request a much higher level of priority. ■

CHAPTER TEN

Recruiting, Training, and Supervision

Importance of This Chapter

The new controller must rely to a great extent on the knowledge base of other accounting staff who have been with the company for some time. In order to maintain a reasonably functional department, she must ensure that key staff stay in the department and new staff of sufficient quality are hired. Consequently, this chapter is extremely important as a source of tips for recruiting, promoting, and retaining accounting staff.

If the accounting staff is carefully selected, properly trained, and motivated, the controller will enjoy a huge productivity advantage over a controller who does not pay attention to these factors. The inevitable results of not doing so are slipshod work, high employee turnover, and massive inefficiency due to the time needed to constantly recruit and train new employees. Consequently, the recruiting, training, and supervision functions are crucial to the success of a controller.

It is unfortunate, but business schools rarely give any formal training in this most important area, so controllers must pick up the requisite knowledge through either hands-on experience, a mentor, or additional training. This chapter is also a valuable source of information on the topic, but should be used as an overview. More detailed information can be obtained from books that deal entirely with business management.

 ## RECRUITING SOURCES

This section describes a number of sources a controller should consider when searching for candidates for accounting positions. There are three key factors involved in selecting a recruiting source, and these factors are discussed for each of the possible recruiting sources:

1. **Recruiting cost**. The cost of recruiting an accounting person can range from $100 for an advertisement on a web site to one third of the hired person's salary, which is a typical charge if the person is hired through a search firm. The recruiting cost tends to have a low level of importance if the recruiting task must be completed at once and a higher one if there is a long time line involved. Also, the lower-cost approaches tend to involve extra time by the controller to screen recruits, whereas more expensive approaches, such as using a search firm, tend to require less screening time, because this task is completed by the intermediary. In short, a cheap recruiting method takes longer and requires more effort than an expensive approach.

2. **Recruiting quality.** The quality of the person hired tends to go up if there is a long time interval for the recruiting process. This is because a controller can take the time to obtain a large pool of candidates, interview them at his or her leisure, and spend the extra time needed to review their references. The reverse is generally true if there is a time crunch involved. However, these assumptions are generalizations, for it is also possible to run into a perfect candidate on the first day of a search.

3. **Recruiting time.** As noted in the first two factors, the time allowed to conduct a recruiting campaign will usually result in higher costs if there is little time available, because a controller must resort to expensive sources. Also, there is a chance that the quality of candidate recruited will be lower if the recruiting period is short, because there is only enough time to meet with and evaluate a limited pool of candidates.

Once a controller has determined which of these three factors (or a combination thereof) are paramount in the search for a specific candidate, it then becomes an easier matter to select the correct recruiting source. For example, if a controller needs a new payroll clerk immediately, even if there is a high cost involved, it is best to go straight to a search firm, which will charge an inordinately high price but will present a set of qualified candidates in as little as a day. However, if there is no rush to fill a position, the search firm may be the last source consulted. The recruiting sources are:

- **Auditing and consulting firms.** It is common for a controller to hire from the ranks of the auditing and consulting firms that work for the company. This approach is very inexpensive, because the controller probably already knows the best performers within these firms and just calls them to see if they are interested in a position. This can also result in a fast hire, so there is a very short time line involved. The quality of the person hired also tends to be high, because the audit or consulting firms have already done the prescreening when *they* hired these people. In short, this is an excellent way to bring in topnotch personnel quickly and at low cost.

- **Campus recruiting.** A good recruiting source for lower-level positions is the college campus. However, it is difficult to determine the quality of the people hired, because they have never worked before. Also, this tends to require a very long lead time, since candidates must be recruited months in advance; thus, this approach is useful only for filling positions that are constantly needed and for which accurate hiring projections can be made. It is also expensive to send personnel to colleges for recruiting and costly to bring in candidates for additional interviews.

- **Employees.** One of the best sources of recruits is current employees. This approach works best when a company offers recruiting bonuses to employees. This incentive turns the entire employee group into an enthusiastic horde of recruiters. They have the additional advantage of recruiting their own friends, which typically results in a great deal of prescreening by the employees, resulting in a high quality of applicant. This also tends to be a fast way to gain recruits. The only problem is that the recruiting bonuses paid to employees can be rather large, usually exceeding $1,000 and sometimes going higher than $5,000 for each person hired.

- **Former employees.** A controller should go to great lengths to maintain contact with quality employees who have left the company. Sometimes, the reasons why they left (higher pay, better positions, etc.) are not good enough, and they may be willing to return to the company. This approach is not only quick and inexpensive, but best of all, it results in highly qualified candidates who require minimal interviewing before being hired back. This is one of the best recruiting methods, though it typically accounts for only a very small proportion of the people hired into the accounting department.

- **Internet postings and advertisements.** A common recruiting method is to use a job posting site on the Internet. This can involve either posting a job or reviewing posted resumes. Either alternative is inexpensive but requires screening an inordinate number of potential recruits to find a few promising candidates. It is a quick recruiting method, but the average quality of applicant tends to be low.
- **Professional organizations.** This approach involves meeting qualified candidates through the meetings of professional organizations. It requires a great deal of "face time" by a controller or other members of the accounting staff, who must attend many organizational functions to meet with potential recruits. Though there is a minimal direct cost, the amount of labor by the accounting staff can be excessive. Also, it takes many months of attending meetings to build up a lengthy list of potential recruits. However, this can result in high-quality candidates who have been prescreened through the organizational meetings. Due to the time involved, this is a little-used recruiting method.
- **Search firms.** This is the most expensive recruiting approach, for search firms typically charge between one quarter and one third of a hired person's first-year salary as their fee. However, there are good reasons for using this method. One is that the search firms conduct their own screening of candidates, which results in a higher quality of applicant. Also, most search firms maintain a lengthy backlog of resumes, and so can bring in many candidates on short notice. Thus, the quality of recruits and the speed with which they can be brought to the controller may offset the high cost of this alternative.
- **Unsolicited applications.** The lowest-cost recruiting method is to receive an unsolicited application, because there is no advertising cost at all. Also, if a company stores these applications, there is no wait time needed to collect resumes, since they are all kept on file. However, despite these favorable points, unsolicited applications tend to result in the lowest possible quality of candidate. This is because there is no screening mechanism built into the process, which results in lots of interviews by the controller to separate the chaff from the wheat.

There are a variety of ways to recruit qualified accounting candidates, based on the key factors of time, cost, and quality of recruit. A controller can pick a selection of recruiting methods from this list to create a mix of methods that enhance the chance of bringing in the right recruits within the required time frame and at the right cost.

FACTORS TO CONSIDER WHEN RECRUITING

There are a number of applicant attributes to consider when recruiting. An applicant should possess as many of them as possible to a high degree, for any lack may lead to an excessive degree of turnover, poor job performance, or complaints by other people who work with the recruit. The key attributes fall into the categories of technical ability, communication skill, and stability. In more detail, they are:

- **Integrity.** The accounting department has some control or influence over the disposition of assets, the reporting of financial information, and the use of controls. If a person lacks integrity, a controller may find that assets go astray, financial information is incorrectly reported, or controls are not enforced. The resulting havoc occurs because accounting personnel were not concerned about doing the right thing. Instead, accounting employees must care about their reputation for honesty and objectivity, which causes them to point out unethical considerations or actions to higher management even if such things are not illegal but perhaps only misleading or unfair. Due to the extreme importance of this factor, any hint of minimal integrity on the part of a candidate should immediately disqualify that person from receiving a job offer.
- **Process knowledge.** The accounting function is similar to manufacturing in that it involves highly predictable process flows that must be carefully organized in order to reach peak levels of efficiency. Clearly, it is of great use if new employees already have these skills, so it is useful to include process flow questions in an interview. To determine whether an applicant has these skills, interview questions should cover an applicant's knowledge of and experience in implementing and using accounting best practices. Applicants with this kind of background are most likely to create an efficient and effective accounting department.

The Importance of Integrity

It is not a long stretch of the integrity concept to view the accounting department as the one department where the level of ethics needs to match that of a minister or priest. The reason is that a lack of ethics can lead to wildly inaccurate reported financial information, which in turn tends to color the operations of the entire company. Consequently, any hint of ethical impropriety is an excellent reason *not* to hire someone.

- **Certification review.** If an applicant holds one of the major accounting certifications (e.g., certified public accountant, certified management accountant, or certified internal auditor), the company should contact these certifying organizations. There are two reasons for doing so. First, the company should verify that the applicant actually has earned the certification and that it has not lapsed. Second, the company should ask if there have been any warnings (of which there are various levels, such as license suspensions or revocations) issued by the certifying organization to the applicant for misconduct in the past. Any such occurrences should be grounds for considerable additional investigation prior to issuing a job offer. Usually, given the level of trust required in an accounting position, it is not a good risk to hire someone to whom a warning has been issued.
- **Communication skills.** An invaluable attribute is excellent communication skills. In order to succeed, a candidate should be able to actively participate in meetings with other employees, clearly summarize and present information, and create understandable written reports. It ultimately means having others understand what you want to tell them. This can be difficult when financial people communicate with nonfinancial people, because the complexity and jargon of the profession must be replaced with simple business language.
- **Drive.** Though a candidate may have an overwhelming impressive set of credentials, strong interpersonal skills, great integrity, and fine background experience, none of these factors will be of much use if the person lacks the drive to complete work in a timely manner and take the initiative in undertaking new projects. This is the key underlying factor impacting a person's ability to be promoted into new and more difficult positions. It is also one of the most difficult issues to fully understand when interviewing a candidate. To do so, a considerable portion of the interviewing time should cover a candidate's underlying goals and objectives—a strong goal orientation is a sure sign of a strong drive to succeed.
- **Technical capability.** An accounting recruit must have the basic accounting knowledge that can be imparted only through a regular course of training, which can include a bachelor's or MBA degree. Possessing such a degree from an accredited university should form the basis of a minimal technical qualification. If the person does not have such a degree, then further evaluation is necessary to ensure that the person can adequately complete any assigned work. Bringing an untrained person into a professional job, no matter how good the other qualifications, will probably result in that person's becoming dissatisfied and discouraged and eventually leaving the company or requiring unusual amounts of management attention.

- **Teamwork skills.** An applicant must be able to function with the rest of the group. It is easier to identify characteristics that will inhibit integration rather than those that will guarantee it. If a candidate, who should be on his or her best behavior, comes across as abrasive, it is reasonable to expect that this person will have a negative influence on the work group. This behavior will likely turn off fellow workers and require an excessive proportion of the controller's management attention. Both results will detract from the quality of performance of the work group as a whole. For evidence of teamwork skills, the interviewer can question the candidate about leadership roles. This can be leadership in school activities if the person is coming from college, or civic or work-related activities if the person has some experience outside of college.
- **Turnover likelihood.** Because it is a time-consuming and expensive process to hire a professional, it follows that the people who are hired should have a high probability of staying with the company. There are many considerations in trying to assess a candidate's staying potential. From the candidate's perspective, some of the considerations are the likelihood of being satisfied with his or her professional responsibilities, prospects for advancement, and degree of comfort with the culture of the organization. From the company's perspective, some of the considerations are the person's ability to handle changing environments, acceptance of retraining, and ability to relocate as necessary. Evaluating these considerations may be the most difficult assessment of all for a recruiter to make.

FACTORS TO CONSIDER WHEN PROMOTING

A controller can do a wonderful job of recruiting the best possible staff and still experience high staff turnover due to a poor promotion policy. This section discusses two kinds of promotion, as well as the reasons for engaging in one type versus the other.

The most common kind of promotion is one that shifts a staff person sideways through the hierarchy of the accounting department. This type of promotion is intended to expand a person's skill base. For example, a person who is fully experienced in the billing area can be shifted to accounts payable in order to gain experience in how that functional area operates. The same approach can be used to add to the experience of the staff in other areas, such as collections, fixed assets, taxes, or producing the financial statements. This type of promotion can be given to the entire accounting staff, which rotates among the various functional areas. Generally, it reduces turnover, because the controller is giving all employees a chance to acquire new skills. However, the reverse can also happen if a staff person does not want to shift to a new skill area and may even quit if the change is implemented. A controller must watch out for this problem by carefully interviewing the staff about prospective switches to new areas. If it is clear that a person has "maxed out" and no longer desires to learn new tasks, then it is best to leave that employee alone in order to avoid any turnover.

A less common type of promotion is of the vertical variety, in which someone is shifted upward in the corporate hierarchy. This will always be less common, for there are far fewer positions available at the management level than at the clerical level. Promotion to a management position is based on the presence of an entirely different set of skills than are used as the basis for a sideways promotion. A controller must be extremely careful in evaluating employees for promotion to a management spot, for any missing skills may not only result in the departure of the person being promoted (who was probably an excellent performer at the lower, clerical level), but also of the staff reporting to that person, and will likely result in a great increase in the time required by the controller to handle the situation.

What are the key skills needed by someone being promoted to management? Certainly, it is necessary to have a reasonable knowledge of accounting theory and practice, but the primary emphasis is no longer in these areas. Instead, the main focus is on people skills: communication, team building, reviews, and interviews, as well as planning and control. The mind-set of anyone in this position is to effectively coordinate the activities of the underlying personnel, *not* to continue doing the work that took place prior to promotion. This is an extremely difficult transition for many people in the accounting profession, for it is filled with a large proportion of people who are introverted and process oriented, which results in a good clerk but a poor manager. The best approach for a controller who has just promoted someone to management is to realize the most likely traps into which the former clerk can fall and to provide constant monitoring and advice. This should be intensive during the first few days of the promotion, thereby giving the promotee the best possible chance of succeeding in the new position.

▨ IMPORTANCE OF REDUCED TURNOVER

The bane of many accounting departments is the turnover of the accounting staff. It results in staff turmoil, inefficient transaction processing, and lots of wasted time on the part of the controller. This section describes the impact of turnover, and how to prevent it from happening.

Some company departments assume that high employee turnover is a common fact of life, and that they must continually deal with bringing in a high percentage of new employees every year. This is true for many low-skill areas, such as assembly, where the entire workforce can turn over in one year. Alternatively, a highly skilled profession with lots of stress, the consulting industry, also has very high turnover, typically in the range of 25 percent to 33 percent per year. However, the accounting area should not be an excessively high-stress area, so it should not have the turnover rates common in consulting. It also requires a significant level of skill, so its turnover rates should not match those of an assembly operation. Instead, a controller should target a turnover rate well below 20 percent, and preferably only half that amount. This means that the average accountant should stay in the controller's department a minimum of five years, and preferably ten.

By keeping the staff turnover rate as low as possible, a controller can avoid many problems that result in gross inefficiencies, poor customer service, high error rates, and increased costs. These problems are:

- **Add poorer methods.** A new recruit may have his or her own ways of dealing with transactions, which may not be as efficient as the ones developed during the tenure of the person being replaced. When this happens, the efficiency level of the position drops for some time, until the new person has reviewed and evaluated how work is completed and improved operations based on that experience.

- **Increased costs.** Not only must a controller pay for recruiting costs to replace someone (e.g., web site advertisements, search firm fees, and travel expenses), but there are the added and less clearly defined costs of training new employees and correcting the inevitable mistakes that they will make as they learn their jobs. In addition, the controller must pay for replacement staff to fill in during the period when the old employee has already left the company and the new one has not yet started.

- **Increased inefficiency.** The typical new hire, unless vastly experienced, will not reach the efficiency levels of the person being replaced for at least six months. This inefficiency will appear in several ways: the extra time required to complete tasks, the extra temporary help needed to support the person, and the time of other staff people needed for training. For some recruits, performance never reaches the level attained by the previous employee, in which case the controller may be forced to move the new hire to another position, or else let the person go and then spend even more time looking for *another* replacement.

- **Increased time by the controller.** The recruiting process is a very time-consuming one, and the time a controller puts into it takes away from other tasks, such as preparing and evaluating financial statements, undertaking new cost-reduction projects, or analyzing various accounting-related proposals from around the company.
- **Loss of specialized knowledge.** Every company has a unique set of processes. When a company loses an employee, it also loses that person's knowledge of the processes. When a new person arrives to replace the outgoing person, some of that specialized knowledge may be lost, or at least it may take many months before it is assimilated from the other members of the accounting department. If turnover is extremely high, there may be so few "old timers" left in the department that this specialized knowledge is permanently lost.
- **Risk of an inappropriate hire.** Bringing in a new person carries with it the risk of hiring someone who is hiding a past of improper behavior, who may attempt to take company assets once in a position to exercise control over assets (a common enough position in the accounting department). Another risk is that a controller may find that the person hired is so inappropriate for the position that termination is the only answer, and then find that the new employee has sued the company for wrongful termination. No matter how correct the controller's actions may be in getting rid of the employee, the company must still expend a large amount of money to defend itself against litigation.

Obviously, there are many reasons to avoid turnover. However, in today's environment of highly mobile employees who feel little association with a single company, how is it possible to drive turnover down to such low levels that a controller no longer has to deal with its effects?

The answer is to meet the needs of employees. They may not feel any closer association with the company (a difficult proposition), but they will react well to an enlightened style of management that is revealed by the factors noted in the following list, such as flex hours, slightly higher rates of pay, and recognition programs. A controller will find that these factors will vastly reduce turnover by giving employees no possible reason to leave the company. The ways to reduce turnover are:

- **Clarify jobs and related procedures.** There is nothing more irritating for a new employee than to be unceremoniously dumped into a new job without any clue regarding what the job entails or how to perform tasks. This lack of information causes a great deal of stress for a new employee, who must essentially build a job description from scratch, probably making mistakes along the way. It is also difficult to get a good performance review if there is no baseline job description against which to be measured. A controller can avoid this degree of uncertainty by supplying each new employee with an accurate job description that is supplemented by detailed procedures that clearly describe how each required job element can be completed. An example of such a job description is shown in Exhibit 10.1.

▪ **Improve communications**. Employees want to know what is going on. For example, a controller can meet with the accounting staff every month, after financial statements are published, and go over the company's results with them. This gives the staff a good feel for how the company is doing, what they can do to improve the situation, and (above all) it tells the staff that the controller is not trying to hide anything from them. This sets the tone for an open and constructive dialogue between the controller and the staff; if the controller is willing to impart information to them, they will be more comfortable with bringing information to the controller.

Money Can Buy Happiness

One of the first things a new controller should do is review the condition of all computer and office equipment in the department, as well as the version number of the software being used. Then gain approval of a replacement budget and become involved in upgrading the most archaic items. The staff will be especially appreciative if the controller personally shows up with a new flat-panel monitor, computer, and so on. ▪

▪ **Increase pay.** Many companies have a policy of paying employees the median pay rate for their job classifications. Though this ensures that a company is not paying too much for its staff, this policy does not take into account the total cost of employment. If a company loses employees to competitors who are willing to pay somewhat more than the median pay rate, it must then incur substantial additional costs to recruit and train a replacement. When this recruitment cost is added to an employee's median pay rate, it becomes apparent that a company should actually pay somewhat *more* than the median rate in order to avoid the costs of turnover.

▪ **Look for a history of job longevity.** A controller can avoid turnover up front by hiring only recruits with a history of staying with their previous companies for long periods. This avoids potential employees who are more likely to walk out for minor reasons over which a controller may have little control.

EXHIBIT 10.1   Sample Job Description

Position: Assistant Controller

Report To: Controller

Review Dates:

1. 01/20   Quarterly Review
2. 04/20   Quarterly Review
3. 07/20   Quarterly Review
4. **10/20 Annual Review**

Pay Change Criteria:

1. If issue financial statements within 5 days of month-end.
   - OK performance: ___% if reach 5 day close by end of 20XX.
   - Good performance: ___% if reach 5 day close by September 20XX.
   - Great performance: ___% if reach 5 day close by July 20XX.
2. If achieve accounts receivable turns of 9.0.
   - OK performance: ___% if reach 9 turns by end of 20XX.
   - Good performance: ___% if reach 9 turns by the end of September 20XX.
   - Great performance: ___% if reach 9 turns by the end of July 20XX.

Overview of Tasks:

Timing	Description
Daily	Collect accounts receivable
Daily	Maintain general ledger accounts
Daily	Receive and apply cash receipts
Daily	Run batch jobs and backups
Daily	Clear checks for accounts payable and accounts receivable
Daily	Reconcile invoices with customers
Daily	Take deposits to bank
Monthly	Calculate monthly quality bonus
Monthly	Complete bank reconciliations
Monthly	Conduct internal audit tasks
Monthly	Create variance report
Monthly	Prepare borrowing base reports
Monthly	Prepare financial statements
Monthly	Prepare tax returns
Monthly	Prepare workers' compensation insurance reports
Monthly	Track fixed assets
Monthly	Track mold shop expenses
Yearly	Create documents for annual audit
Yearly	Update archives

Development Areas:

1. Financial statement preparation
2. Activity-based costing
3. Report writer training

- **Meet special employee needs.** Employees may have special needs, such as flex time, so that they can handle various aspects of their personal lives that might otherwise interfere with company business. A controller should consider these needs and modify employee work routines (within reason) so that employees can continue to work for the company. It is important not to allow too many exemptions to specific employees, because this may engender ill will among other employees who do not appreciate the special favors being extended to a minority of them.

- **Recognize employee efforts.** Some employees make exceptional efforts on behalf of the companies where they work, yet receive no recognition for these efforts. After going to extra lengths to help the company, an employee should receive some special recognition, which makes that person want to stay with the company—not because they are making more money or have a fancy title, but because they feel appreciated. This type of recognition can take a variety of forms, such as tickets to sports events, plaques, public recognition, or an employee-of-the-month parking spot.

- **Review employees frequently.** Employees want to know where they stand in terms of performance, potential advancement, and the impression given to coworkers. It is difficult for an employee to make meaningful changes to work habits in a timely manner if this information is communicated only once a year, during the annual review. Instead, a controller should schedule informal quarterly reviews to supplement the annual review, plus more frequent feedback if there are issues that require immediate corrective action. By giving frequent reviews, a controller not only ensures improved behavior by employees, but also a better sense by staff of how they are doing, which reduces their level of uncertainty.

Keep a Stash of Gift Certificates

The author has had considerable success for years by rewarding excellent performance with gift certificates. Whenever an employee does something especially well, he or she receives one on the spot. I usually have a variety of gift certificates on hand, so I can most closely match the certificate to the recipient. Representative stores for which I keep certificates on hand include a restaurant, home furnishings, sports equipment, and building supplies. ■

Thus there are a number of techniques for avoiding turnover, which tend to emphasize clear job descriptions for employees, frequent communications, and paying attention to special employee needs. By taking these steps, a controller can greatly reduce the costs of turnover and increase the productivity of the accounting department.

IMPORTANCE OF DEVELOPING CAREER PLANS FOR EMPLOYEES

Even though accountants are known to be a thoroughgoing and detail-oriented group, most do not engage in a sufficient degree of career planning. This results in a considerable amount of movement between jobs, as they go in search of perceived incremental improvements to their positions, presumably resulting in better titles, greater responsibilities, and more pay. This behavior also results in a great deal of turnover, which, as noted throughout this chapter, is anathema to any controller. This section describes how to lock in employees for long periods of time by assisting them in developing career plans.

For the typical accountant, there is no specific career plan, and for only the rare few is it even committed to paper. A more common career plan is to acquire some sort of certification or college degree early in the career and then use these credentials to gradually work up through the ranks at a corporation until reaching the pinnacle of success, the chief financial officer (CFO) position. Because only a small proportion of accountants can reach this position (after all, there are not many CFO positions available), every accountant needs a great deal of preplanning to assist in achieving this goal, or to aim for goals culminating in different positions. The controller can assist with this difficulty by meeting each staff person, comparing the aspirations to the existing set of experience and skills, and determining where there must be improvements for that person to reach whatever the goal may be. This plan should clearly define required skills, a time line for achieving them, and specific action steps to be taken by the staff person as well as the controller to ensure that those steps are reached. For example, an accounts payable staff person may have no experience with payroll. To acquire it, the controller can commit to assigning the staff person as a backup to the regular payroll person for the next year. In exchange, the payroll person will become the backup for the accounts payable person for the same period. This ensures that both employees acquire more knowledge and experience.

Why would a controller go to some lengths to ensure that the entire accounting staff will eventually be in a position to replace the controller? There are several reasons. First, putting every staff person on a solid career path will lock them into working for the company for a long time. For example, encouraging employees to take reimbursed college courses will keep them with the company until a degree is acquired, which can easily take six years. Also, rotating a staff person through all possible accounting areas takes a number of years, especially if the company is a large one. In both cases, a controller can effectively reduce (if not eliminate) turnover by keeping the entire staff busy with various kinds of training programs. The second reason is that very few accounting employees really have the wherewithal to become a CFO; instead, they will be promoted to the point where the job responsibilities match their abilities, and they will stop. By using career planning and reviewing progress, it will become obvious to both the staff person and the controller when this point is reached, and the controller can then shift the motivational focus to retaining that person in the same position for as long as possible. Third, a mature controller will realize that an accountant who has the ability to eventually become a controller or CFO should be allowed to do so. Rather than getting mad at an employee who has been thoroughly trained by the controller, it is best to throw a farewell party for the person and maintain relations when the person moves on to other organizations. This not only maintains goodwill between the controller and the former staff person, but also makes it easy for the person to return someday, or to refer other people to the controller for various positions. Finally, a controller can use career planning to determine the timing of changes in the department. For example, if it is obvious that a qualified subordinate should go outside the company to take a controller position elsewhere, the controller can use the career plan to make a rough estimate of when this might occur (or even discuss the issue with the subordinate), and then make plans to promote other people in an orderly fashion to fill in the post that is about to be vacated. In short, career planning reduces turnover while promoting employees to the maximum level and allowing the controller to plan for employee advancement in an orderly manner.

Some controllers include career planning in an employee's annual review. This is a mistake, because the annual review is supposed to cover issues that the employee is *required* to do, whereas a career planning session discusses items that are *optional*—an employee may take additional steps to advance his or her career, but those steps can be taken at the discretion of the employee. For example, a goal that might be discussed during an annual review is the ability of an employee to issue financial statements within a specified time period and to determine a course of remedial action if that goal has not been met. A career planning session discusses any steps an employee has taken along his or her career path, and what assistance the controller can give in furthering that person's aspirations. In short, a controller adopts the role of a supervisor when using an annual review to cover immediate performance issues, but must switch roles to be a mentor and coach when covering career planning issues.

A key part of career planning is sharing the salary ranges of targeted positions with the accounting staff. There is considerable motivation in knowing that there is a large increase in pay associated with gaining a higher-level accounting position. Telling employees about market rates for desired positions can also keep them from making a mistake in pursuing a position that does not yield a significant pay increase in proportion to the amount of work required to attain the position. You may think that there is some risk in appearing to promise specific pay rates to employees well in advance of their being placed in those positions, so it is important to tell employees up front that prospective pay rates fall within fairly wide pay ranges, and that they can expect to begin at the lowest levels of the pay rates and gradually gain additional compensation as they gain experience and skill.

A controller should encourage the accounting staff to earn certifications. There are many accounting certifications, all of which require a considerable amount of training before you can pass the required examinations. By taking the training, an employee can improve his or her skill set, which directly benefits a company by bringing more expertise to its accounting operations. To encourage the acquisition of certifications, a controller should actively pursue the purchase and distribution of study materials, as well as pay employees for the time off needed to take the tests. To really encourage acquiring certifications, a controller can even offer one-time bonuses or pay raises to those who have successfully completed their examinations. The most common certifications for an accounting person to earn are:

- Certified Public Accountant (CPA)
- Certified Management Accountant (CMA)
- Certified Internal Auditor (CIA)
- Certified Production and Inventory Manager (CPIM)
- Certified Purchasing Manager (CPM)

Some of the certifications listed do not directly cover accounting topics. Instead, they address such areas as production, logistics, and purchasing. It is useful for an accounting person to acquire these extra certifications, because there is great value in having a broad knowledge of how a wide array of processes function throughout a company.

IMPORTANCE OF COMMUNICATIONS WITH EMPLOYEES

The title of this chapter includes the words "training" and "supervision." Communicating with employees comprises a key element of both activities. A controller should include a variety of modes of communication with the accounting staff, which can vary in frequency based on the type of communication. This section notes the different types of communication, as well as the offsetting risks of losing some confidential information to competitors.

There are several distinct types of communications that a controller should use. One consists of *operational information*. This type of information describes company performance, and that of the accounting area in particular. It can include such performance information as the number of days to issue financial statements, accounts receivable turnover, and the dollar amount of accounts payable discounts that were not taken. It is crucial to impart this information regularly, because the accounting staff needs it to determine its own performance, as well as to form a basis for requesting additional improvements in the future. The information is best presented in a historical context, so that there are a string of performance figures that clearly show a trend line of performance; this is best presented in a chart or on a whiteboard, so that the information is presented visually, not verbally.

Another type of communication consists of *financial information*. Since one of the primary functions of the accounting staff is to generate information that is summarized in the financial statements, it makes sense to show them the result of all that work—the financial statements. Many company managers shy away from the prospect of revealing company performance to employees, especially if performance is poor, but one of the best ways to motivate employees is to give them this information; then they are more likely to pitch in and suggest ways to improve performance. The only type of financial information that you can legitimately withhold from employees is salary data, because this is considered confidential by most managers, not to mention most employees. Financial information can also include the budget, which can be shared with the staff without divulging payroll information.

Another type of communication is of *general information*. This can be directives issued by senior management (such as news about a company merger), notes about the work schedule (such as when the company will observe holidays), or similar information. Though the most minor forms of general information can be communicated by such media as voice mail, e-mail, or the venerable memo, more important information, for which employees may have questions, is best communicated in person. The timing of the information may also have a bearing on the form of communication used. For example, a notice regarding when an official holiday will be taken is easily communicated by memo if done a month in advance, but may require an in-person discussion if it is being communicated one day in advance, because this may interrupt work schedules and require some negotiation with the staff regarding taking alternate holiday time. Thus, the form of communication used to impart general information depends on the lead time used, as well as the likelihood of answering questions from the staff.

Learn Through Lunch

The author has made a point of taking a mix of different staff out to lunch at least once a week for years. This tends to be the best place to learn about what is really going on all over the company. Employees are more likely to unwind and talk about a wide range of topics in this setting, where they would be less inclined to do so in the more formal office environment. This is also a good chance to be with junior staff people who would otherwise have little face time with "the boss." ■

An additional type of communication is of *personal performance information.* This is a form of communication that many controllers do not perform well. The worst case is when controllers essentially ignore the accounting staff, never giving them any feedback on their performance. This tells the staff nothing about how they are doing, and in the absence of information, they tend to assume the worst. The next worst form of communication is going over performance only during an annual review. Though many controllers consider this to be a sufficient interval for giving feedback, it is actually far too infrequent. There may be a problem with performance early in the review period, which a controller notes for the annual review but does not mention to the employee until the actual review. This means that the staff person is performing improperly for nearly a year before getting any feedback! Many controllers delay in giving feedback because they do not relish the charged emotional atmosphere that frequently results. However, waiting until the review and churning out a long list of faults tends to exacerbate the situation and results in a difficult review. By far the best way to issue personal performance information is by wandering through the accounting area on a daily basis and giving feedback in small doses to everyone. This gets the staff used to continual feedback and results in a vastly more relaxed working environment. In short, the frequency of feedback is very important when relaying personal performance information.

This section has focused on feeding as much information as possible to the accounting staff, on the assumption that a well-informed staff is a satisfied one. However, the response of senior management to this approach is frequently that of the risk to the company—what if a dissatisfied employee takes the information to a competitor or issues it to the press? Of course this can happen, but usually only when relations with the staff are so bad (perhaps due to a lack of information) that employees are actively looking for a way to harm the company. In this case, the controller is well advised to look for employment elsewhere, since the working environment is exceptionally difficult. When staff relations are good, the risk of disseminating information outside the company is much lower. To provide additional coverage to the company, all financial information can be marked as classified, which gives the company some recourse to legal action if it finds that information has left the company. Usually, it is much more beneficial to issue information to the staff than to worry about the much smaller risk that the information will get out to the general public or to competing firms.

The recurring recommendations in this section have been to give lots of information to the accounting staff, and to do so as frequently as possible. This is very important for maintaining good staff morale and usually results in a better performance. Many old-time controllers who were brought up in an environment of "closed books" will have a hard time with this approach, especially if it requires lots of face time with employees. Nonetheless, the controller who invests time in his or her staff will reap considerable rewards in terms of a happy, well-informed, and productive department.

HOW TO MOTIVATE EMPLOYEES

Motivating employees clearly improves employee morale as well as department performance, but motivation should be based on a multilayered motivation scheme that covers the long, medium, and short term. By using this multilayered approach, employees are presented with a richer environment in which to work, which is more satisfying for them, and gives them many good reasons for staying with the company. This section discusses multilayered motivational systems.

A long-term motivational system is based on the career plan. As noted earlier, in the "Developing Career Plans" section, the controller should discuss career options with all accounting employees and devise a progression of steps that will last for a number of years, culminating in greatly increased levels of experience and expertise for them. This is an excellent long-term motivator, but it does not grab the attention of the typical employee on a day-to-day basis, because it is typically comprised of course work that happens only after working hours or involves occasional seminars or job switches. Something more is required that will make motivation a more immediate issue.

A mid-range motivational system is the annual performance goal. Many controllers set up goals for each employee to reach, which are used in determining pay raises or bonuses at the end of the year. Examples of these goals are increasing accounts receivable turnover through greater attention to collections, taking all purchase discounts, and issuing financial statements by a specified date. These can even be tied to a specific pay raise. For example, accounts receivable turnover of 8.0 can be awarded with a 2 percent raise, while a turnover rate of 10.0 will result in a 3 percent raise. This type of motivational system is an excellent way to focus the attention of the staff on key improvement goals, while rewarding them as well. Though this is a good motivator, especially when used in concert with the longer-range career plans, it still does not focus day-to-day attention on the tasks at hand. That requires a short-range motivation system.

A short-range motivation system is one that grabs and holds the attention of the accounting staff every day. This system is much more difficult to arrange than the long-term and mid-range motivational systems, and also requires much more work by the controller to keep it operational and meaningful. The reason for the excessive level of attention is that the motivational targets must be changed from time to time to avoid boredom, while the types of awards must also be changed for the same reason. When constructing short-term goals, it is best to create group goals so that the entire team wins, rather than just one person. The targets are not necessarily intended to cause any long-term change. Instead, they should be fun and make employees feel better about coming to work. For example, a clean desk week may leave no lasting impression or enhance company performance, but it will give the staff something to focus their attention on in the very short term. Also, the rewards for reaching such goals should involve the group, such as a free team lunch or a block of tickets to a sporting event. The reward should always act to bring the group together by treating them as a unit, not split them apart by giving different awards to different people. Thus a short-range motivational system is targeted at employee morale, not at reaching any quantifiable goals.

In summary, employees can be motivated with three types of motivation systems. The first is the long-range career plan, which requires minimal attention by the controller to maintain. The second is annual performance goals; this is the most common motivational system employed by controllers and also requires minimal work to maintain. Finally, there should also be brief, team-based contests or targets in the very short term (e.g., weekly) to grab the attention of the accounting staff and add some spice to the work experience. This short-term system requires the most work by the controller but also greatly contributes to a more pleasant work environment, which is a prime factor in motivating employees.

CHAPTER ELEVEN

Controller's Role in Investor Relations

Importance of This Chapter

If there is no Chief Financial Officer (CFO), the controller is likely to be in charge of investor relations. This group can include directors, senior managers, and a variety of outside interests, all of whom can variously sue the company or be ready sources of more funds, so it calls for a considerable amount of circumspection and skill in dealing with them. This chapter covers a number of key areas in determining the information needs of various constituencies as well as how to disclose information to them.

Very little has been written about the controller's role in investor relations (IR). This is partially because many controllers, by all outward signs, are not actively engaged in this function—at least as far as the public is concerned. In Chapter 2 IR activities of the controller are included in the category of "Additional Controller Functions." To many outsiders with an interest in investments, the controller is variously regarded as the "inside man," the number cruncher, the figure man, or the introverted accountant. To be sure, many of these same representatives do not have a real understanding of what the controller should do or can do.

In contrast to this view of the controller, in discussions with security analysts, they have expressed opinions to the author concerning a preference for talking about financial matters with the controller because "he has the facts" (while many of the non-accounting-trained public relations persons do not). Certainly, if the chief accounting officer wishes to climb the financial ladder or aspire to a broader executive career, experience in the IR arena may be very useful.

In reaching some conclusion concerning those duties the controller might perform in the IR function, a review of the following facets may help in ferreting out those activities for which the controller might be suited, and which he or she might enjoy:

- The objectives or purpose of the IR function
- The nature of the function
- The principal vehicles used to convey financial information
- The nature of the "customer"
- What type of information is desired and limits on its disclosure
- Some brief observations about organization structure in this field

OBJECTIVES OF THE INVESTOR RELATIONS FUNCTION

In a general sense, it may be said that the principal purpose of the IR function, regardless of who performs it, is the enhancement of shareholder value. Is this not a familiar term? The stated purpose by the perpetrators of some hostile takeovers is "to enhance shareholder value;" the defense against such actions, as voiced by some CFOs of the targets, is an effort "to enhance shareholder values by increasing the price of the common stock." As a matter of fact, one of the purposes of sound financial policy is to enable the company to raise funds, on an acceptable basis, to meet its needs, so as to enhance the long-term interests of the shareholder; and a related corollary is to cause the entity to be so well regarded in the financial marketplace that its stock will command an acceptable price/earnings ratio.

Some chief executive officers (CEOs) might still regard the IR function as a simple financial reporting activity, with no intent to affect the stock price. But many CFOs will bluntly state that the objective is to maximize the market price so as to minimize the cost of equity capital. Executives of brokerage houses will acknowledge that a continuing IR program helps prepare the market for an initial public or secondary offering and influences the credit ratings of fixed-income securities. Certainly, the importance of the stock price is not lost on those CEOs engaged in selloffs, acquisitions, or other restructurings. In the view of the author, these enumerated purposes, however described, translate into an objective of enhancing shareholder value.

In today's environment, companies must compete for investment capital—whether in the bond market or the equity market. But to secure recognition, the story of the enterprise must be told. Just as the advantages and uses of a company's service or product must be described and marketed, so also information about the value of an entity's securities and its financial prospects must be disseminated, understood, and accepted.

EVOLVING NATURE OF THE FUNCTION

IR is an evolving activity. About 30 years ago, it often was a part of the public relations department, perhaps viewed as a somewhat specialized communication function. In the 1950s through the 1960s and into the early 1970s, with the rapid growth of employee retirement funds, many blue-chip companies, including General Electric, used skilled communicators to "educate" portfolio managers and brokerage intermediaries about the investment merits of the company's stock. By the mid-1970s, when many individual investors abandoned the stock market, when the market was dominated by large institutions, when many less-than-blue-chip companies felt they were neglected by the brokers and investing institutions, and when the need for more capital intensified, many managements became more aggressive and began directly contacting potential investors, both institutional and individual, who were willing to take more risks and were often receptive to growth situations and better-than-average returns. The individuals representing these companies were variously communication specialists and security analysts. In this time frame, with the growth of dividend reinvestment plans, self-registration, and an increased recognition of the need to plan and sell new security issues, the IR function became more marketing oriented.

These changes also induced changes in the nature of the IR specialist. While communicators (public relations) and security analysts had predominated, gradually more and more individuals well acquainted with finance assumed a greater role. The customers became far more sophisticated about what they needed. So the IR function evolved into a combination of two disciplines—communications and finance.

Accordingly, in this century, the IR function must not only communicate effectively about past performance, but it must more closely align itself with the strategic plans of management and tell its customers more about corporate goals and the entity's strengths and weaknesses.

COMMUNICATION VEHICLES FOR INVESTOR RELATIONS

At this point, a recap of the several vehicles now commonly used to communicate with "IR customers" may be helpful. Each is directed to a somewhat different audience, and each typically conveys a disparate or varied message—but always with an investor-related aspect. They are distinct in words and tone from the typical product or service advertising originating with the advertising or marketing department. The methods used to communicate investor-related messages, in no special order, include:

- Annual report to shareholders
- Quarterly reports to shareholders (and the financial community)
- Annual meeting with shareholders
- Reports to the Securities and Exchange Commission (SEC)
  - Annual Report Form 10-K
  - Quarterly Report Form 10-Q
  - Current Report Form 8-K
- Regular or special meetings with security analysts, institutional investors, brokers, and large individual investors—often arranged in cooperation with one of the several associations or societies for analysts
- Institutional advertising in periodicals (financial or general interest)
- Corporate announcements of special interest to investors or potential investors:
  - New products or services
  - Management changes
  - Acquisitions and/or divestments
  - Reorganization attempts, such as restructuring, unfriendly takeovers
- Webcasts dealing with financial matters
- Individual meetings with government representatives and the stock exchanges concerned with financial matters (Internal Revenue Service, SEC, etc.)

Electronic Investor Communications

A simple and essentially free form of communication with investors is to issue them an electronic version of the company newsletter (usually in PDF format). Many organizations already convert their newsletters into electronic format and e-mail them to a variety of suppliers and customers, so adding investors to the e-mail list is all the work that is needed. ▪

INVESTOR RELATIONS MESSAGE RECIPIENTS

Broadly and technically speaking, the IR function must service an unusually complex and diverse audience. For example, here is a typical listing (with some overlapping) of the vast potential "customers:"

- Investors and potential stock investors (small)
- Large institutional stock investors and potential investors
- Security analysts
- Credit-rating agencies
- Financial advisory services
- Brokerage firms
- Bond-rating agencies
- Bank loan officers
- Bondholders
- Financial press
- Portfolio managers
- Acquisition candidates
- Government agencies dealing with financial matters (federal, state, and local)
- Employees

Having said this, it should be realized that three broad groups with which the IR activity is *primarily* and continuously directed are (1) security analysts, (2) stockbrokers, and (3) large institutional, investors. Practically speaking, and as discussed later, some of these information-seeking persons would deal directly with the CFO—that is, the bank loan officer handling most of the company's current bank borrowings, the bond-rating agency, or credit-rating agency—in some kind of one-on-one desired meeting that is heavily and technically financial in nature.

Many of the members of the three principal groups mentioned—security analysts, stockbrokers, or institutional, or other large investors (or their representatives)—are quite sophisticated financially. Each of the three groups may, and usually does, have different information needs; and each may be motivated, for different reasons, to discuss the financial affairs of the entity.

INFORMATION NEEDS OF THE FINANCIAL ANALYST

The management of a company usually desires that it be perceived in its most favorable light—hopefully without exaggeration, and as objectively determined. While communication with all segments of the IR audience on this matter is important, perhaps the key person is the financial analyst, also called the security analyst. He is in a position to influence a large cross-section of investors. It therefore especially behooves the IR executives to know what information the analyst needs and how he will probably use it. It is imperative that the financial executive involved (CFO or controller) properly interpret the information for this analyst and not merely infer certain conclusions. In most instances, the analyst desires information so that he can reasonably predict earnings (and hence market price, potential of the stock dividend rate, etc.).

A most important source of information for the security analyst is management presentations generally made to large institutional investors, brokers, or investment bankers, as well as the analysts themselves. The information gained from such meetings, plus that distilled from annual and quarterly reports or Form 10-Ks and the like, together with discussions among other analysts and other articles about the company and the industry, enable the analyst to reach certain conclusions about the entity and aid in helping him predict financial performance.

These analyst meetings present an unusual opportunity for the company to portray itself in its best light. They not only permit the company to make *factual* presentations, but also to subjectively influence the analyst about the depth of management and long-term objectives of the company. Moreover, they enable management to directly answer the questions of the group and fully explain troublesome events, such as complicated footnotes to the annual report and so forth.

Each industry and each company has certain factors that are important to its well-being and growth. For example, in the aerospace business, the order backlog is of significance, as well as the status of various contracts or programs. In other companies, product development might be of major interest.

Facts and opinions should be divulged within the limits of prudent disclosure. Such meetings with analysts are not just public relations events. Solid and specific information is needed.

While each entity has its own requirements, here is an outline of five general suggestions about presentation content to analysts for a well-established, reputable company.

1. To give a sense of an experienced, in-depth, and well-qualified management:

    (a) The CEO should be present and give the principal talk—about prospects, style of management, management development programs, market position, and so on.
    (b) The key executives should be introduced and usually should make some short comments about their areas of responsibility.
    (c) Perhaps the organizational structure and incentive system and the like should be discussed.

2. To provide an insight into the long-term prospects of the entity, the following subjects might be covered by a knowledgeable executive (CEO, executive vice-president, senior vice president of finance, or controller):

    (a) The system or method of strategic planning
    (b) The short-term or annual plan process and the related control system
    (c) Some examples of long-range objectives that have been achieved
    (d) The long-range outlook for the industry or selected products or markets
    (e) The status of market penetration or dominance for some key products
    (f) Important research and development programs underway (whether specific quantified projections or plans should be divulged may depend on the individual circumstances.)

3. To provide a broad financial picture, including the financial strength of the company, perhaps a slide presentation (graphs and charts) could be given that would identify:

    (a) Status of orders on hand
    (b) Trend of sales by product line
    (c) Margins by product line or organizational units, and trends thereof
    (d) Financial position through comments about a condensed balance sheet, with emphasis on key ratios or relationships
    (e) The trend of long-term indebtedness, times debt service is covered, debt capacity, and so on

    (f) The trend of cash flow by important segments: from operations, investing activities, and financing activities, and perhaps cash flow per share from operations

    (g) Trends on equity and earnings:
- Growth in equity
- Equity relationships (ROE)
- Earnings per share
- Return on assets

    (h) By simple explanation and illustration, any aspect of the financial statements that often causes confusion (inventory, valuation method, tax accruals, reserves, etc.)

    (i) Perhaps some comparative ratios with industry or selected competitors

    (j) Company posture regarding acquisitions or diversification

4. The chief marketing executive probably should make a presentation that would describe and illustrate major new products or major revenue procedures and the sales prospects for the next year or two

5. Other executives, as appropriate, might discuss any timely topics, such as:

    (a) Employee relations

    (b) Cost reduction programs

    (c) Process improvements

    (d) Information resource management

    (e) Quality control changes

    (f) Any major troublesome contracts or publicity items and the like

The objective should include a demonstration of financial conservatism, stability, and the ability to raise capital when needed. Interpretation of what the figures mean should be given; it should not be left to the unaided judgment of the analyst.

In fact, the executives deeply involved in the process should know their audiences and determine what they need to know, so that the analysts (and others) may make a proper evaluation of the entity.

These are some key points that should be covered. Experience at meetings with analysts, including their questions, will provide guidance as to other subjects of interest.

Above all, the presentations by management and the responses to questions raised by the analysts must be open, frank, and responsive to the information needs. Any sense that management is not forthright and will not truthfully answer reasonable questions will cause analysts to choose not to follow the company's progress.

INFORMATION NEEDS OF OTHER GROUPS

The financial analysts and large investors of all groups, as might be expected, do the most probing. Their approach is highly analytical. Usually, when a company can adequately communicate with this group, it can deal effectively with most others.

These other players have varying interests, some of which involve answers to the items raised in the preceding sections. Perhaps the typical individual shareholder is most concerned with the general progress of the company and the prospect of continued and increasing dividend payments. A highly skilled financial background is not required to meet her inquiries. At the other extreme, a bank loan officer will be interested in the prospects of repaying the loan on time; and it might be proper to make available to him the annual budget for the next year or two, and perhaps the long-range financial plan. Bond-rating agencies may be exposed to past and prospective debt service coverage and related matters. Credit agencies, who have the published annual report available, may direct their questions to the content of the balance sheet items and prospective earnings. Many other investors may be interested in the significance of certain litigation, or product development. The required financial knowledge of the IR person will depend on the types of questions and the inquisitor's knowledge and interest.

DISCLOSURE POLICY

In providing information to or communicating with analysts, brokers, investors, or others, a matter to be resolved is: What constitutes proper and adequate disclosure? Typically, management is concerned about excessive disclosure that may harm the company. On the other side of the question, there should be sufficient disclosure to enable the analysts and others to discern shareholder value. Hence, the problem is one of weighing the benefits versus the costs.

However, the dangers of excessive disclosure include:

- Loss of competitive advantage through early disclosure of new products or marketing strategy or other strategic information
- Exposing the entity to litigation by reason of allegedly providing insider information, or attempting to foreclose competition or otherwise violate antitrust laws

- Generating earlier competitive reaction, or even new competitors, than would otherwise be the case
- Revealing strengths or weaknesses that might invite an unfriendly take-over attempt

Most analysts would prefer to get information first or early, but normally there is no benefit to them in causing long-term share decline. And most appreciate the need to protect competitive information.

While there is a danger in excessive disclosure, there are sometimes unrecognized costs of insufficient disclosure. Some of these are the following, resulting in a share price lower than normally might be the case:

- Failure to provide adequate data may encourage analysts and others to avoid the company and fail to follow its progress.
- Lack of information may cause unpleasant or unexpected surprises—something the financial community abhors.
- If management does not maintain good relations with analysts and investors, it usually takes much longer for positive developments to become known and reflected in the stock price.
- Most importantly, lack of firsthand knowledge, such as that secured through personal contact, prevents analysts and other interested parties from "kicking the tires"—from assessing the depth and quality of management, the adequacy of the company's controls, its ability to cope with change, as well as the quality of the product and services.

Impact of Regulation FD

The Securities and Exchange Commission has issued Regulation FD, stating that a company cannot issue information to a small subset of the investment community, thereby potentially giving those people an investment advantage over the general public. Some companies have reacted to this regulation by halting all contact with financial analysts and issuing a flood of general press releases, while others have elected to issue the minimal amount of required information to the investment community. So far, it appears that the issuance of more information is winning out. ▪

The IR group and management must thoroughly weigh what constitutes a proper balance in its disclosure policy.

ORGANIZATION STRUCTURE FOR INVESTOR RELATIONS

A successful IR program must, as previously mentioned, permit the exercise of two skills by company executives: the ability to (1) communicate effectively and (2) ferret out and comprehend the financial significance of operating trends and relationships, together with the composition of the various elements in the financial statements and their significance or impact. Company representatives must clearly, and often in sophisticated or knowledgeable financial terms, discuss highly technical financial issues with a great many types of investors or potential investors. What organizational structure best fills or facilitates this execution?

Several structures may be observed in operation, but one truth is paramount: There must be a coordinated approach; the company must speak with one voice. Thus, confusion is created if the vice president of sales discusses the potential financial impact of a new product to a group of distributors as having certain results, and the financial vice president describes a quite different financial impact with a group of financial analysts.

Assuming adequate and effective coordination among the company's spokespersons as to the presentation of financial data, what organizational structure is desirable? One answer is, "The one that is effective."

The external or investing public of a company is viewed by many top executives as consisting of several parts of the whole. The result is a dichotomy of views about proper organization:

▪ In some companies there is no single executive who is responsible for the external IR (as distinguished from employee relations). Basically, each major executive meets with his or her audience (e.g., a research audience, a marketing audience, a manufacturing group, a financial group). However, whenever financial content is involved, it would be cleared with the proper financial executive.

▪ In other entities, a single executive is held accountable for the IR function. Under this latter scenario, the IR activities might be a segment of the public relations department (renamed an IR department). Also, under such a plan the finance department, including the controller, would be considered an internal function—a resource to be made available to those responsible for IR activities.

▪ Some other organizational structures divide the responsibility into two segments: (1) The activity relating to preparation of the annual and quarterly reports to shareholders, institutional or financial advertisement, small shareholder inquiries, and the like, is handled by the public relations department (and coordinated with finance)—the so-called mass media facet; (2) the unit relating principally to contacts with security analysts, large institutional or individual investors, investment bankers, rating agencies, and so forth—that audience assumed to possess considerable financial knowhow—is handled by an IR unit reporting to the CFO or a financial officer. Presumably the members of this unit have a financial background (CPAs, accounting, investment banking) but have also been trained in communication skills.

The type of "customer" determines the unit most likely assigned the task. There must be coordination with the public relations segment or unit.

Finally, one other factor should be mentioned as a possible participant in the IR activity, and that is a professional IR agency. While such a firm often may be used by small companies, sometimes they can also be helpful consultants to medium-sized and larger entities in properly organizing the IR function.

The proper organizational structure for a specific company will depend, again, on the interests, ability, and personality (and perhaps financial interest) of the officers and executives who are actual or potential participants—consistent with management philosophy, style of management, available time, and so forth.

ROLE OF THE CONTROLLER AND OTHER PRINCIPALS

Having provided only a very general background on the sources of financial information about the company, the type of inquirers, and suggestions about management presentations to the security analysts in particular, the basic question is, "What should be the role of the controller?"

As is often true, what functions an officer performs depends on several factors, including his or her ability, personality, and interests, along with the interest and capabilities of the other officers, as well as the size of the company, management organization structure, management style, and so forth. If there is a CFO as well as a controller, the duties will be shared. And in those instances where the CEO feels he himself should play a major role in IR, that will further divide the effort. If the controller is a good financial analyst, certain activities will tend to be assigned to this position; and if the chief accounting officer is, in addition, a good presenter or communicator, then still other duties are likely to fall in this direction.

For the typical medium-sized to large company, where the CEO is somewhat active in IR, and where the CFO tends to spend some time with IR activities, a likely split of functions might be listed as:

Controller

1. An *information resource* or source for any *financial* data for those officers and executives who need it for IR purposes including:
   (a) Financial statements reflecting actual results and/or condition of the entity and/or any segments, such as
      (i) Income statement
      (ii) Statement of cash flows
      (iii) Balance sheet

   (b) Relevant financial *analyses* of actual data and trends of these statements, as required for IR purposes, such as
      (i) Inventories
      (ii) Accounts receivable
      (iii) Long-term debt, by category of debt
      (iv) Plant and equipment, by location
      (v) Relevant ratios, including comparisons with industry and competitors
      (vi) Detail and type of revenue and expenses by appropriate segment

   (c) Financial statements and related analyses representing *planned* or *forecasted* results or condition, both the annual plan and long-range plan, for the consolidated entity and any segment. (These data should be available, but often should not be disclosed to the analyst groups, etc.)

   (d) Relevant *graphs* and tabulations showing financial trends and relationships, actual and projected. Basically, all financial data (whether to be presented to outsiders, or simply used as background or a reference source) should be prepared under the supervision of, or by, the controller, subject to appropriate suggestions or constraints by the CFO or CEO.

2. As required, an *interpreter* of the financial data, when asked to do so by other major officers or executives present, to the appropriate IR audience

(groups, individuals [analysts, investors], financial information sources such as Dun & Bradstreet, bank loan officers, etc.).

3. A *communicator* of financial information to individuals and groups entitled to receive it, under the applicable working rules. This would include presentations to groups or individual analysts, investors, or brokers, and so forth, as well as answering their questions. It might be that the controller would (1) make presentations in the absence of the CFO, and (2) give talks to small groups regularly, with the CFO (or even the CEO) handling the larger or more important meetings. Certainly, if the controller is a good communicator he or she should be trained to be the alter ego of the CFO.

4. Either prepares or reviews for accuracy and completeness any financial commentary in such financial documents as the annual report to shareholders, quarterly report to shareholders, Forms 10-K, 10-Q, and so on.

5. A *reviewer* for content and accuracy of all news releases, special announcements, and publications of the IR activity (and those of other executives) dealing with *financial/accounting* matters. As applicable, the controller would make his or her recommendations or comments to the CFO, unless she is authorized to make the final decision in the event of disagreement or needed major changes.

When the controller is de facto the CFO, he or she would exercise the duties listed previously, plus those of the CFO enumerated next.

Put Your Role in Writing!

There are few areas in which a new controller can get into more trouble with senior management than in the area of IR. Knowing that he is new, an investor may contact the controller and attempt to extract information about the company. The fallout from this situation can require a great deal of time by senior managers to fix. To avoid the problem, sit down with the CFO or president as soon as possible and define exactly what the controller is or is not allowed to do with investors. Write down the results and send back a copy, so there is evidence of what was agreed upon. ■

Chief Financial Officer

1. Should be the principal communicator of financial policy and the reasons therefore, financial status, and operating trends and relationships to major groups, including the leading security analysts of the industry, major

brokerage houses, and large investors—actual or potential—whether institutional or individual.

2. Should be the principal spokesman or negotiator, subject to approval of the CEO and/or board of directors, as may be applicable, in connection with the actual and imminent raising of capital—whether equity or indebtedness. Thus, he or she would be the principal contact with investment bankers, large commercial bankers, lessors, and institutions, using such advice and assistance deemed necessary.

3. Should delegate to the controller any of the above duties and any lesser ones relative to IR when deemed to be in the interest of the company, and assuming the controller is experienced and capable.

4. Should review all major published financial documents (annual report to shareholders, quarterly reports, financial news releases) and receive comments from the controller for accuracy, completeness, adequate disclosure, and the like.

5. If the IR department is a part of the financial organization, should direct its activities, establish appropriate disclosure policies, and develop a competent and professional IR staff to handle those functions not assigned to the CEO or the controller or himself.

If the IR activities are under the cognizance of the CEO or the public relations officer, the CFO should make appropriate recommendations on suggested improvements.

Chief Executive Officer

1. Preside over major meetings with security analysts, large investors, and the like, and present the background and related information on such important matters as:

    (a) Company mission, purpose, goals and objectives, and so forth
    (b) Competitive position of the company
    (c) Major operating accomplishments in recent periods
    (d) Direction company is headed
    (e) Any forthcoming major events that can be announced (management changes, acquisitions, divestments, etc.)

    Additionally, he should answer the questions of the audience on major public matters and the like. By bearing and knowledge he should demonstrate that he is, indeed, the CEO.

2. Meet, on a one-to-one basis or with a few individuals only, any major investor, opinion maker, banker, and so on, who wishes to see him. Discuss major points as in 1 above.

3. As appropriate in IR meetings, refer financial questions to the vice president of finance or controller, and certain operating questions to the operating executive present.
4. As to important financing matters, meet with other major players, as deemed proper: commercial bankers, investment bankers, rating agencies, institutional investors, and so on. He should lend support to the proposed transactions, provide relevant background about the company, and answer questions directed to him.
5. Ascertain that the messages in any important public statements (e.g., the annual report, quarterly financial reports, financial-type news releases) are as he thinks they should be, or understand why not.
6. Address important company matters and the annual meeting of shareholders.

SOME SUGGESTED FINANCIAL MARKET OBJECTIVES

The objectives of the company with respect to financial markets will depend on what condition appears to need improvement or change. In the experience of

Buy Back Shares from Small Investors

An emerging best practice for IR is to buy back shares from investors owning only a few shares of stock. By doing so, the company can save money tracking fewer investors and mailing out fewer annual reports. The savings can be considerable if there are many thousands of small investors. ▪

the author, here are some typical objectives, one or more of which might apply to a particular entity:

▪ Increase the P/E ratio to X, or to the Standard & Poor's (S&P) 500 level, or to the best in the industry.
▪ Lengthen the average stock holding period by attracting more long-term investors.
▪ Reacquire some portion of the present outstanding shares through stock repurchase programs.

- Increase the average daily share sales volume, so that institutions can buy or sell in a given day without significantly moving the stock price.
- Reduce volatility by expanding the shareholder base.
- Build shareholder demand (by diversifying the shareholder base).
- Create a greater demand for company bonds or other debt securities.
- Reduce the proportion of shares held by institutional investors.

While consistent earnings growth, based on good products and capable marketing, and a sound financial position, are fundamental in attaining and maintaining many of these objectives, another aid is to target particular markets and properly communicate relevant financial information. Which targets need to be reached will require an analysis of the present shareholder types, and so forth. A few comments on this phase follow.

SOME SUGGESTED METHODS

A successful IR program involves providing reliable, consistent, timely, and truthful information about the company on such matters as depth of management, developments as to products and markets, probable trend of sales and earnings, and some guidance on company financial objectives—not only to the usual array of stock brokers, security analysts, and individuals, but more especially to carefully selected institutions that probably would be a desirable type of shareholder—who could aid in meeting the objectives set out in the investor relations agenda. Some suggestions include:

1. *Maintain a current, well-documented background book which is available to all key executives, and for all key contacts with the investing groups.*
   Such an information source would provide these benefits:
   (a) The reader will have a better idea of what subjects are matters of concern to an investor or potential investor.
   (b) The executives will have a consistent and uniform response to queries.
   (c) The reader will be updated on the current developments in the company which should be communicated to the investing public.

   In terms of content, aside from the financially relevant information on the company itself, the data book might contain information about potential investor contacts: location, position, investment patterns, availability for conference calls, and so on.

2. *Be certain that all key internal officers are current on new and important developments and that the investor significance is understood.*

With such a background, the likelihood is reduced of making offhand comments that can be misinterpreted.

3. *Establish close one-on-one relationships with selected institutional investors where particular investor relations objectives can be furthered.*

It already has been mentioned that increasing the investor base by the addition of long-term investors will lengthen the average holding period. Creating closer relations with institutional investors also may reduce volatility. Volatility occurs or increases because large segments of the shareholder population decide to take the same action at the same time, for example, to sell the company's shares. If large shareholders are kept informed about the company, this may decrease the tendency to follow the actions of other investors. These long-term investors may buy more shares while the short-horizon investors may be selling—thus creating a balance in the marketplace and maintaining the stock price.

The program for contacting large institutional investors or potential investors can include periodically scheduled visits (once or twice a year) to the financial centers (New York, Boston, Chicago, San Francisco, etc.) to meet particular institutional investors and security analysts.

4. *Consider the possibility of conference calls to selected investors or security analysts.*

This has the advantages of (a) making one call instead of numerous ones, (b) releasing the data to many sources at the same time, and (c) keeping the message more consistent. A disadvantage arises of making it more difficult to answer all the questions of every analyst.

5. *In some circumstances, increase contacts with noninstitutional investors.*

Noninstitutional investors are generally more likely to hold on to their shares for extended periods, so catering to these investors can reduce the volatility of the company's stock price.

CHAPTER TWELVE

Taxation Strategy

Importance of This Chapter

Taxation is an area cluttered with land mines for the new controller, usually involving tax late fees and penalties. However, there are also opportunities to save a considerable amount of money through the use of such tax tools as net operating loss (NOL) carryforwards, inventory valuation techniques, and the use of transfer pricing. This chapter makes the new controller aware of these types of issues.

The obvious objective of tax strategy is to minimize the amount of cash paid out for taxes. However, this directly conflicts with the general desire to report as much income as possible to shareholders, since more reported income results in more taxes. Only in the case of privately owned firms do these conflicting problems go away, since the owners have no need to impress anyone with their reported level of earnings and would simply prefer to retain as much cash in the company as possible by avoiding the payment of taxes.

For those controllers intent on reducing their corporation's tax burdens, there are five primary goals to include in their tax strategies, all of which involve increasing the number of differences between the book and tax records, so that reportable income for tax purposes is reduced. The five items are:

1. **Accelerate deductions.** By recognizing expenses sooner, you can force expenses into the current reporting year that would otherwise be deferred. The primary deduction acceleration involves depreciation, for which a company typically uses MACRS (an accelerated depreciation methodology acceptable for tax reporting purposes) and straight-line depreciation, which results in a higher level of reported earnings for other purposes.

2. **Take all available tax credits.** A credit results in a permanent reduction in taxes, and so is highly desirable. Unfortunately, credits are difficult to find, though a company might qualify for the research and experimental tax credit, which is available to those companies that have increased their research activities over the previous year. The only type of expense that qualifies for this credit is that which is undertaken to discover information that is technical in nature, and its application must be intended for use in developing a new or improved business component for the taxpayer. Also, all of the research activities must be elements of a process of experimentation relating to a new or improved function, or that enhances the current level of performance, reliability, or quality. A credit cannot be taken for research conducted after the beginning of commercial production, for the customization of a product for a specific customer, for the duplication of an existing process or product, or for research required for some types of software to be used internally.

   There are more tax credits available at the local level, where they are offered to those businesses willing to operate in economic development zones, or as part of specialized relocation deals (normally available only to larger companies).

3. **Avoid nonallowable expenses.** There are a few expenses, most notably meals and entertainment, that are completely or at least partially not allowed for purposes of computing taxable income. A key company strategy is to reduce these types of expenses to the bare minimum, thereby avoiding any lost benefits from nonallowable expenses.

4. **Increase tax deferrals.** There are a number of situations in which taxes can be shifted into the future, such as payments in stock for acquisitions, or the deferral of revenue received until all related services have been performed. This can shift a large part of the tax liability into the future, where the time value of money results in a smaller present value of the tax liability than otherwise would be the case.

5. **Obtain tax-exempt income.** The controller should consider investing excess funds in municipal bonds, which are exempt from both federal

income taxes and the income taxes of the state in which they were issued. The downside of this approach is that the return on municipal bonds is less than the return on other forms of investment, due to their inherent tax savings.

There is no single tax strategy that will be applicable to every company, since the tax laws are so complex that the controller must construct a strategy that is tailored to the specific circumstances in which her company finds itself. Nonetheless, there are a number of taxation areas that a controller must be aware of when creating a tax strategy using the preceding five goals. Those areas are listed in alphabetical order through the remainder of this chapter, ranging from the accumulated earnings tax to unemployment taxes. The controller should carefully peruse these topics to see if they should be incorporated into her overall tax strategy.

ACCUMULATED EARNINGS TAX

There is a double tax associated with a company's payment of dividends to investors, because it first must pay an income tax from which dividends *cannot* be deducted as an expense, and then investors must pay income tax on the dividends received. Understandably, closely held companies prefer not to issue dividends in order to avoid the double taxation issue. However, this can result in a large amount of capital accumulating within a company. The Internal Revenue Service (IRS) addresses this issue by imposing an accumulated earnings tax on what it considers to be an excessive amount of earnings that have not been distributed to shareholders.

The IRS considers accumulated earnings of less than $150,000 to be sufficient for the working needs of service businesses, such as accounting, engineering, architecture, and consulting firms. It considers accumulations of anything under $250,000 to be sufficient for most other types of businesses. A company can argue that it needs a substantially larger amount of accumulated earnings if it can prove that it has specific, definite, and feasible plans that will require the use of the funds within the business. Another valid argument is that a company needs an amount of accumulated earnings sufficient to buy back the company's stock that is held by a deceased shareholder's estate.

If these conditions are not apparent, then the IRS will declare the accumulated earnings to be taxable at a rate of 39.6 percent. Also, interest payments to the IRS will be due from the date when the corporation's annual return was originally due. The severity of this tax is designed to encourage organizations to issue dividends on a regular basis to their shareholders, so that the IRS can tax the shareholders for this form of income.

 ## CASH METHOD OF ACCOUNTING

The normal method for reporting a company's financial results is the accrual basis of accounting, under which expenses are matched to revenues within a reporting period. However, for tax purposes, it is sometimes possible to report income under the cash method of accounting. Under this approach, revenue is not recognized until payment for invoices is received, while expenses are not recognized until paid.

The cash basis of accounting can result in a great deal of manipulation from the perspective of the IRS, which discourages its use, but does not prohibit it. As an example of income manipulation, a company may realize that it will have a large amount of income to report in the current year, and will probably have less in the following year. Accordingly, it prepays a number of supplier invoices at the end of the year, so that it recognizes them at once under the cash method of accounting as expenses in the current year. The IRS prohibits this type of behavior under the rule that cash payments recognized in the current period can relate only to current-year expenses. Nonetheless, it is a difficult issue for the IRS to police. The same degree of manipulation can be applied to the recognition of revenue, simply by delaying billings to customers near the end of the tax year. Also, in situations where there is a sudden surge of business at the end of the tax year, possibly due to seasonality, the cash method of accounting will not reveal the sales until the following year, since payment on the invoices from customers will not arrive until the next year. Consequently, the cash method tends to underreport taxable income.

In order to limit the use of this method, the IRS prohibits it if a company has any inventories on hand at the end of the year. The reason for this is that expenditures for inventory can be so large and subject to manipulation at year-end that a company could theoretically alter its reported level of taxable income to an enormous extent. The cash basis is also not allowable for any C corporation, a partnership that has a C corporation for a partner, or a tax shelter. However, within these restrictions, it is allowable for an entity with average annual gross receipts of $5 million or less for the three tax years ending with the prior tax year, as well as for any personal service corporation that provides at least 95 percent of its activities in the services arena.

The IRS imposes some accrual accounting concepts on a cash-basis organization in order to avoid some of the more blatant forms of income avoidance. For example, if a cash-basis company receives a check at the end of its tax year, it may be tempted not to cash the check until the beginning of the next tax year, since this would push the revenue associated with that check into the next year. To avoid this problem, the IRS uses the concept of *constructive receipt*, which requires one to record the receipt when it is made available to one without restriction (whether or not it is actually recorded on the company's books at that time). Besides the just-noted example, this would also require a company to record the interest on a bond that comes due prior to the end of the tax year, even if the associated coupon is not sent to the issuer until the next year.

Removing the Cash Basis

Though the IRS allows companies to use the cash basis of accounting, it is certainly not generally accepted accounting principles (GAAP), and so requires the new controller to adjust the accounting records for financial reporting purposes. Given the extra work involved, it is best to plan for a near-term conversion to the accrual basis of accounting.

INVENTORY VALUATION

It is allowable to value a company's inventory using one method for book purposes and another for tax purposes, except in the case of the LIFO inventory valuation method. In this case, the tax advantages to be gained from the use of LIFO are so significant that the IRS requires a user to employ it for both book and tax purposes. Furthermore, if LIFO is used in any one of a group of financially related companies, the entire group is assumed to be a single entity for tax reporting purposes, which means that they must all use the LIFO valuation approach for both book and tax reporting. This rule was engendered in order to stop the practice of having LIFO-valuation companies roll their results into a parent company that used some other method of reporting, thereby giving astute companies high levels of reportable income and lower levels of taxable income at the same time.

MERGERS AND ACQUISITIONS

A key factor to consider in corporate acquisitions is the determination of what size taxable gain will be incurred by the seller (if any), as well as how the buyer can reduce the tax impact of the transaction in the current and future years. In this section, we will briefly discuss the various types of transactions involved in an acquisition, the tax implications of each transaction, and whose interests are best served by the use of each one.

There are two ways in which an acquisition can be made, each with different tax implications. First, you can purchase the acquiree's stock, which may trigger a taxable gain to the seller. Second, you can purchase the acquiree's assets, which triggers a gain on sale of the assets, as well as another tax to the shareholders of the selling company, who must recognize a gain when the proceeds from liquidation of the business are distributed to them. Because of the additional taxation, a seller will generally want to sell a corporation's stock, rather than its assets.

When stock is sold to the buyer in exchange for cash or property, the buyer establishes a tax basis in the stock that equals the amount of the cash or fair market value of the property transferred to the seller. Meanwhile, the seller recognizes a gain or loss on the eventual sale of the stock that is based on its original tax basis in the stock, which is subtracted from the ultimate sale price of the stock.

It is also possible for the seller to recognize no taxable gain on sale of a business if it takes some of the acquiring company's stock as full compensation for the sale. However, there will be no tax only if *continuity of interest* in the business can be proven by giving the sellers a sufficient amount of the buyer's stock to prove that they have a continuing financial interest in the buying company. A variation on this approach is to make an acquisition over a period of months, using nothing but voting stock as compensation to the seller's shareholders, but for which a clear plan of ultimate control over the acquiree can be proven. Another variation is to purchase at least 80 percent of the fair market value of the acquiree's assets solely in exchange for stock.

When only the assets are sold to the buyer, the buyer can apportion the total price among the assets purchased, up to their fair market value (with any excess portion of the price being apportioned to goodwill). This is highly favorable from a taxation perspective, since the buyer has now adjusted its basis in the assets substantially higher; it can now claim a much larger accelerated depreciation expense in the upcoming years, thereby reducing its reported level of taxable income and reducing its tax burden. From the seller's perspective, the sale price is allocated to each asset sold for the purposes of determining a gain or loss; as much of this as possible should be characterized as a capital gain (since the related tax is lower) or as an ordinary loss (since it can offset ordinary income, which has a higher tax rate).

The structuring of an acquisition transaction so that no income taxes are paid must have a reasonable business purpose besides the avoidance of taxes. Otherwise, the IRS has been known to require tax payments on the grounds that the structure of the transaction has no reasonable business purpose besides tax avoidance. Its review of the substance of a transaction over its form leads the controller to consider such transactions in the same manner and to restructure acquisition deals accordingly.

There is a specialized tax reduction available for the holders of stock in a small business, on which they experience a gain when the business is sold. Specifically, they are entitled to a 50 percent reduction in their reportable gain on sale of that stock, though it is limited to the greater of a $10 million gain or ten times the stockholder's basis in the stock. This exclusion is reserved for C corporations and applies only to stock that was acquired at its original issuance. There are a number of other exclusions, such as its inapplicability to personal service corporations, real estate investment trusts, domestic international sales corporations, and mutual funds. This type of stock is called *qualified small business stock*. The unique set of conditions surrounding this stock make it clear that it is intended to be a tax break specifically for the owners of small businesses.

NET OPERATING LOSS CARRYFORWARDS

Since income taxes can be the largest single expense on the income statement, the controller should carefully track the use and applicability of NOL carryforwards that were created as the result of reported losses in prior years. An NOL may be carried back and applied against profits recorded in the two preceding years, with any remaining amount being carried forward for the next 20 years, when it can be offset against any reported income. If there is still an NOL left after the 20 years have expired, then the remaining amount can no longer be used. You can also irrevocably choose to ignore the carryback option and use it only for carryforward purposes. The standard procedure is to apply all of the NOL against the income reported in the earliest year, with the remainder carrying forward to each subsequent year in succession until the remaining NOL has been exhausted. If an NOL has been incurred in each of multiple years, then these should be applied against reported income (in either prior or later years) in order of the first NOL incurred. This rule is used because of the 20-year limitation on an NOL, so that an NOL incurred in an earlier year can be used before it expires.

The NOL is a valuable asset, since it can be used for many years to offset future earnings. A company buying another entity that has an NOL will certainly place a high value on the NOL and may even buy the entity strictly in order to use its NOL. To curtail this type of behavior, the IRS has created the Section 382 limitation, under which there is a limitation on its use if there is at least a 50 percent change in the ownership of an entity that has an unused NOL. The limitation is derived through a complex formula that essentially multiplies the acquired corporation's stock times the long-term tax-exempt bond rate. To avoid this problem, a company with an unused NOL that is seeking to expand its equity should consider issuing straight preferred stock (no voting rights, no conversion privileges, and no participation in future earnings) in order to avoid any chance that the extra equity will be construed as a change in ownership.

A Good Time for Tax Advice

Because Section 382 can have such a severe impact on the amount of an acquiree's NOL that an acquirer can use, be sure to obtain qualified tax advice regarding this issue whenever a potential acquiree has an NOL. The resulting advice can alter the legal structure of the transaction and possibly allow the acquirer to still use some portion or all of the NOL. ▪

If a company has incurred an NOL in a short tax year, it must deduct the NOL over a period of six years, starting with the first tax year after the short tax year. This limitation does not apply if the NOL is for $10,000 or less, or if the NOL is the result of a short tax year that is at least nine months long and is less than the NOL for a full 12-month tax year beginning with the first day of the short tax year. This special NOL rule was designed to keep companies from deliberately changing their tax years in order to create an NOL within a short tax year. This situation is quite possible in a seasonal business where there are losses in all but a few months. Under such a scenario, a company would otherwise be able to declare an NOL during its short tax year, carry back the NOL to apply it against the previous two years of operations, and receive a rebate from the IRS.

NEXUS

A company may have to complete many more tax forms than it would like, as well as remit taxes to more government entities, if it can be established that it has nexus within a government's area of jurisdiction. Consequently, it is very important to understand how nexus is established.

The rules vary by state, but nexus is generally considered to have occurred if a company maintains a facility of any kind within a state, or if it pays the wages of someone within that state. In some locales, the definition is expanded to include the transport of goods to customers within the state on company-owned vehicles (though nexus is not considered to have occurred if the shipment is made by a third-party freight carrier). A more liberal interpretation of the nexus rule is that a company has nexus if it sends sales personnel into the state on sales calls or trains personnel there to educate customers, even though they are not permanently based there. To gain a precise understanding of how the nexus rules are interpreted by each state, it is best to contact the department of revenue at each state government.

If nexus has been established, a company must file to do business within the state, which requires a small fee and a refiling once every few years. In addition, it must withhold sales taxes on all sales within the state. This is the most laborious issue related to nexus, since sales taxes may be different for every city and county within each state, necessitating a company to keep track of potentially thousands of different sales tax rates. Also, some states may require the remittance of sales taxes every month, though this can be reduced to as little as once a year if the company predicts that it will have minimal sales taxes to remit, as noted on its initial application for a sales tax license.

Some states or local governments will also subject a company to property or personal property taxes on all assets based within their jurisdictions, which necessitates even more paperwork.

Though the amount of additional taxes paid may not be that great, the key issue related to the nexus concept is that the additional time required to track tax liabilities and file forms with the various governments may very well require additional personnel in the accounting department. This can be a major problem for those organizations in multiple states and should be a key planning issue when determining the capacity of the accounting department to process tax-related transactions. Some organizations with a number of subsidiaries will avoid a portion of the tax filing work by accepting the nexus concept only for those subsidiaries that are clearly established within each governmental jurisdiction, thereby avoiding the tax filing problems for all other legal entities controlled by the parent corporation.

PROJECT COSTING

A company that regularly develops large infrastructure systems such as enterprise resource planning (ERP) systems for its own use will usually cluster all costs related to that project into a single account and then capitalize its full cost, with amortization occurring over a number of years. Though this approach will certainly increase reported income over the short term, it also increases income taxes. If the avoidance of income taxes is a higher priority for the controller than reported profits, then it would be useful to separate the various components of each project into different accounts and expense those that more closely relate to ongoing operational activities. For example, a strong case can be made for expensing all training associated with a major system installation, on the grounds that training is an ongoing activity.

Another approach is to charge subsidiaries for the cost of a development project, especially if the charging entity is located in a low-tax region and the subsidiaries are in high-tax regions. This transfer pricing approach would reduce the reported income in high-tax areas, effectively shifting that income to a location where the tax rate is lower. However, these cost-shifting strategies must be carefully documented with proof that the systems are really being used by subsidiaries, and that the fees charged are reasonable.

A variation on the last approach is to create a data center in a tax haven that stores and analyzes company data and then issues reports back to other corporate divisions for a substantial fee. This approach has to involve more than simply locating a file server in a low-tax location, since the IRS will claim that there is no business purpose for the arrangement. Instead, a small business must be set up around the data center that provides some added value to the information being collected and disseminated. This approach is especially attractive if a company acquires another entity with a data center in a low-tax location and simply shifts its own facilities to the preestablished location.

PROPERTY TAXES

Local governments use property tax assessments as one of their primary forms of tax receipt. Personal property taxes are assessed based on a company's level of reported fixed assets in the preceding year and typically are paid once a year. In order to minimize this tax, the accounting department should regularly review the fixed asset list to see which items can be disposed of, thereby shrinking the taxable base of assets. Also, by increasing the capitalization limit, fewer items will be classified as assets, and so will also not be taxed.

Audits Are for Property, Too

Property taxes can be a considerable expense each year, and yet too many controllers simply accept the figures presented by the local government without argument. Instead, the new controller should conduct a fixed-asset audit and eliminate from the property tax role any assets that are no longer on the premises, and then go a step further and schedule continuing annual fixed-asset reviews on a fixed date. Also, if fixed assets are clearly not being used, dispose of them as soon as possible. The net result will be lower property taxes.

Local taxing authorities can also impose a tax based on any real property owned by a business. The buildings and land that fall into this category will be appraised by the local assessor, with the resulting assessment being multiplied by a tax rate that is determined by the local government. The assessment can be challenged. If a recent assessment change results in a significant boost in the reported value of a business's real property, it is certainly worthwhile to engage the services of a private assessor to see if the new valuation can be reduced.

If a business rents its property, the tax on real property can be either absorbed by the landlord or passed through to the business, depending upon the terms of the lease. If subleasing from another business, the property tax can be either absorbed by that entity or passed through to the business, again depending on the terms of the lease.

S CORPORATION

The S corporation is of considerable interest to the controller, because it generally does not pay taxes. Instead, it passes reported earnings through to its shareholders, who report the income on their tax returns. This avoids the double taxation that arises in a C corporation, where a company's income is taxed, and then the dividends it issues to its shareholders are taxed as income to them a second time. The amount of income is allocated to each shareholder on a simple per-share basis. If a shareholder has held stock in the corporation for less than a full year, then the allocation is on a per-share, per-day basis. The per-day part of this calculation assumes that a shareholder still holds the stock through and including the day when the stock is disposed of, while a deceased shareholder will be assumed to retain ownership through and including the day when he or she dies.

An S corporation has unique taxation and legal protection aspects that make it an ideal way to structure a business if there are a small number of shareholders. Specifically, it can be created only if there are no more than 75 shareholders, if only one class of stock is issued, and if all shareholders agree to the S corporation status. All of its shareholders must be either citizens or residents of the United States. Shareholders are also limited to individuals, estates, and some types of trusts and charities. Conversely, this means that C corporations and partnerships cannot be shareholders in an S corporation. The requirement for a single class of stock may prevent some organizations from organizing in this manner, for it does not allow for preferential returns or special voting rights by some shareholders.

There are a few cases where an S corporation can owe taxes. For example, it can be taxed if it has accumulated earnings and profits from an earlier existence as a C corporation, and its passive income is more than 25 percent of total gross receipts. It also can be liable for taxes on a few types of capital gains, recapture of the old investment tax credit, and LIFO recapture. If any of these taxes apply, then the S corporation must make quarterly estimated income tax payments. On the other hand, an S corporation is not subject to the alternative minimum tax.

If the management team of an S corporation wants to terminate its S status, the written consent of more than 50 percent of the shareholders is required, as well as a statement from the corporation to that effect. If the corporation wants to become an S corporation at a later date, there is a five-year waiting period from the last time before it can do so again, unless it obtains special permission from the IRS.

SALES AND USE TAXES

Sales taxes are imposed at the state, county, and city level—frequently by all three at once. It is also possible for a special tax to be added to the sales tax and applied to a unique region, such as for the construction of a baseball stadium or to support a regional mass transit system. The sales tax is multiplied by the price paid on goods and services on transactions occurring within the taxing area. However, the definition of goods and services that are required to be taxed will vary by state (not usually at the county or city level), and so they must be researched at the local level to determine the precise basis of calculation. For example, some states do not tax food sales, on the grounds that this is a necessity whose cost should be reduced as much as possible, while other states include it in their required list of items to be taxed.

A company is required to charge sales taxes to its customers and remit the resulting receipts to the local state government, which will split out the portions due to the local county and city governments and remit these taxes on the company's behalf to those entities. If the company does not charge its customers for these taxes, it is still liable for them and must pay the unbilled amounts to the state government, though it has the right to attempt to bill its customers after the fact for the missing sales taxes. This can be a difficult collection chore, especially if sales are primarily over the counter, where there are few transaction records that identify the customer. Also, a company is obligated to keep abreast of all changes in sales tax rates and charge its customers for the correct amount; if it does not do so, then it is liable to the government for the difference between what it actually charged and the statutory rate. If a company overcharges its customers, the excess must also be remitted to the government.

The state in which a company is collecting sales taxes can decide how frequently it wants the company to remit taxes. If there are only modest sales, the state may decide that the cost of paperwork exceeds the value of the remittances and will require only an annual remittance. It is more common to have quarterly or monthly remittances. The state will review the dollar amount of remittances from time to time and adjust the required remittance frequency based on this information.

All government entities have the right to audit a company's books to see if the proper sales taxes are being charged, and so a company can be theoretically subject to three sales tax audits per year—one each from the city, county, and state revenue departments. Also, since these audits can come from any taxing jurisdiction in which a company does business, there could be literally thousands of potential audits.

The obligation to collect sales taxes is based on the concept of *nexus*, which was covered earlier in this chapter. If nexus exists, then sales taxes must be collected by the seller. If not, the recipient of purchased goods instead has an obligation to compile a list of items purchased and remit a use tax to the appropriate authority. The use tax is in the same amount as the sales tax. The only difference is that the remitting party is the buyer instead of the seller. Use taxes are also subject to audits by all taxing jurisdictions.

If the buyer of a company's products is including them in its own products for resale to another entity, then the buyer does not have to pay a sales tax to the seller. Instead, the buyer will charge a sales tax to the buyer of *its* final product. This approach is used under the theory that a sales tax should be charged only one time on the sale of a product. However, it can be a difficult chore to explain the lack of sales tax billings during an audit, so sales taxes should be halted only if a buyer sends a sales tax exemption form to the company, which then should be kept on file. The sales tax exemption certificate can be named a resale certificate instead, depending on the issuing authority. It also can be issued to government entities, which are generally exempt from sales and use taxes. As a general rule, sales taxes always should be charged unless there is a sales tax exemption certificate on file—otherwise, the company will still be liable for the remittance of sales taxes in the event of an audit.

Review Nexus Every Year

The controller is in charge of sales taxes, so it can be a considerable embarrassment to be required to pay a fine for nonpayment of taxes. To avoid this problem, review nexus concerns every year to see if new company locations, deliveries, or other activities will make the company liable for sales tax collections and remittances. If there is a checklist of accounting actions to implement following an acquisition, include on it the company's registration for a sales tax license in the new location. ▪

TRANSFER PRICING

Transfer pricing is a key tax consideration, because it can result in the permanent reduction of an organization's tax liability. The permanent reduction is caused by the recognition of income in different taxing jurisdictions that may have different tax rates.

The basic concept behind the use of transfer pricing to reduce one's overall taxes is that a company transfers its products to a division in another country at the lowest possible price if the income tax rate is lower in the other country, or at the highest possible price if the tax rate is higher. By selling to the division at a low price, the company will report a very high profit on the final sale of products in the other country, which is where that income will be taxed at a presumably lower income tax rate.

For example, Exhibit 12.1 shows a situation in which a company with a location in countries Alpha and Beta has the choice of either selling goods in Alpha or transferring them to Beta and selling them there. The company is faced with a corporate income tax rate of 40 percent in country Alpha. To permanently avoid some of this income tax, the company sells its products to another subsidiary in country Beta, where the corporate income tax rate is only 25 percent. By doing so, the company still earns a profit ($60,000) in country Alpha, but the bulk of the profit ($125,000) now appears in country Beta. The net result is a consolidated income tax rate of just 28 percent.

The IRS is well aware of this tax-avoidance strategy and has developed tax rules that do not eliminate it, but that will reduce the leeway that a controller has in altering reportable income. Under Section 482 of the IRS Code, the IRS's preferred approach for developing transfer prices is to use the market rate as its basis. However, very few products can be reliably and consistently compared to the market rate, with the exception of commodities, because there are costing differences between them. Also, in many cases, products are so specialized (especially components that are custom-designed to fit into a larger product) that there is no market rate against which they can be compared. Even if there is some basis of comparison between a product and the average market prices

	Country Alpha Location	Country Beta Location
Sales to subsidiary:		
Revenue	$1,000,000	
Cost of goods sold	850,000	
Profit	$ 150,000	
Profit percentage	15%	
Sales outside of company:		
Revenue		$1,500,000
Cost of goods sold		1,000,000
Profit		$ 500,000
Profit percentage		33%
Income tax percentage	40%	25%
Income tax	$ 60,000	$ 125,000
Consolidated income tax	$ 185,000	
Consolidated income tax percentage	28%	

EXHIBIT 12.1 Income Tax Savings from Transfer Pricing

for similar products, the controller still has some leeway in which to alter transfer prices. The IRS will allow you to add special charges that are based on the cost of transferring the products, or extra fees, such as royalty or licensing fees that are imposed for the subsidiary's use of the parent company's patents or trademarks, or for administrative charges related to the preparation of any documentation required to move products between countries. It is also possible to slightly alter the interest rates charged to subsidiaries (though not too far from market rates) for the use of funds sent to them from the parent organization.

If there is no basis on which to create prices based on market rates, then the IRS's next most favored approach is to calculate the prices based on the *work-back method.* Under this approach, you begin at the end of the sales cycle by determining the price at which a product is sold to an outside customer, and then subtract the subsidiary's standard markup percentage and its added cost of materials, labor, and overhead, which results in the theoretical transfer price. The work-back method can result in a wide array of transfer prices, since a number of different costs can be subtracted from the final sale price, such as standard costs, actual costs, overhead costs based on different allocation measures, and overhead costs based on cost pools that contain different types of costs.

If that approach does not work, then the IRS's third most favored approach is the *cost plus method.* As the name implies, this approach begins at the other end of the production process and compiles costs from a product's initiation point. After all costs are added before the point of transfer, one then adds a profit margin to the product, thereby arriving at a transfer cost that is acceptable to the IRS. However, once again, the costs that are included in a product are subject to the same points of variation that were noted for the work-back method. In addition, the profit margin added should be the standard margin added for any other company customer, but they can be quite difficult to determine if there are a multitude of volume discounts, seasonal discounts, and so forth. Consequently, the profit margin added to a product's initial costs can be subject to a great deal of negotiation.

An overriding issue to consider, no matter what approach is used to derive transfer prices, is that taxing authorities can become highly irritated if a company continually pushes the outer limits of acceptable transfer pricing rules in order to maximize its tax savings. When this happens, a company can expect continual audits and penalties on disputed items, as well as less favorable judgments related to any taxation issues. Consequently, it makes a great deal of sense to consistently adopt pricing policies that result in reasonable tax savings, are fully justifiable to the taxing authorities of all involved countries, and that do not push the boundaries of acceptable pricing behavior.

Another transfer pricing issue that can modify a company's pricing strategy is the presence of any restrictions on cash flows out of a country in which it has a subsidiary. In these instances, it may be necessary to report the minimum possible amount of taxable income at the subsidiary, irrespective of the local tax rate. The reason is that the only way for a company to retrieve funds from the country is through the medium of an account receivable, which must be maximized by billing the subsidiary the highest possible amount for transferred goods. In this case, tax planning takes a back seat to cash flow planning.

Yet another issue that may drive a company to set pricing levels that do not result in reduced income taxes is that a subsidiary may have to report high levels of income in order to qualify for a loan from a local credit institution. This is especially important if the country in which the subsidiary is located has restrictions on the movement of cash, so that the parent company would be unable to withdraw loans that it makes to the subsidiary. As was the case for the last item, cash flow planning is likely to be more important than income tax reduction.

A final transfer pricing issue to be aware of is that the method for calculating taxable income may vary in other countries. This may falsely lead you to believe that another country has a lower tax rate. A closer examination of how taxable income is calculated might reveal that some expenses are restricted or not allowed at all, resulting in an actual tax rate that is much higher than originally expected. Consultation with a tax expert for the country in question prior to setting up any transfer pricing arrangements is the best way to avoid this problem.

UNEMPLOYMENT TAXES

Both the state and federal governments will charge a company a fixed percentage of its payroll each year for the expense of unemployment funds that are used to pay former employees who have been released from employment. The state governments administer the distribution of these funds and will compile an experience rating on each company, based on the number of employees it has laid off in the recent past. Based on this experience rating, it can require a company to submit larger or smaller amounts to the state unemployment fund in future years. This can become a considerable burden if a company has a long history of layoffs. Consequently, you should consider the use of temporary employees or outsourcing if this will give a firm the ability to retain a small number of key employees and avoid layoffs while still handling seasonal changes in work loads. Also, if a company is planning to acquire another entity, but plans to lay off a large number of the acquiree's staff once the acquisition is completed, it may make more sense to acquire the acquiree's assets and selectively hire a few of its employees, thereby retaining a pristine unemployment experience rating with the local state government.

The federal unemployment tax is imposed on a company if it has paid employees at least $1,500 in any calendar quarter, or had at least one employee for some portion of a day within at least 20 weeks of the year. In short, nearly all companies will be required to remit federal unemployment taxes. For the 2011 calendar year, the tax rate is 6.2 percent of the first $7,000 paid to each employee; this tends to concentrate most federal unemployment tax remittances into the first quarter of the calendar year. In many states, you can take a credit against the federal unemployment tax for up to 5.4 percent of taxable wages, which results in a net federal unemployment tax of only 0.8 percent.

If a company is shifting to a new legal entity, perhaps because of a shift from a partnership to a corporation, or from an S corporation to a C corporation, it will have to apply for a new unemployment tax identification number with the local state authorities. This is a problem if the organization being closed down had an unusually good experience rating, since the company will be assigned a poorer one until a new experience rating can be built up over time, which will result in higher unemployment taxes in the short term. To avoid this problem, you should contact the local unemployment taxation office to request that the old company's experience rating be shifted to the new one.

About the Author

Steven Bragg, CPA, CMA, CIA, CPIM, has been the chief financial officer or controller of four companies, as well as a consulting manager at Ernst & Young and auditor at Deloitte & Touche. He received a master's degree in finance from Bentley College, an MBA from Babson College, and a bachelor's degree in economics from the University of Maine. He has been the two-time president of the Colorado Mountain Club, is an avid alpine skier and mountain biker, and is a certified master diver. Mr. Bragg resides in Centennial, Colorado, with his wife and two daughters. He has published the following books through John Wiley & Sons:

Accounting and Finance for Your Small Business
Accounting Best Practices
Accounting Controls Best Practices
Billing and Collections Best Practices
Controller's Guide to Costing
Controller's Guide to Planning and Controlling Operations
Controller's Guide: Roles and Responsibilities for the New Controller
Controllership
Cost Accounting
Design and Maintenance of Accounting Manuals
Essentials of Payroll
Fast Close
Financial Analysis
GAAP Guide
GAAP Implementation Guide
Inventory Accounting
Inventory Best Practices
Just-in-Time Accounting
Managing Explosive Corporate Growth

Outsourcing
Payroll Accounting
Payroll Best Practices
Sales and Operations for Your Small Business
The Controller's Function
The New CFO Financial Leadership Manual
The Ultimate Accountants' Reference

Subscribe to Steve's FREE accounting best practices newsletter, podcast, and blog at www.stevebragg.com. His podcast is also available through iTunes.

Index